W9-BZZ-759

DUKE HAMILTON IS DEAD!

Also by Victor Stater

Noble Government: The Stuart Lord Lieutenancy
and the Transformation of English Politics

DUKE HAMILTON IS DEAD!

A Story of Aristocratic Life and Death in Stuart Britain

VICTOR STATER

ⓌⓌ *Hill and Wang*

A division of Farrar, Straus and Giroux

New York

Hill and Wang
A division of Farrar, Straus and Giroux
19 Union Square West, New York 10003

Distributed in Canada by Douglas & McIntyre Ltd.
Printed in the United States of America
Designed by Jonathan D. Lippincott
Family trees designed by Jeffrey L. Ward
First edition, 1999

Library of Congress Cataloging-in-Publication Data
Stater, Victor Louis, 1959–
    Duke Hamilton is dead! : a story of aristocratic life and death in
Stuart Britain / Victor Stater. — 1st ed.
        p.   cm.
    Includes bibliographical references (p.   ) and index.
    ISBN 0-8090-4033-6 (alk. paper)
    1. Hamilton, James Douglas, Duke of, 1658–1712—Death and burial.
2. Inheritance and succession—Great Britain—History—18th century.
3. Aristocracy (Social class)—Great Britain—History—18th century.
4. Aristocracy (Social class)—Great Britain—History—17th century.
5. Mohun, Charles Mohun, Baron, 1677–1712—Death and burial.
6. London (England)—Social life and customs—18th century.
7. Great Britain—History—Stuarts, 1603–1714—Biography.   8. Great
Britain—Politics and government—1702–1714.   9. Dueling—England—
London—History—18th century.   10. Nobility—Great Britain—
Biography.   11. Nobility—Scotland—Biography.   I. Title.
DA483.H315S73   1999
941.06'092—dc21
    [b]   98-42907

A concerted effort has been made to obtain permission for the use of copy-
righted material. Please see the list of sources on page 321 for details.

CONTENTS

Acknowledgments   xi

English Monarchs and Family Trees   xv

Introduction   3

1   *A Season of Youth*   11

2   *Evil Inheritance*   65

3   *Lawyers and Politicians*   104

4   *The Revolution*   154

5   *The Duel*   203

6   *The Aftermath*   239

Conclusion   282

Notes   291

Bibliography   310

Sources of Illustrations   321

Index   323

LIST OF ILLUSTRATIONS

1. James, fourth Duke of Hamilton, as a young man *26*
2. Charles, fourth Baron Mohun, aged about thirty *38*
3. Boconnoc, Cornwall, the Mohun family's ancestral home *39*
4. Anne Bracegirdle *44*
5. Westminster Hall, home of the law courts and venue of Mohun's murder trials *52*
6. The Old Hall at Gawsworth, Cheshire, home of the Fitton family, inherited by the Earls of Macclesfield, and disputed by Mohun and Hamilton *67*
7. A scene from Hogarth's *Rake's Progress*, set in a private room at the Rose Tavern in London, c. 1730s *98*
8. The château at Saint-Germain, home of Hamilton's mentor, the exiled James II *128*
9. St. James's Square, Hamilton's London home after 1708 *144*
10. Queen Anne in the House of Lords, 1710 *150*
11. The gatehouse of St. James's Palace, London, during the reign of Queen Anne *159*
12. A bird's-eye view of Whitehall, about 1720 *160*
13. A London coffeehouse, about 1710 *164*
14. Gawsworth's New Hall, built by Lord Mohun after 1702 *182*
15. Hamilton after he became a Knight of the Garter and Master of the Ordnance, 1712 *199*
16. John Churchill, first Duke of Marlborough *204*
17. Marlborough House, London *206*
18. Trade card of a master swordsman *222*
19. A view of the western edge of London, about 1730; in the background, Buckingham House, right, and Westminster Abbey, left *231*
20. Price's Lodge in Hyde Park *232*
21. A contemporary depiction of the duel, showing Maccartney murdering Hamilton *235*
22. The old church of St. Martin-in-the-Fields, where Mohun was buried *262*

ACKNOWLEDGMENTS

This book began as a broad investigation of the unification of England and Scotland in 1707. As I continued my research, I found myself becoming more and more interested in what was initially merely a fascinating story: the life, and more particularly the death, of a central figure in the Anglo-Scottish Union, James, fourth Duke of Hamilton. He was a crucial player in the events surrounding the Union, and his end, in a duel with the notorious rake Charles, fourth Baron Mohun, sparked my imagination. Several historians had already reconstructed a good deal of both men's lives. In the 1920s literary historian Robert Forsythe told Lord Mohun's story, and in the 1970s Rosalind Marshall examined the household of Hamilton's mother, the Duchess Anne, in minute and fascinating detail. In the 1950s Raymond Richards wrote a wonderful history of the Manor of Gawsworth, part of the property Mohun and Hamilton fought over. Thirty years ago Harry Dickinson wrote an article about the duel itself. All these works have been important in shaping my view of the subject, and I am greatly indebted to these authors.

My own account of the Mohun-Hamilton struggle is based on research in archives and libraries as far-flung as San Marino, California, and Haddington, Scotland, and I have accumulated a store of debts that I can never repay, but must acknowledge. The staffs of the Public Record Office in London and the Scottish Record Office in Edinburgh bore with great patience my requests for never-consulted classes of legal records, my bemusement at eighteenth-century legal form, and my fouling the tables and air with the soot and coal dust that time had deposited on the documents. The staff at the British Library bent the rules and allowed a foreign scholar in a hurry to consult more documents than he had a right to, and the staff at Lennoxlove House in Haddington endured a personal invasion of their premises with admirable grace and aplomb. In the United States I owe thanks to the librarians and staff of the Middleton Library at Louisiana State University, the Firestone Library in Princeton, and especially the Widener Library at Harvard University.

The aid and comfort provided by friends and colleagues have made my work seem effortless—indeed, for some of them it may have appeared that all the effort was on their part, rather than mine. John Fielding acted as chauffeur and sounding board, carting me hither and yon in England as I chased down sites connected with my two lords. Peter Lake's brilliant critical sense never failed me, and Tom Cogswell generously read the manuscript and offered me the benefit of his advice. Sandy Solomon cast a poet's eye over Chapter 1 and taught me more than a few things about how to write. I am especially indebted to Mark Kishlansky, who made a fruitful semester of reading and research in Cambridge possible by clearing out of his library study and listening to my monologues about Mohun, Hamilton, land law, and late Stuart politics. Two other friends have a particular claim upon my gratitude. Angus, the fifteenth Duke of Hamilton, warned me when we first spoke that he was "not very ducal." He was correct, for throughout the research of this book he has been a prince: unfailingly generous of his time, hospitality, and interest. He made his family papers available to me at short notice and kindly put me up in his family home. I could not have asked for better treatment. I am no less grateful to Charles Royster. Throughout this project Charlie has acted as unpaid research assistant, editor, and cheerleader. Nothing I could say would be adequate repayment for the hours he has devoted to this book; a glance through the end notes will give the reader only a barely adequate sense of the magnitude of Charlie's assistance. And if the reader enjoys the prose offered in these chapters, he must also thank Royster, whose editorial skills did much to render them readable.

The list of others who have helped me in this project could continue ad infinitum, but some cannot be left out: Maribel Dietz, Christine Kooi, Paul Paskoff, John Rodrigue, Chuck Shindo, and

Meredith Veldman have all conspired to make the history department at Louisiana State University the best place in the world to work. Lauren Osborne, my editor, is another whose assistance has been critical. She has been a supporter of this project from nearly the beginning, and her suggestions for revisions have helped make this a much better book. Lauren's patience and good sense have rescued me from more than a few editorial blunders. Elaine Chubb, who undertook the arduous task of copy-editing the manuscript, has done superb work. She rescued me from many errors, large and small, and for that I am grateful.

My family deserves far more gratitude than I could express; my wife, Sue Marchand, has always been my wisest counsel and staunchest friend. Our son, Charles Albert, arrived just as this work was being completed, but he has enlivened the final preparations of the manuscript in ways I cannot enumerate but will always appreciate. My parents have always supported the eccentricities of their eldest son, and the only regret I have is that my father did not live to see this work in print. It is to them that I dedicate this book.

ENGLISH MONARCHS
1485–1714

HOUSE OF TUDOR

Henry VII	*1485–1509*
Henry VIII	*1509–1547*
Edward VI	*1547–1553*
Mary I	*1553–1558*
Elizabeth I	*1558–1603*

HOUSE OF STUART

James I (VI of Scotland)	*1603–1625*
Charles I	*1625–1649*
Interregnum	*1649–1660*
Charles II	*1660–1685*
James II	*1685–1689*
William III & Mary II (joint monarchs)	*1689–1694*
William III (sole monarch)	*1694–1702*
Anne	*1702–1714*

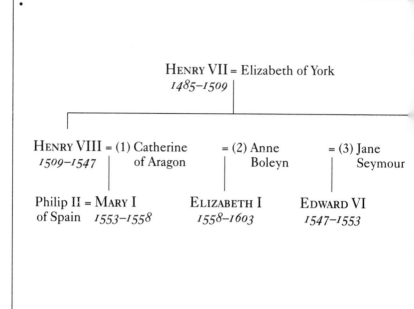

HENRY VII = Elizabeth of York
1485–1509

HENRY VIII = (1) Catherine   = (2) Anne   = (3) Jane
1509–1547   of Aragon   Boleyn   Seymour

Philip II = MARY I   ELIZABETH I   EDWARD VI
of Spain   *1553–1558*   *1558–1603*   *1547–1553*

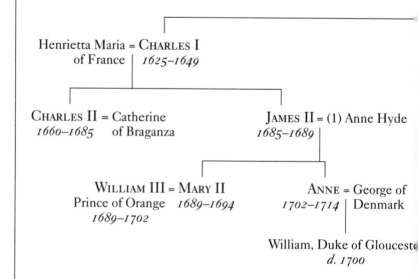

Henrietta Maria = CHARLES I
of France | *1625–1649*

CHARLES II = Catherine   JAMES II = (1) Anne Hyde
1660–1685   of Braganza   *1685–1689*

WILLIAM III = MARY II   ANNE = George of
Prince of Orange   *1689–1694*   *1702–1714* | Denmark
1689–1702

William, Duke of Glouceste
d. 1700

English Monarchs

Showing the Stuart and Hanoverian Succession

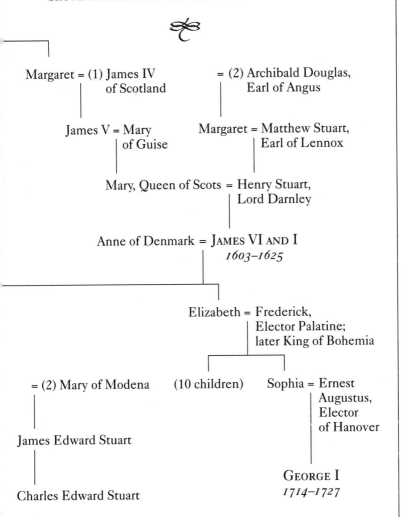

Margaret = (1) James IV of Scotland   = (2) Archibald Douglas, Earl of Angus

James V = Mary of Guise   Margaret = Matthew Stuart, Earl of Lennox

Mary, Queen of Scots = Henry Stuart, Lord Darnley

Anne of Denmark = JAMES VI AND I
1603–1625

Elizabeth = Frederick, Elector Palatine; later King of Bohemia

= (2) Mary of Modena   (10 children)   Sophia = Ernest Augustus, Elector of Hanover

James Edward Stuart

Charles Edward Stuart

GEORGE I
1714–1727

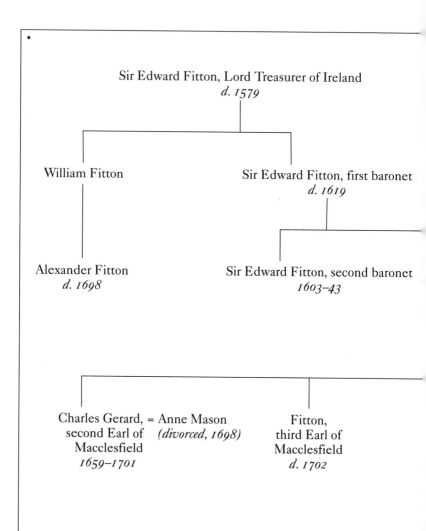

Sir Edward Fitton, Lord Treasurer of Ireland
d. 1579

William Fitton

Sir Edward Fitton, first baronet
d. 1619

Alexander Fitton
d. 1698

Sir Edward Fitton, second baronet
1603–43

Charles Gerard, = Anne Mason
second Earl of   *(divorced, 1698)*
Macclesfield
1659–1701

Fitton,
third Earl of
Macclesfield
d. 1702

THE
FITTON-GERARD-MOHUN-HAMILTON
CONNECTION

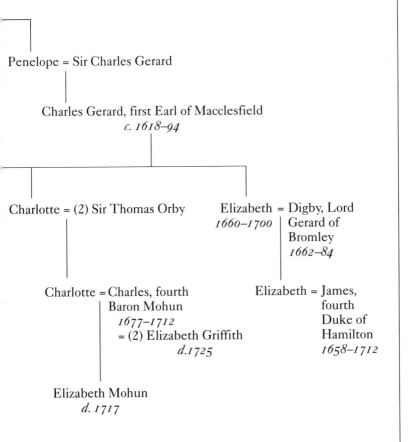

Penelope = Sir Charles Gerard

Charles Gerard, first Earl of Macclesfield
c. 1618–94

Charlotte = (2) Sir Thomas Orby

Elizabeth = Digby, Lord
1660–1700 Gerard of
Bromley
1662–84

Charlotte = Charles, fourth
Baron Mohun
1677–1712
= (2) Elizabeth Griffith
d.1725

Elizabeth = James,
fourth
Duke of
Hamilton
1658–1712

Elizabeth Mohun
d. 1717

DUKE HAMILTON
IS DEAD!

Introduction

TO be born into an aristocratic family in late-seventeenth-century Britain was to be fortunate indeed. The handful of aristocrats who sat in Charles II's House of Lords had few social rivals. Ordinary people, engaged in the struggle for survival, growing the food served at aristocratic tables or laboring to produce the luxurious garments that clothed aristocratic backs, might be forgiven for thinking of the lords and their ladies as Olympian figures. Like the gods of old, they cut a swath through the mortal world of labor, dispensing fortune and tragedy alike from their expensive coaches; noble patronage might raise an artisan to fame and fortune, but a peer's enmity could bring ruin. In the countryside, aristocrats dominated their neighborhood, providing social and political leadership; even gentlemen of fortune hankered for their noble neighbors' condescension. In the capital, peers set the fashions; Londoners scrutinized their dress and gossiped about their personal lives. They competed with one another for royal favor at court and maneuvered feverishly to maintain their power in the King's Council or in the Upper House of Parliament, careless of the consequences for their social inferiors.

To live within this charmed circle ensured a life of luxury and ease, of power and prestige denied to nearly all the rest of the King's subjects. And yet in the decades following the Stuart Restoration (the return of the monarchy, under Charles II) in 1660 and ending with the death of Charles II's niece Queen Anne in 1714, many peers felt themselves beleaguered as never before. Social and economic change threw many old verities into question and advanced rivals to aristocratic dominance: new forms of wealth challenged the primacy of the land. Shrewd English and Scots merchants carried home the riches of Asia and the Caribbean to feed a consumer market that grew larger and more socially diverse year by year. Worldwide war with France spurred the development of ever more sophisticated forms of capital: the "moneyed interest" so despised by traditionalists built fortunes for men who in previous generations would have contented themselves with far more modest aspirations. "So that *power*," wrote Swift, "which according to the old maxim, was used to follow *land*, is now gone over for money."[1] Nobles were not reluctant to compete upon these new playing fields—they invested in the national debt, snapped up shares in the East India and Darien Companies, and sometimes even indulged in colonial adventures in the newly settled lands of North America. But their former easy dominance of the levers of economic power became more difficult to maintain as more and more rivals crowded to the fore, men like the notorious Thomas Pitt, whose ruthless exploitation of the Indies made him the first of the "nabobs."

Many peers struggled against mounting debts, yet were obliged to contract still more debt in order to maintain their social positions. When every shopkeeper could afford the utensils required to serve tea and even the porters in the street ate West Indian sugar, nobility was bound to get increasingly expensive. Elaborate tableware, luxurious linens, bigger and more stylish houses—all seemed increasingly necessary and were often purchased on credit. Debts—many owed to tradesmen or City money men—piled up, forcing aristocrats to press their tenants for higher rents, requiring them to compromise the paternalism that tradition demanded toward their inferiors.

Financial extravagance combined with the appearance of so many new claimants to gentility encouraged extravagant behavior as well. Contemporaries complained of the increase of immorality and incivility in the later seventeenth century. Blasphemy, gambling, drunkenness, infidelity, and violence seemed worse than anyone could remember. "We became," Bishop Gilbert Burnet recalled, "deeply corrupted in principle: a disbelief in revealed religion and a profane mocking at the Christian faith . . . became avowed and scandalous."[2] Divines and moralists warned their fellows of the impending wrath of God. Queen Mary II patronized the good work of the Societies for the Reformation of Manners. Still, manners continued unreformed: every night taverns rang with the shouts of drunken gentlemen and nobles. The streets and back alleys of the capital swarmed with prostitutes and cutthroats in search of fashionable prey. Samuel Johnson remembered his early-eighteenth-century boyhood in the provincial city of Lichfield, where "all the decent people . . . got drunk every night and were not the worse thought of."[3] Legend has it that the lawyers of Lincoln's Inn, hosting Charles II, were so drunk by the time the King arrived for his meal that they were incapable of standing. Charles, whose moral example left his more godly subjects speechless with exasperation, promptly joined the party and dispensed with the formality altogether—a privilege Lincoln's Inn maintains to this day.[4]

Alcohol and blurred lines of social demarcation led to a dramatic increase in violence among the nobility. Aristocrats battered their inferiors, they battered their wives, and they beat one another with increasing frequency. In 1701 the Countess of Anglesey, a bastard daughter of James II, accused her husband of savagely mistreating her: he kicked her down the stairs, pinched her until her arms and breast were black with bruises, and in a fury told a servant, "I will make my wife humble. She is a king's daughter but I will make her as humble as a kitchen wench!"[5] And nobles practiced violence beyond the home as well. The second Duke of Grafton, a grandson of Charles II, beat a coachman in the middle of a London street, while the Duke of Leeds shot his son's steward.[6] The duel, seemingly out of fashion in the sterner days of Oliver Cromwell, revived and flourished under the later Stuarts. Gentlemen and nobles fought over two hundred duels in Charles II's reign alone, and the custom continued unabated into the eighteenth century.[7] Few peers lived their lives without at some point entering the field of honor, as either a second or a principal. Many were seriously wounded, and some died, fighting over what we today would consider trivial matters: an argument at court, a careless word spoken at a gaming table, or a disputed point of precedence.

Commonplace disagreements arising in the course of everyday life led many peers into deadly conflict, but at least as many disputes had their origins in political differences. The rise of party politics in England added still more tension to aristocratic lives, for with his seat in the Lords a peer was a politician by birth. Moreover, the tumultuous history of seventeenth-century Britain made politics a dangerous game. From 1642 to 1646 Royalist supporters of Charles I fought against his Parliamentarian enemies in a vicious civil war. Parliament's victory, sealed by the King's execution in 1649, was ultimately succeeded by the military dictatorship of Oliver Cromwell. Peers bore a disproportionate share of the costs of these struggles, and political violence threatened their lives and fortunes for the rest of the century.

The disintegration of Cromwell's Protectorate following his death in 1658 did nothing to restore stability, nor did it return when Charles II received a joyous welcome in London on his May birthday two years later. Political divisions founded upon civil war loyalties reemerged in the 1670s. Tories, harkening back to the absolutist royalism of Charles I, resisted the attempts of

Whigs to limit the power of the Crown and to alter the succession by excluding Charles II's Roman Catholic brother (and heir), James, Duke of York, from the throne. The Exclusion Crisis of 1679–81 solidified party differences. Tories, defined by their loyalty to the legitimate succession and the established Church of England, struggled against Whigs, who favored limits on monarchical power, were violently anti-Catholic, and sympathized with Protestant dissenters from the established Church. Both sides identified their opponents with the bugbears of the recent past: Tories were often stigmatized as pro-Catholic supporters of arbitrary government, while Whigs were painted with the brush of rebellion and regicide.

These political differences went well beyond the realm of Parliamentary politics. Led by Charles II's bastard son the Duke of Monmouth, radical Whigs led an unsuccessful rebellion in 1685 against the newly crowned James II and his Tory supporters. Hundreds died on the battlefield at Sedgemoor and the hangman dispatched hundreds more. But nemesis arrived for James only three years later. Many peers feared the King's pro-Catholic policies, and James soon found himself the exiled pensioner of France's Louis XIV, his throne usurped by his son-in-law William of Orange, now King William III. Some Tories, inflexibly wedded to the legitimate succession, followed their master into exile or led opposition to the new government at home, and were condemned as "Jacobites" (those who supported James II and the "legitimate" succession through his son, James Edward Stuart). Even Tories who made their peace with William were excluded from power and often threatened with government oppression.

The struggle between Whig and Tory divided all the political nation, but for those at the top the stakes were highest. The dramatic shifts of political fortunes represented by the Restoration, exclusion, Monmouth's rebellion, and the 1688 Revolution taught a grim lesson: losers lost everything. Penury, exile, and even death were the potential rewards of a poor political choice.

Almost constant war with France from 1689 until 1713 further sharpened the conflict; the war militarized the nobility, who served the state as generals and colonels and who internalized the violent ethos of the camp. Until the death of Queen Anne in 1714 and even after the accession of her German cousin George I, political differences among British peers sparked personal enmity and public feuds.

Complicating matters still further was the ancient hatred that divided the Scots and English. Although they had shared a royal family since 1603, they shared little else. An essential part of making Britain truly "great" and standing up to the aggression of a confident Louis XIV was a solution to the divisions separating the two kingdoms. As long as the Stuarts ruled both kingdoms, which were still technically independent states, the problem of British unity could be discreetly ignored. But the childlessness of William and Mary and Queen Anne's inability to provide an heir reopened the question of the Anglo-Scottish relationship. If the 1701 Act of Settlement provided for Hanover's ruling family to inherit the English throne, it had nothing to say about Scotland. Who would reign in Edinburgh after Queen Anne died? As in every other matter of political importance, this, too, divided Whigs and Tories and added yet another volatile element to an already inflammable mixture. The peers who provided much of the leadership in the late-Stuart British monarchy faced daunting problems, and there was no consensus about how to resolve them.

The decades surrounding the turn of the eighteenth century were crucial in the formation of what historians have often called the "aristocratic century." Crushed by the ruthless power of the Tudor monarchs, the English nobility entered the Stuart age far less triumphantly than they had the previous century. In 1485 Thomas, Lord Stanley, placed Richard III's battered crown upon Henry VII's head on Bosworth Field, but in succeeding years royal authority brought aristocratic kingmaking to heel. It was not until the arrival of the Stuarts in 1603 that the peerage began its long march back to power. After sacrificing their all on behalf of Charles I, by 1688 the nobles were once again prepared to make kings. William of Orange's invitation came from a group of powerful nobles, and James's failure had much to do with the refusal of peers—both Whig and Tory—to support him at the crucial moment. The British nobility emerged from this time of troubles remarkably well: they met the challenges of social and economic change and mastered them. They defeated the centralizing tendencies of ambitious Stuart kings and consolidated their hold upon the reins of political power through the House of Lords. But the course of this triumph was neither smooth nor linear: there were many lessons to be learned.

Describing the creation of an aristocratic century is not easy, but a focus upon the lives of two British peers sheds light on what is an undeniably complex story. Born on the same April day nineteen years apart, James Douglas Hamilton, fourth Duke of Hamilton, and Charles Mohun, fourth Baron Mohun, experienced all the shifting fortunes of their class and struggled to cope with the challenges facing all their peers.[8] They shared much: both soldiers, both rakes, both ambitious politicians. And yet they were separated by an enmity that grew over the course of time into murderous hatred: one a Scot, one an Englishman; one Tory, one Whig. Both desperately in need of cash to sustain their political careers, they clashed over the possession of an estate large enough to solve their worries.

Mohun and Hamilton grew up in a world where traditional values were under siege and their own position in society was threatened by debt and a political system dominated by party. The salvation they and so many of their contemporaries sought came in the form of wealth and political power. The lessons they learned in the course of their rivalry would be crucial for the revival of aristocratic dominance in the eighteenth century: mastering the art of parliamentary politics, deploying the resources of the law, and exploiting the opportunities created by new forms of wealth. Mohun and Hamilton's careers touched every element of the late-Stuart aristocratic experience: the moral crisis of the day, political conflict, war, and economic stress.

But despite its utility as a window upon a society under great pressure, their struggle was nevertheless an intensely personal one. Charles and James were real men who struggled with real problems: looming bankruptcy, Jacobite treason, demanding wives and creditors, and even murder figure in their story. Both spent their lives fighting for a place at the center of the British aristocratic world, facing difficulties that overwhelmed others but moving relentlessly forward, rising despite adversity. Their personalities and the choices they made led them very nearly to their goal, and in the process their lives became inextricably, and fatefully, connected. The rivalry ended abruptly, on a cold November morning in 1712, as they brought their hopes and fears onto the field of honor and fought one last battle for the place each believed he deserved.

ONE

A Season of Youth

GODLINESS went out of fashion when the Stuarts returned from their Continental exile in the spring of 1660, and though there was no shortage of people to lament the immorality of the times, the royal example encouraged misbehavior. The Queen Mother, Henrietta Maria, her life blighted by the execution of her husband, Charles I, knew a great deal about the failings of the new generation, and especially those of her rakish boy, the King. The English were often scandalized by Charles II's irregular life: the news that the man who claimed to be, "by the grace of God," King of England, France, Scotland, and Ireland had been creeping through a Whitehall garden in the pursuit of yet another loose woman was hardly likely to reassure anxious moralists about the state of their society. In this climate two women whose son and grandson would later be linked prepared to send their children to court.

Anne, Duchess of Hamilton, and Catherine, Lady Mohun, were in some respects opposites.* The duchess, a devout Presbyterian,

---

* In ascending order, the peerage consisted of five ranks: baron, viscount, earl, marquess, and duke. All but dukes were referred to in ordinary speech as "Lord": "Lord Mohun" and "Lord Clarendon," even though Mohun was a baron and Clarendon an earl. In most cases wives derived their titles from their husbands, although rarely, as

wife of one of Scotland's most powerful men as well as a power in her own right, was possibly the richest woman north of the Scottish border. Her lands stretched across Scotland's waist from Edinburgh to Glasgow, and her house, which dominated the Clyde Valley just south of Glasgow, was imposing enough to be called Hamilton "Palace." Lady Mohun, on the other hand, was the widow of Warwick, second Baron Mohun, a nobleman of distinctly minor importance whose family lived in relative modesty in Cornwall. Her peculiar Norman name, though it argued for the antiquity of her husband's family, invariably perplexed strangers, who never pronounced it correctly—"Moon"—on the first try. Her odd name aside, Lady Mohun's Catholic faith would certainly have disgusted the duchess—the seventeenth-century Presbyterian horror for all things Catholic was only matched by the Catholic's equal revulsion for Presbyterians. Fortunately, the two women probably never met, because in their old age neither of them cared to travel to London.

And yet these women, so different in some ways, shared more than an antipathy toward the court and its corrupt London home. Like virtually every noble family in the British Isles, the Hamiltons and the Mohuns paid a high price during the civil wars of the mid-century. Both families had sided with Charles I, and Parliament's victory over the King's forces had left them in serious trouble. Lord Mohun, who raised a regiment of infantry at his own expense, found himself and his estate subject to punitive fines and taxes in the aftermath of defeat. The Duchess of Hamilton suffered still more. Parliament executed her father in 1649, an ironic martyrdom, for the King had not only distrusted him but even jailed him for his suspect loyalty. Her uncle, the second Duke of Hamilton, died in the service of Charles II not two years

---

with Anne, Duchess of Hamilton, a woman held a title in her own right. Complicating matters still further is the fact that the forms of address had not yet been completely fixed in the late-Stuart period; one sometimes sees references, for example, to "Lord Hamilton," despite his rank as a duke.

later, killed in the disastrous Royalist defeat at Worcester. The duchess inherited her uncle's title, but with it came the unwelcome attention of the Commonwealth's authorities, who seized her property and expelled her from her house. Both women endured the years of Cromwell's regime under the threat of penury.

The Restoration of Charles II ended the immediate threats from a hostile government: the political climate changed dramatically from the moment the handsome young King landed at Dover to the frantic cheers of his subjects. But the legacy of the wars remained. Weakened estates and political divisions dogged the kingdom's noble families, many of whom were bitterly disappointed by Charles II's inability to make their losses whole. Nevertheless the prospect of renewed royal favor drew the ambitious to London, where they prowled around the King's person, competing for power and place. This unrelenting search for courtly success, conducted by many with an ugly ruthlessness that was the despair of contemporary moralists, ultimately drew the families of Lady Mohun and the duchess together.

Lady Mohun's eldest son, Charles, was probably the first to arrive in the metropolis. Born in 1649, the year of Charles I's execution, Charles grew up in straitened circumstances, and at his father's death in 1665 he inherited large debts with his title.[1] Though the family's lands in Cornwall and Devon must have brought in a substantial income, mostly from rents, nearly all the money went to creditors, including the annual £1,000 the second baron left his wife. These heavy charges, to say nothing of the high cost of living fashionably in London, reduced the third Lord Mohun to near desperation. Like many of his peers, he financed his lifestyle through a constant round of debt: mortgages, bonds, and credit extended by merchants provided the food, housing, and consumer goods that he and much of the English aristocracy and gentry relied upon to distinguish themselves in an increasingly prosperous society. In the 1660s a laborer in the fields or a porter in the streets of London lived on less than £20 a year, and a gentleman could live comfortably on an annual income of a few hundred pounds. Many merchants and tradesmen found their own incomes rivaling those of the gentry in the boom following the Restoration. But nobility demanded spending well beyond that expected from others; a peer's social standing depended upon high living—and what constituted "high living" was changing quickly, as gentlemen competed to outspend their lowborn rivals.

The second Duke of Buckingham, to take only one example among many, piled up debts of well over £160,000 in the 1660s and '70s before his creditors finally called a halt to his spending.* He was not alone in being tempted by new houses, coaches, horses, art, and clothes. Fortunately, deficit financing could maintain a peer at a far higher level of consumption than his income warranted, but the system depended upon lenders' confidence. Shopkeepers sold to their noble clients on credit to boast of their high-class clientele, and to augment their profits. Knowing the risks, merchants routinely inflated their prices for ordinary goods by as much as 100 percent. They kept a wary eye upon their customers' estates and income. When they concluded that a borrower was overextended, they stopped the flow of goods, and the embarrassed noble faced a scramble for cash.

Like that of his peers, therefore, Mohun's social position depended upon the judgment of an array of men and women who ranked far below him: tailors, grocers, vintners, and even washerwomen. They conspired to maintain his extravagant life only as long as they could be sure that he was creditworthy. While they

---

* Translating the value of money across the centuries is notoriously difficult, but some idea of the size of Buckingham's debts might be gained from the fact that the sum would support 8,000 laborers and their families for a full year—enough to populate a large provincial town. To take an example from higher up the social scale, the sum could enable 1,280 urban tradesmen to live quite comfortably, on £125 each annually. To put it another way, the duke's debts would have bought 19,200,000 pounds of beef or no less than 153,600,000 farthing loaves of bread, the staple of the poor.

might pull their hats off when they presented their bills, this cast of characters nevertheless had considerable power over his reputation. Mohun's first direct experience of this power came in 1667, when one of his creditors, patience at an end, sued for a debt of £300. Thereafter Mohun's financial standing threatened to vanish like a mirage: shopkeepers and other lenders rushed to secure their debts. He could not be arrested for debt himself (a longtime privilege of peers, the monarch's hereditary counselors) but this did not save him from the constant din of complaining tradesmen. Family servants were arrested, and the door of his London lodgings resounded with the knocks of importunate lenders.[2]

In these circumstances there was only one thing that any self-respecting peer could do: find a rich wife. Marriage to an heiress was one of the few ways, apart from royal favor, that an impecunious nobleman could recover from financial catastrophe. Status-conscious fathers often traded cash for social standing, and many peers were more than willing to oblige in the pursuit of ready money. Certainly Lord Mohun was. His search for a well-endowed wife was under way by about 1670, but was hampered by his reputation. Three years earlier there had been a scandal when John Dolben, Bishop of Rochester, was alleged to have "put his hand into the opening in the front of the hose of Lord Mohun, a boy on account of his age, but not on account of the beauty of his face."[3] More important, however, was the paucity of Mohun's income. Most annoying of all was the money siphoned away from his property by his mother, who obstinately refused to part with a penny of her jointure or, better still, die. Instead, she continued to live piously in her now increasingly ramshackle Cornish home while her son's debts mounted. At last, in an effort to make himself a more attractive candidate for marriage, Mohun was reduced to suing his own mother. In February 1671 he claimed before the House of Lords, the highest court in the land, that Lady Mohun's willfulness threatened to deprive him of his estate. Despite what he called his repeated "dutiful applications" to her, the old lady clung obstinately to the deeds and papers he claimed he needed to maintain his rights. It would seem that the Lords were skeptical of Mohun's tender regard for his mother, however, because they refused to act on his petition.[4]

This result no doubt caused Mohun to redouble his efforts to find a wife, but it did nothing to strengthen his bargaining position with prospective fathers-in-law. It was not until 1673 that the search finally paid off. The Earl of Anglesey's daughter Phillippa was, as subsequent events would illustrate, a burden her father was eager to unload. Not that the earl was himself beyond reproach—the diarist Samuel Pepys wrote that Anglesey was "one of the greatest knaves in the world," and James, first Duke of Ormonde, a good judge of character, said that he was no better than a common thief.[5]

As far as Arthur, Earl of Anglesey, was concerned, though, the proposed match was a great opportunity. In April 1672 he wrote in his diary that Lord Mohun had "moved me with great civility" for Phillippa's hand—an application as unexpected as it was welcome. Even more pleasant were Mohun's words on the next day, when the young lord repeated his request, "leaving everything else to myself, whether I gave anything or nothing." As Phillippa was the Earl's only child, Mohun must surely have expected a substantial settlement—but he expected too much if he was relying on Anglesey's sense of fairness. Mohun's pledge was most welcome: the heavy cost of a daughter's dowry could substantially weaken an aristocrat's estate, and no doubt Anglesey was delighted to find Phillippa's suitor to be so reasonable.[6] Mohun's barony would ordinarily entitle him to a dowry of at least £5,000, but undoubtedly Anglesey used Charles's weak financial position to his own advantage.

We do not know what sort of bargain the wily old earl extracted from his new son-in-law, just that Phillippa and Charles were married sometime before September 1674. It is clear that from the first they were desperately unhappy together. Mohun was probably disappointed in his wife's financial settlement, and he was clearly displeased by her strong will. On Phillippa's side there was the problem of a husband who brought with him a multitude of debts and a taste for debauchery. They moved into a house in Drury Lane, a fashionable but not too expensive address, and proceeded to make each other extremely miserable.

Seventeenth-century Londoners lived intimately; houses even in streets like Drury Lane were fitted tightly together and neighbors knew a great deal about what went on next door or across the narrow street. Everyone who could afford them kept servants, who were both cheap and ubiquitous, and who passed on local news with the regularity, if not the reliability, of a modern newspaper. Lord and Lady Mohun's neighbors must have buzzed with tales of their life together. Exactly what caused the titanic rows between the two remains a matter for surmise: his carousing with notorious men like the Duke of Buckingham and Lord Lovelace, her sharp tongue, and their mutual debts could have sparked more than a few domestic battles. Lord Anglesey found himself forced to act as a peacemaker time and again. In September 1674 Anglesey recorded a violent dispute he had with Phillippa over her most recent marital spat. She and Charles were "most desperately out" once more, and he placed most of the blame upon his daughter, who told him that "she would be a common whore" before she submitted to her husband's will. Seventeenth-century fathers were hardly used to such defiance from their children, and Lord Anglesey was in a passion: "if she had not been married I had beat her, I did call her 'impudent baggage' and said she carried herself like a whore and left her with resolution to see her no more."

There is clearly more to this story than meets the eye, however, because part of Anglesey's complaint against Phillippa was that although Mohun had "sworn never to strike her nor give her ill words," she refused to be reconciled with her husband. The promise itself implies that he had already abused her. In any event, a father's love for his daughter eventually reasserted itself. In less than three months Anglesey was writing: "Spent most of the day in reconciling my daughter Mohun and her husband, and supt with them and left them in bed."[7] As bitterly divided as Charles and his wife often were, however, they could at times stand shoulder to shoulder in the face of mutual enemies: their creditors. Time did nothing to ease the financial pressures on the young couple, and the demands of disgruntled merchants and shopkeepers grew more insistent.

In October 1676 Phillippa turned away two aggressive duns with the promise that they would be paid as soon as her husband's rents arrived from the country. The women departed grumbling, and then nursed their grievances over brandy at a local grog shop. Encouraged by the alcohol, they concluded that their previous meek acceptance of Lady Mohun's promises had been a mistake that must immediately be rectified. Somehow—probably through the promise of a share of the loot—they persuaded four men, three Irishmen and a soldier in the Life Guards, to return to Drury Lane for a showdown. These assistants, all armed and at least as drunk as their employers, accompanied them to the Mohun doorstep. There the women barged their way upstairs to have it out with her ladyship, leaving their protectors in the street. Perhaps they were unaware of Phillippa's own determined nature, but few words were exchanged before the scene shifted from reason to chaos: the voices upstairs rose to a screech as the shopwomen attacked Phillippa, who returned as good as she got. Meanwhile, the men downstairs set up a raucous cry for Lord Mohun: "Where is my lord, the son of a bitch!" "By God we'll do his business for him!" Alarmed by the outbreak of what appeared to be a riot in his own home, Charles dashed for his sword and pistols. As his wife battled the women in the drawing room—they had now progressed to spitting at their noble customer—Lord Mohun was more seriously engaged below. With the aid of one of his servants he withstood the initial assault from the thugs. In the close quarters of the hall and stairway, Mohun defended himself against his opponents' drawn swords. As the men pressed forward into the house, he fired a shot, blasting a hole through the hat of one of his assailants, and he would very probably have hit another had his second pistol not misfired. By now the assailants had attracted the attention of the entire neighborhood, and thought it best to withdraw. The final outcome of the Battle of Drury Lane was a nick on Lord Mohun's hand, a seriously wounded hat, and one later casualty, a family servant caught and beaten by one of the thugs sometime after the main assault.[8]

Mohun's resort to deadly weapons was hardly surprising. Male gentility was defined by the bearing of arms, and most gentlemen were prepared to use them—not only in defense of their homes from impromptu collection agents, but also in defense of their honor. Englishmen had been dueling for a century, but duels increased dramatically after the Restoration. Consecutive monarchs had tried, and failed, to eliminate them, and after 1660 duels became more common than ever. In a society where a stray comment could be taken as a personal affront, where men routinely drank alcohol from the time they awoke until they at last staggered home to bed, and where every gentleman wore a razor-sharp sword at his side, violence was to be expected. When engaged in what was called an "affair of honor," there could be no turning back. Even though society evolved elaborate rules of civility designed to obviate the need for dueling, contemporary social reality made these rules more and more difficult to follow. A political disagreement or even a minor fracas over a seat in church could spark a deadly conflict, and civility was abandoned in the defense of honor. For a gentleman to refuse a challenge amounted to the surrender of his rank, and impecunious, status-conscious young peers like Lord Mohun were among the most vulnerable. Their shaky finances and social uncertainty imperiled their high position, and many men such as Mohun grew exceedingly sensitive to perceived insults.

Perhaps in part because of his own insecurity, financial and otherwise, Mohun seems to have gone out of his way to associate
with the most extravagant, flamboyant, and violent of his peers.
His closest companions included Lord Wharton's heir, infamous
for demonstrating his contempt for the Church of England by
defecating in a parish pulpit; Lord Mordaunt, for whom debauchery was more a career than a hobby; and his political mentor, the
Earl of Shaftesbury. Shaftesbury campaigned to deny the Duke of
York, Charles II's Catholic brother, his right to succeed Charles,
who had no legitimate children. Shaftesbury's political radical-
ism—as strident as any seen since the days of the Commonwealth—attracted a coterie of young peers like Mohun and his
hot-tempered friend William, Lord Cavendish. They had little to
lose and much to gain from a new political dispensation, and, in
keeping with the recklessness of their mentor, Mohun and his
friends were quick to draw a sword.

Politically tinged violence could erupt anywhere, even at court.
Charles II's entertainments were open to virtually anyone of
respectable appearance, and his own taste for pleasure ensured
that balls in the rambling palace at Whitehall were lively, well-
attended affairs. The atmosphere at Whitehall was usually over-
heated. Hundreds of anxious courtiers strove daily for recognition
there, competing with rivals for the favor of the King and his ministers. But in the late 1670s, as political tensions between the enemies and supporters of the Duke of York escalated, competition
intensified. In November 1676 Mohun's friend Cavendish quarreled at a court ball with John Power, an Irish officer in the service
of Louis XIV of France. To Cavendish, working for the arch-
Catholic King of France seemed hardly better than serving
Antichrist, and in his encounter with John Power he may have
said so. No gentleman, least of all an Irish soldier, could bear such
an affront without response, and a duel was arranged for November 17. Cavendish chose his friend Mohun as his second.

Serving as a second in a late-Stuart duel meant more than ensur-
ing fair play. Seconds often engaged in the fighting themselves,

usually against their opposite numbers. Theoretically a duel was combat bound by rules designed to make it less deadly and more civilized than mere assault; in practice the rules often became irrelevant when men fought for their lives. Cavendish and Power's struggle rather surprisingly stuck to the classic rules: both principals and their seconds drew their weapons and fought; ultimately, Mohun and Cavendish disarmed Power and his second, another Irishman named Edward Birmingham. Honor satisfied, apparently without injury to any of the combatants, the gentlemen began to leave the field. It was at this point that the unpredictability of the contemporary code of honor asserted itself. Mohun exchanged words with Power, once again swords were drawn, and this time more than pride was wounded. Power was clearly an experienced swordsman, and Mohun, for all his bravado, was no match for him. Furious at being bested by Lord Cavendish, Power fought this time with deadly skill. Mohun was "run into the guts," as Power's sword passed through his opponent's lower belly into his thigh.[9]

Any kind of wound was a serious matter in the seventeenth century. Though medical knowledge was advancing, thanks to the discoveries of William Harvey and others, even aristocrats who could afford the most expensive medical treatment were more often harmed than cured by a doctor's attentions. Mohun was carried home to Drury Lane, where a pregnant Phillippa called in the physicians and awaited their verdict. On November 26 a newsletter* reported a fatal wound, but others in the know said that the news was good: serious as the case was, the doctors thought that their patient might recover—his vital organs seemed to have been spared.

Mohun now waited in his cold bedroom for his wound to heal. London winters were never comfortable before the advent of

---

* Newsletters were the ancestors of the modern newspaper. Subscribers received a handwritten letter through the post catching them up on news and gossip at home and abroad at a cost of a few pennies a letter. During this period they coexisted with a growing number of printed newspapers, some weekly, although later daily titles appeared. Eventually newspapers came to dominate the market.

central heating. Houses, even substantial ones like the Mohuns', were uninsulated: their bricks drew the fitful heat provided by smoky coal fires right out of the building, and the windows routinely let blasts of cold air sweep in around rattling panes. The patient spent the winter of 1676–77 muffled in his bedclothes, suffering the expensive ministrations of his doctors as well as the damp cold. However harsh the cold, the company cannot have been any more pleasant, given the history of Mohun's relationship with his wife. Phillippa, in the middle of her pregnancy, was undoubtedly little inclined to spend much time comforting him. To her rage and her father's alarm, Mohun received Lord Shaftesbury for a series of mysterious conferences—devising unjust wills, Lady Mohun suspected. But there was no need as yet for wills; the presence of his mentor seems to have had a positive effect on Mohun's condition. By late January 1677 Shaftesbury was confidently predicting the imminent return of his young ally to the House of Lords. He and the Duke of Buckingham demonstrated their confidence by promising one hundred pounds each to fund a spectacular party celebrating their friend's recovery. Two hundred pounds, in a world in which a few shillings paid for the most expensive meal in town, would undoubtedly have purchased a party memorable even by Restoration standards.

Unfortunately, Shaftesbury's plans were repeatedly put off. Mohun remained in his bed even after Lady Mohun brought in a French doctor to take over the case. He was still in his bed when his son and heir, named Charles after his father, was born on April 11. An ill-tempered English physician claimed that foreign incompetence was the cause of Mohun's slow recovery, but whatever the reason, Mohun was still doing poorly at summer's end.* In fact he did not leave his bed until eight o'clock on the morning of September 29, 1677, when at long last he died. His body was

---

* When Restoration doctors were not killing their patients, they were usually accusing their colleagues of killing them.

buried three days later under the floor at the east end of the church of St. Martin-in-the-Fields, not far from his home in Drury Lane.[10]

The third Lord Mohun left a bitter legacy to his infant son and two-year-old daughter, Elizabeth. Now there were two widows to support from the income of an already limited estate; the family's parlous financial situation was certain to get still worse. The third lord's response to the economic and social pressures of the Restoration was not unusual: many sought to camouflage the weakness of their positions through extravagance and radical politics, but the price of their behavior to their descendants was steep. Staggering debts and a propensity for violence were the infant Charles's principal inheritance. The new Lord Mohun would grow up fatherless, the son of a mother who manifested complete indifference to his fate. And Lady Catherine Mohun's grandson would inherit even less of her strict piety than had her debauched and unlamented son.

The Duchess of Hamilton's own impious heir would have known little more about the third Lord Mohun than what he read in the newsletters as he whiled away his time in college and on the grand tour that followed. Hamilton, born April 11, 1658, was almost a decade younger than the senior Mohun, and the two probably never met. Nor could he have imagined how fatally intertwined his life would become with that of the tiny fourth lord when he, the good-looking young heir to the duchy of Hamilton, made his first appearance at court in 1679. James Douglas-Hamilton, who during his father's lifetime bore the lesser family title of Earl of Arran, arrived in London determined to play a role in the courtly competition for place and power. Unlike Lady Catherine's son, he began his career with considerable advantages. Mohun was a mere baron, his courtly connections slender, and his fortune even more limited. Arran, on the other hand, was heir to a powerful political family and a fortune second to none in Scotland. Even though he was financially dependent upon his parents—who were not as rich as many

English aristocratic families—his prospects gave him a standing that Mohun, for all his efforts, could never have achieved.

Arran, then, enjoyed easier access to the court than did the third Lord Mohun. Yet in some ways the two men were quite similar: both were disappointments to their parents. From his youth James's parents held up a rigid standard of conduct that he either would not or could not meet. The duke and duchess practiced a Presbyterianism of the sternest sort: sobriety and godliness were what marked a Christian, and lapses were all too likely to be proof of damnation. From the huge stone palace they inhabited on the banks of the river Clyde emanated an austere morality that may have been laudable, but was certainly hard to live by.

As the eldest surviving of the duchess's thirteen children, James bore the heaviest load of expectations. When he was about twelve, his parents packed him off to Glasgow, where he studied first at the local grammar school and then at Glasgow University.* The duchess's father had attended Oxford, but Glasgow was only a few miles from Hamilton, the family had long-standing connections with both schools, and, moreover, here the duchess could keep a close watch on her boy. The Scottish universities were if anything more rigorous than the English, but by the seventeenth century the son of a peer was expected to do little more than acquire a veneer of classical learning and avoid the more public forms of debauchery. In fact, many did neither. Judged from his parents' perspective, James's education was hardly successful. As one of his few surviving letters from his college days indicates, he was no scholar: "my misfortoun has incapacitated me to be a witness to this gentilmens good behaviour," he wrote in a fractured letter of reference.[11] By the standards of the day his

---

* Grammar schools were institutions where boys were given the foundations of a gentleman's education. They would arrive already having learned to read and write, and the curriculum focused upon the classics—Latin grammar and translation in particular. After several years (boys arrived at grammar school anywhere from their eighth to their twelfth year), boys often went on to a university for further study.

education was probably more than sufficient; for the rest of his life he was considered to be a man of some culture and at least a little learning. Unfortunately, his parents cared little for the world's opinion. "Pray consider," Duchess Anne wrote to James toward the end of his scholarly career, "what credit it will be to you that after four years being at the college you come from it a dunce."[12]

Arran's mother and father worried about the "low company" he kept, and feared that he might get into the habit of extravagant spending. Despite their disappointments, however, they obviously cared very much for their son, who often talked them into indulgences that probably went against their better judgment. They allowed James a two-year-long European grand tour, though his expenses were limited to £600 annually, considerably less than many young English noblemen spent. Arran returned from the Continent with a good knowledge of French and a greater appreciation of foreign ways. His father, however, was convinced that the tour had been a terrible mistake: James still wasted his time with objectionable characters, and his tour abroad had spoiled him for a less-sophisticated life in Scotland.[13] It was with considerable trepidation that in 1679 the duke and duchess, knowing his extravagance, allowed their son to establish himself in London amid the sins of King Charles's court.

Whatever his parents' view of Arran's education, he had obviously learned something about courtly behavior, because the King honored James immediately with court office: he was appointed a gentleman of the bedchamber in January 1679. The office was neither very profitable nor very important, but it was a sign that the King had looked upon the young man with some favor. Gentlemen of the bedchamber were, in essence, the King's companions. They took turns waiting on his commands, sleeping in the palace to be nearby if ever Charles wanted attention. Charles was nearly thirty years older than Arran, but he was still a vigorous man. When he went out into St. James's Park for one of

1. James, fourth Duke of Hamilton, as a young man

his galloping strolls, whoever was on duty was obliged to keep stride and provide witty repartee if occasion required. The job was sometimes wearisome, but it offered some compensations. Because the King spent most of his nights with one or another of his mistresses, gentlemen of the bedchamber were usually left free to pursue their own love affairs after the sun set.

James wasted no time emulating his royal master; within a few years he had become the father of at least three bastard children by two different women. Rampant sexuality was standard practice at court, and Arran was determined above all to be a man of fashion. His parents' disapproval was obvious, but, after all, the King himself had an impressive brood of illegitimate children. As with his education, James conformed to the contemporary cultural standard rather than godly morality and managed to alienate his parents still further.[14]

Arran was undeniably a success at court, sexually and politically. Yet success had its price: it bred envy in his rivals. We know that he fought a duel with at least one other courtier, the third Lord Mohun's old friend Lord Mordaunt. The cause remains obscure, but the peers fought on the outskirts of London at Greenwich, and both were wounded.[15] And success cost a great deal of money. Clothes, jewelry, horses, food, and drink came pouring into Arran's household in return for bonds, promises to pay, and, very rarely, cash. His father the duke complained bitterly and threatened to cut him off. But London creditors knew that eventually Arran would be the master of one of Scotland's largest estates, and they continued to advance him money and goods—at a markup suitable to the risk involved, of course.

Despite the creeping burden of debt, Arran had every reason to be well satisfied with his life in the capital. He was a friend and confidant not only of the King but of Charles's brother James, the heir presumptive. His debts were of little concern as long as they served to aid his progress at court. A wise courtier would see twenty pounds spent on a new periwig or a thousand on jewels for the King's mistress as an investment in his own future, certain to be repaid many times over. The Crown had many lucrative offices in its gift; true, as a gentleman of the bedchamber Arran earned little or nothing of immediate value, but the position was a first step on a ladder that could lead very high.

The wisdom of Arran's investment was confirmed when in 1683 Charles dispatched him to Paris as ambassador extraordinary. His mission, which was to offer congratulations upon the birth of Louis XIV's grandson, affirmed his high standing at court. Unfortunately, this honor was an expensive one, for an ambassador was rarely reimbursed for even a small part of his expenses, and no ambassador could afford to skimp on ceremony and extravagance. But the King's confidence was worth more than money, and James, whose admiration for France had not dimmed since his grand tour, was delighted to go.

The court of Louis XIV was far more magnificent than that presided over by Charles II, and Arran was in his element at Versailles. That vast palace, only recently completed, was a glittering reminder of the prizes awaiting the successful courtier. Marble, gold leaf, priceless tapestries, and solid silver furniture decorated what was already the center of the civilized world, and James, far from the disapproving eyes of his parents, threw himself into life there. He mastered the intricate ceremony that was designed to raise the Sun King above ordinary mortals—bowing to the King's food as it made its stately way through the halls of the palace to the royal table, gazing reverently at the morning levee, where Louis was solemnly dressed from his stockings to his elaborate wig by the highest nobles in the land. And, as he did in London, Arran charmed his royal host. Though perhaps a dunce in his mother's eyes, he was obviously fluent enough in French for the King to regard him as an interesting companion. Louis appointed him one of his aides-de-camp and took him on two campaigns in 1684, during which the ambassador learned a little bit about soldiering.

Arran returned triumphant to England in February 1685 with the good wishes of King Louis, whose envoy was instructed to push for the young man's advancement at court. Charles obliged happily, and not only reinstated Arran as a gentleman of the bedchamber but at last gave him a post of some pecuniary value: Master of the Wardrobe. The Wardrobe was an ancient office, originally responsible for nothing more than the monarch's garments. Over the centuries the position grew in importance because it was so close to the heart of the royal household: the incumbent dispensed money for the upkeep of the King's clothes as well as for many other incidentals, such as jewels. We must not imagine James fussing about in a large royal closet on the lookout for moths or bargains in ermine, however. Once little more than a minor clerk, by Charles II's day the master was an important official whose duties were handled by paid assistants, but who nevertheless was in a position to profit through the operation of an office with a large budget. James, Earl of Arran, had at last broken into the golden circle at court.

Six years of assiduous—and expensive—work had raised Arran to eminence, and the unexpected death of his royal patron Charles II almost immediately after his return to court amounted to little more than an inconvenience. The new King, James II, was if anything even better disposed to the charming Scot. James had struggled for years to defend his right to the throne despite his Catholicism, and Arran's family's well-known Presbyterianism had done nothing to reduce his personal loyalty to the new King. Arran's devotion to James must, however, have further strained relations with his parents, who were deeply anti-Catholic and fearful of the King's plans for the realm. Once again Arran found himself at odds with his family, pursuing a course they instinctively deplored.[16]

The Duke and Duchess of Hamilton were not the only ones who viewed the accession of a Papist as a catastrophe; Shaftesbury's surviving followers continued to nurse their grievances and plan for better days, and within a few months James's regime was challenged by a full-scale rebellion. Charles II's bastard son the Duke of Monmouth landed in the west of England with a small group of followers and a plan to depose his uncle, who he charged had poisoned the old King and usurped the throne. The duke's attempted coup ended dismally at the Battle of Sedgemoor, where the King's well-trained and professional forces mowed down an army of poorly fed and poorly armed rebels. Arran commanded one of the royal regiments that crushed the revolt, and probably had no sympathy for Monmouth's frantic pleas for mercy before he was inexpertly butchered by a nervous headsman on Tower Hill.*

The earl's reward for his display of steadfast loyalty was command of a regiment of cavalry—a very lucrative responsibility. Regimental colonels enjoyed much more than simply their generous pay. They received allowances from the government to provide their men with uniforms and equipment and also distributed their wages. That a certain proportion of these funds stuck to the colonel's fingers was only to be expected. Men such as Arran had invested a great deal in their pursuit of royal favor, and no one denied that a regiment could be doled out as at least partial compensation. If a colonel was prudent and employed agents whose regard for the King's purse and a soldier's welfare came after the prosperity of their commander, a handy sum could be earned at the expense of the Treasury. That such practices were technically illegal bothered virtually no one, provided the funds siphoned away were within reason.

Arran's star continued to rise under James II's influence. The financial rewards of office were made all the sweeter by obvious signs of the King's favor. In 1687, in an effort to gain the loyalty of increasingly troubled Scottish peers, James revived the Order of the Thistle. This order of knighthood, defunct for many years, was to function as an exclusive club for powerful Scots nobles and was modeled after the English Order of the Garter, the most coveted of all the chivalric orders. Arran was one of the first entitled to add the coveted initials "K.T." to his name.

By 1688 the Earl of Arran had found himself a new father in King James II. Though the Duke of Hamilton, Arran's real father, was very much alive, the King provided his surrogate son all that the duke had been so reluctant to offer: money, power, and, above all, approval. In the duke's eyes Arran's flaws were many and

---

* The executioner's first blow landed on the duke's shoulder instead of his neck, and it took several more panic-stricken swings of the ax to sever Monmouth's head.

obvious, but James seemed to dote on an altogether different young man. Where the Hamiltons saw extravagance the King saw generosity. What the Hamiltons called frivolity the King called high spirits. What the Hamiltons considered mendacity the King believed was merely a facility for polite conversation. It is hardly surprising that the earl, now thirty years old, preferred the attentions of the King to those of his natural father.

Unfortunately, while Arran was one of James's favorites, the rest of the nation chafed under the royal parent's regime. James's Catholicism, deeply felt and sincere as it was, hardly comforted his subjects. The King's intentions toward the Protestant Church of England, of which he was the official head, were never very clear, but his people feared the worst. Louis XIV had only just brutally suppressed Protestantism in his realm, and everyone knew that no kingdom had ever successfully harbored two competing faiths. The French example, which relied upon liberal doses of persecution and brutality, was foremost in the minds of British Protestants. They feared that the King's easy victory over Monmouth's rebellion had persuaded him that God intended His truth—Catholicism—to be restored to the British Isles. For his people such a policy was anathema: for them Catholicism meant slavery and the stench of the roasting flesh of Protestant martyrs.

Tension reached its height after the long-dreaded birth of a son and heir to the King in the summer of 1688, and conspiracies to end the Catholic regime began to form. We can be certain that the Earl of Arran was not taken into the confidence of the plotters. When William, Prince of Orange, James's son-in-law and self-appointed savior of British Protestantism, landed in England on November 5, 1688, Arran leaped to the King's defense.* Although

---

* William of Orange's interest in the affairs of the Stuart family was personal. His mother, Princess Mary, was herself a Stuart, the oldest daughter of Charles I. After the death of William's father, William II of Orange, Charles II had been one of the boy's guardians. On November 4, 1677, William married his guardian's niece, another Princess Mary, elder daughter of James, Duke of York, thereby binding himself to the heir presumptive to the throne.

his father welcomed William's arrival enthusiastically and organized support for the revolution in Scotland, Arran stood with the
King. As the nation girded for civil war in November, Arran was
rarely far from James's side and he remained loyal even as the
King's support began to collapse. Defections from the army, led
by James's former favorite John Churchill, later Duke of Marlborough, and finally the desertion of his own younger daughter,
Princess Anne, shattered the King's confidence. Even as James
fled to France in December, Arran, still pledging loyalty, was
among the last of a small band of supporters to part from him.

In January 1689, still hoping to do James service, Arran argued
passionately against offering William the throne. Speaking to a
group of Scots peers and gentlemen at Whitehall, he said, ". . . I
cannot violate my duty to my master the King. I must distinguish
between his popery and his person . . ." James's absence in France,
alleged by some to be a de facto abdication, was nothing of the sort;
it ". . . can no more affect our duty, than his longer absence from us
in Scotland has done all this while." In Arran's view King James
should be called back from France to preside over "a free Parliament for the securing our religione and property, . . . which in my
humble opinion will at last be found the best way to heal our
breaches."[17]

Despite Arran's pleas, the triumphant Prince of Orange, soon to
be King William III, was already established on the scene of Arran's
former glory. The new court was crowded with people who had
been excluded from the seat of power for years—many of them the
erstwhile friends and comrades of the third Lord Mohun. The
experience must have been wrenching for a man whose adult life
had been spent in the service of the old regime and who had prospered, both financially and spiritually, from it. Nevertheless, on this
occasion Arran lived up to his reputation for boldness. He was
among the first to meet William after the King's departure, and he
greeted the Prince with a calculated insult, saying that he was there
only thanks to the orders of "the King my master."

In early 1689, as King James settled into Louis XIV's surplus château at Saint-Germain near Paris, the former favorite of a now-hated King felt the cold winds of a new reality. There were more than a few eager to demonstrate their support for the new King by making life difficult for a man whose loyalty to the old was well known and unpopular. On the night of February 21 Arran climbed into one of London's numerous sedan chairs after what was probably an evening of grumbling about William of Orange. He directed the bearers to his lodgings, and the procession set out. Though he was entering middle age by the standards of the time, the nearly thirty-one-year-old earl was not too heavy a burden to bear; years of overindulgence had done little to thicken his body. On the whole the chairmen must have been quite pleased with their passenger—thin and rich was the perfect combination for men in their business. Late on a February night the narrow streets would have been dark and largely empty as they hurried along with their cargo, looking forward to collecting a handsome fare.

Before the sedan chair reached its destination, six heavily armed men sprang out of the darkness, brandishing swords. The frightened bearers dropped their startled customer and ran out of harm's way, while the assassins began skewering the chair with their swords. Even drawing a sword to defend himself must have been impossible for the earl in the narrow enclosed space, which soon bristled with sword blades. One sword, plunging through the side of the chair, grazed his throat. Somehow, in the midst of the roaring and confusion of the attack—with the strangers shouting "Papist dog!" and the chairmen "murder!"—Arran extricated himself from the confined space. Hastily drawing his own sword, he fought back. The furious exchange of blows did not last long. James had only received minor cuts on his hands and head when his servant, dawdling behind on foot, heard the uproar ahead and summoned help in time. The mysterious attackers then fled, leaving Arran in possession of the field and the two terrified chairmen in rueful contemplation of the extensive damage done to their only means of support.

The perpetrators of this attack were never found. In fact, there is little evidence that the attack was investigated at all. Arran's political views made him one of William's least favorite people, and in any case, acts of violence took place on the streets of London every night. No one was going to work overtime to bring this particular band of toughs to justice. The authorities were more interested in Arran's own activities. Supporters of the exiled King had not given up hope that the outcome of the revolution could be reversed. The Earl of Arran was among those in regular contact with Saint-Germain, plotting James's restoration, and William knew it.[18]

Obviously, then, King James's exile was a dramatic turn of fortune's wheel for Arran. It resulted in attempted assassination and imprisonment, for William also sent Arran to the Tower. The arrest came, Jonathan Swift said years later, at the advice of the Duke of Hamilton, whose commitment to the Revolution outweighed his concerns for his own son. The thick walls of the Tower of London became a familiar sight to the earl over the course of the next two years.* Zoo, armory, jewel house, and prison, the Tower had been the terror of failed politicians for generations. Political executions were carried out there; even kings had been murdered within its grim stone confines. The White Tower itself, at the center of the fortress, had guarded the approaches of London for time out of mind—most contemporaries believed that Julius Caesar himself had built it. Unlucky prisoners—those with no money or upon whom the special malice of the government had fallen—led a miserable existence in the dank, cold, and rat-infested lower levels of the prison. With no fires for warmth and little light to see by, these wretched souls often went mad or died.

Arran had certainly fallen very far from his eminence at court, but he had not yet descended into the Tower's dungeons. As a

---

* Arran was imprisoned off and on from about December 1688 to April 1689, when he was freed briefly—but confined again a few weeks later. This time he remained in the Tower for over a year.

high-ranking prisoner of state he lived in somewhat spartan but still-comfortable quarters. There were fireplaces and windows, and servants to take care of his needs. This easy imprisonment was, however, very expensive, for the state did not pay to accommodate its enemies. Everything cost a prisoner more because the keeper of the Tower, as well as most of his underlings, took a hefty cut of everything that went in or out of their charge's lodgings.

By 1689 fate had conspired to reduce James Douglas-Hamilton to a situation similar to that of the boy who was to become his archenemy, the young Lord Mohun. Fatherless, at least in an emotional sense, since the King's flight, overwhelmed by debt (his creditors clamored for sums of more than £10,000), and without a clue about the direction his life should take, Hamilton faced an uncertain and unfriendly future.[19]

At the accession of William III, Lord Mohun's travails were just beginning, as were Arran's. Unlike Arran, Mohun had the promise of youth, and the prospect of royal favor. His father's intimacy with James II's oldest enemies, now William III's strongest supporters, augured well for his rise in the world.

In his earliest years, promise was all the new Lord Mohun seemed to have on his side. He and his sister, Elizabeth, lived with their mother, whose life remained no more peaceful without her husband than when the couple regularly entertained Drury Lane with their battles. In 1678, shortly before Arran's arrival at court as a gentleman of the bedchamber, Lady Mohun found herself once more the center of the fashionable world's attention, and once again the root cause was the malign combination of her debts and her short temper.

Lady Mohun rented lodgings, probably still in Drury Lane, from Anne Love, a widow who kept a shop in the New Exchange. The New Exchange, a few minutes' walk from Drury Lane, contained a variety of shops catering to the metropolis's better sort: silversmiths, milliners, and others supplied the trappings of gentility to their customers, often on credit. There were many women such as Anne Love in London. When their husbands were alive, they acted as junior partners, supervising in the shop and helping customers when times were busy, in addition to their own family duties: raising children, directing servants, and running a kitchen. When her husband died, as many did in a city where more people died than were born every year, Anne Love discovered that she was now in charge of a business. Though many wives had as much experience as their husbands and even more business acumen, they were still women, assumed by society, and especially by their customers, to be less capable and easier to take advantage of than men. We do not know what sort of shop Mrs. Love kept, but she dabbled in real estate, and her properties were genteel.

Unfortunately, a title and a great estate did not necessarily make a tenant more likely to pay her debts; Lady Mohun would have taken honors in a least-desirable-tenant competition. From Phillippa's perspective, the rent she owed—a mere £60—was nothing. Her husband's demise left her with debts of £16,000, and creditors far more significant than Anne Love. For Mrs. Love, on the other hand, £60 was a great deal of money; such a sum could mean the difference between success and destitution for a widow without much capital. Understandably, as the first quarter passed with the rent unpaid, relations between the two women became more and more tense.

Tenant and landlady clashed openly in April 1678. The first quarter's rent was overdue, and Lady Mohun obviously planned to pay the second with promises. Phillippa, whose debts seem not to have hampered her social life, was entertaining two of her friends at cards when Mrs. Love and her daughter made their appearance. The arrival of a pair of duns, and duns of the common sort at that, enraged Lady Mohun, who ordered her footman to toss the women out. Zealous in his mistress's defense, the footman, assisted by a colleague, tried unsuccessfully to remove the now very agitated landladies. The younger Mistress Love was spat upon, while the elder pursued Lady Mohun herself. Mrs.

Love, threatened by a footman with a sword, hurled a large silver candlestick, striking Phillippa on the knee. Eventually the Loves were removed from the house before any more serious injuries had been inflicted, once again giving the residents of Drury Lane an intimate view of life in the Mohun household.

The year-old Lord Mohun was almost certainly unaware of the commotion; more than likely he was in the hands of his nurse. But he was one of the few people in London who did not know all the details of the story. Phillippa brought a formal complaint before the House of Lords. The Earl of Anglesey demanded justice in his daughter's name; she had been "barbarously affronted and abused" and the dignity of the peerage was at stake. It might, however, have been a mistake to link Phillippa, Lady Mohun, and the notion of dignity too closely. When the Lords heard the case, the bruised peeress could hardly claim to be vindicated. Because Lady Mohun's card-playing friends testified that the trouble began when she lost her temper, her complaint fell hopelessly flat. King Charles himself was at the House when the case was heard, and, always interested in the female anatomy, offered to assist the investigation by inspecting the lady's bruise personally. London society derived considerable amusement from the whole abortive affair.[20]

Such was the atmosphere of Mohun's childhood. His father's early death left his estate in the hands of trustees, and Mohun himself was assigned to the guardianship of Sir Charles Orby. Orby's original connection with the Mohun family is unclear, but as the infant lord grew older the connection would become closer. In any event, Orby's main concern must have been the overwhelming debt load on the estate. In their lifetimes both the second and third lords had provided for their families beyond their resources, so that their wills could not be fulfilled without provoking a crisis. By the time of Lady Mohun's imbroglio with Mrs. Love, the second lord's legacies had been unpaid for thirteen years, and to those were added the provisions of the third lord's will.[21]

2. Charles, fourth Baron Mohun, aged about thirty

Raising money on a heavily encumbered estate was never easy. English landed society had one overriding goal, and law, testamentary behavior, and custom all conspired to the same end: keep the estate together, descending intact from one generation to the next.

The "next generation" was narrowly understood to be a sole male heir; under no circumstances could the core of the family property be divided to benefit younger children, for example. While merchants and tradesmen rarely had qualms about dividing their estates, no self-respecting gentleman could contemplate with equanimity the diminution of his family's landed wealth in succeeding generations. Land was what gave a gentleman his status— even when, like Lord Mohun, he spent virtually all his time in London. The great fear of every generation was that the next heir, though improvidence, riotous living, and bad luck, might fritter away the work of his ancestors and sell what had been carefully preserved and passed to him in trust. Consequently, most landed estates were subject to restrictions laid out in wills, trusts, or marriage settlements that placed severe limits upon the heir's freedom to dispose of his property. So it was for the fourth Lord Mohun.

His trustees found that despite the respectable size of the Cornish property, they could not easily discharge the debts attached

3. Boconnoc, Cornwall, the Mohun family's ancestral home

to the estate. After dispensing £1,000 a year to each of the two dowagers, Orby found that the land's income hardly paid the mounting interest on old mortgages. The only solution was an Act of Parliament. A private bill in Parliament was very difficult to obtain as well as very expensive—but it was effective for estates in trouble. Parliament could set aside the restrictions of previous settlements and allow sales of land or other assets to rescue an estate from foreclosure. In April 1679 Sir Charles filed a bill in Lord Mohun's name that would have allowed his guardians to sell timber from his estates to pay off some of the accumulated debts. But nothing was certain when dealing with Parliament, and though both Houses considered the bill, it failed to reach final passage. The estate was still in trouble, and further burdened by the loss of the time and money spent drafting the bill.[22] Debts continued to swell and creditors grew increasingly impatient. Financial catastrophe threatened.

This was only the first of many attempts on the part of Mohun and his family to use the law to rescue themselves from the effects of their own improvidence and ward off assaults upon their property. Charles, the fourth Lord Mohun, obviously grew up in an environment in which instability was the rule. Sir Charles Orby exercised little or no influence upon his ward's behavior in his youth, and it seems clear that his mother's influence was hardly positive. His grandmother Lady Catherine was important principally because of her determination to live forever and thus deprive Charles of £1,000 a year. There is no evidence to tell us where or how Charles was educated; he attended neither Oxford nor Cambridge, which was unusual for a boy of his rank. Someone at least taught him to write a legible italic hand, but writing was not a frequent occupation, to judge from his surviving letters, nor was he known to have much interest in learning or scholarship. Did he see or even meet some of the great minds of the age? John Locke and Isaac Newton were older contemporaries, but if he met them, there is no record of it. How he occupied his time before his teenage years we have no idea, but it is safe to assume that he was often left to his own devices. While the Earl of Arran was cutting a figure at court, Mohun grew up in near obscurity, a condition occasionally illuminated by a flash of his mother's temper or the ongoing difficulties of his estate.

Still, Charles was the son of his parents and a lord of Parliament, so no one would have expected him to be obscure forever. As it happens, he caught the public's eye before he left his teens, rather earlier than most of his peers. In December 1692, months before his sixteenth birthday, he quarreled with twenty-year-old John, Lord Kennedy. As was all too often the case, this dispute began in the course of a drinking bout; the story was unusual only because of Mohun's relative youth. News of the boys' altercation reached William III's ears, and, concerned lest a duel follow, he ordered both of them to stay home. Evidently neither took the King's commands very seriously, for within a week of their initial clash, they fought. The duel, which was relatively brief, left both participants slightly wounded. This was Mohun's first blooding, and it seems that he was not put off by the experience. The consequences were minimal; a day or two of excited gossip ensued, but neither prosecution nor punishment followed.[23] The fatherless boy with the infamous mother must have seen this encounter as an enormously important introduction to the world of adults. His capacity for drink and his ability with a sword would make him a man to be reckoned with: the fourth Lord Mohun had found his niche.

Two days later the excitable teenager became still more famous. London, as Europe's largest city, offered an inexhaustible array of entertainment for its inhabitants, high and low. Lord Mohun had already discovered one of the most popular: drinking. Thousands of taverns, alehouses, and more informal, unlicensed and illegal, establishments served millions of gallons of beer and hundreds of thousands of bottles of wine and spirits to a thirsty multitude every year. But London offered other diversions as well. There were wandering jugglers, puppeteers who delighted crowds on street corners with tableaus of Mr. Punch merrily battering Mistress Judy, dogfights, cockfights, and bare-knuckle prizefights. The theater provided an even more attractive form of entertainment. From the poor apprentice boys who saved or embezzled a few pennies from their shops to gain admission to the gentlemen and ladies who rented boxes for several shillings, everyone went to the theater. Actors and actresses were highly regarded despite (or because of) their unsavory reputations, and many had devoted followers who attended every performance.

Lord Mohun's closest friend, Captain Richard Hill, was just such a devoted theatergoer. Hill was somewhat older than his friend—in December 1692 he had already been in the army for four years. Nevertheless, despite his rank and experience, Hill was no grizzled veteran: commissioned as a lieutenant at the tender age of twelve, he was just sixteen. Adolescent officers were not unusual in the army of William III; commanders regarded commissions as important patronage plums, and distributed them—and the pay that went with them—to relatives or clients, or sold them to gentlemen anxious for regular pay or military experience. The army, swollen to unprecedented size by William's long-running wars with France, had many places of this sort to offer young men like Hill. These officers spent much of their time swaggering through the streets of the capital, roaring late into the night at taverns, and, as in Hill's case, going to the theater.

Both Mohun and Hill haunted London's playhouses; Mohun's attentions made him something of a pest, and the players he afflicted discouraged him by calculated indifference. Hill was even more annoying, particularly after he conceived a passionate love for one of the stage's most popular actresses, Anne Bracegirdle. Nearly twice Hill's age, Mrs. Bracegirdle had been acting for more than a decade when Hill forced his way into her life. She owed her popularity to her considerable talent and her notable beauty. She had dark hair and "a fine set of even white teeth," no small advantage when so many of her contemporaries were plagued with a mouthful of rotten ones, the consequence of the national craze for sugar. Her most famous attribute, though, was her complexion, which a contemporary described as "fresh and blushy." "Whenever she excited herself, she had an involuntary flushing in her breast, neck, and face, having a continually cheerful aspect . . . never making an exit but she left the audience in a state of admiration of her pleasant countenance."[24] She was especially popular for her comic roles, such as Betsy Jiltall, "a cunning, singing, weeping, wheedling, toying, chattering mercenary town jilt" in Thomas D'Urfey's *Love for Money* of 1691.[25]

Anne Bracegirdle had no bigger fan than Richard Hill, who was determined to marry her—or at least keep her as a mistress, for players were understood to have a highly suspect code of morality. Unfortunately, Bracegirdle was atypical in this regard. She lived an eminently respectable life with her mother at rented lodgings in Howard Street, and Hill's puppyish attentions gave her no pleasure. His fruitless efforts to woo his beloved led to increasing frustration and bitterness. Hill became convinced that one of Bracegirdle's colleagues, William Mountford, was a rival. That Mountford was evidently happily married seemed to make little difference to the soldier. The actor was one of the most popular men on the London stage, particularly in comic roles, which meant that he frequently played opposite Bracegirdle. In fact, he had only recently taken the part of Jack Amorous in *Love for Money*, the same play in which Anne was Betsy Jiltall. Interestingly, in that play Amorous and Jiltall are lovers—was Hill unable to distinguish between reality and fiction?

By early December 1692 Hill's obsession threatened to overwhelm whatever limited self-control he possessed. As he and Mohun sat in smoky tavern rooms drinking bottle after bottle of wine, Hill's bitterness grew. Every conversation, drunken or sober, revolved around the problem of Bracegirdle and Mountford. Did

4. Anne Bracegirdle

they sleep together? How could Mountford's hold over her be broken? And in every conversation Hill's resolve to triumph over his
rival hardened. "I do not doubt the success of my amour with Mrs.
Bracegirdle if I were not obstructed by Mountford, whom I design

to be the death of . . . I am resolved to have the blood of Mountford," he whispered into the ear of one of the actor's friends in a
tavern. Ironically, Mohun's own view of Mountford was quite different. He was no slave to the charms of Mrs. Bracegirdle and, in
fact, liked Mountford. He had seen him on the stage many times
and admired his performances in both tragedy and comedy; moreover, Mountford was one of the few actors who did not impatiently
brush off his young admirer.

Still in the grip of his passion, Captain Hill turned up at Bracegirdle's theater, the Theatre Royal in Drury Lane, on Monday,
December 5.[26] He cornered one of the actresses, Mrs. Knight, and
asked her to intercede for him with Anne. She put him off and
tried to persuade him that his suspicions about Mountford were
groundless. The next day he returned, this time with a letter for
Knight to pass on to Anne. Wisely hoping to avoid being dragged
into an affair she knew would be unpleasant, she refused: "I am
not fond of creating myself enemies in the house." More late
evenings of alcohol-fogged brooding with his bosom friend Lord
Mohun eventually showed Hill a way to fulfill his dreams. The
solution was to remove Anne from the influence of William
Mountford. Captain Hill had a plan.

On Friday, December 9, the two friends met at one of their
usual haunts, the Three Tuns Tavern in Chandos Street. There
they perfected the details of their adventure in the company of
Elizabeth Sandys, probably a prostitute, and certainly a woman of
easy virtue. The scheme was very much what one might expect
from a pair of teenagers. Hill bargained with William Dixon, a
coachman, for the hire of a coach and six horses—price, thirty
shillings. They rounded up half a dozen or more pistols, a
woman's cloak (for it was to be a cold night, and it would not do
for Anne to catch a chill), and a file of Hill's own soldiers to serve
as assistants. They would meet at the playhouse after dark, at six
o'clock, find Mrs. Bracegirdle, and kidnap her. A week spent
alone at Barnet, outside London, would surely open her eyes to

Richard's charms. Mountford would not be around to complicate matters, and the beautiful actress would at last see reason.

If the idea was to carry out their plan discreetly, Hill and Mohun failed dismally. In what appears to have been an effort to confuse any prospective pursuers, or perhaps merely an exhibition of juvenile solidarity, the two boys spent much of Friday swapping coats as they bustled about preparing for the evening. They traded coats at least four times that day, to the puzzlement of those who saw them. When they arrived at the theater their antics, far from allaying suspicion, made them stand out even in a colorful audience. During that evening's performance, John Rogers, who collected admission from the audience, noticed that the boys had left their places in the pit—for which they had paid—and had moved up onto the stage. Seating on the stage was customary at the time, and because these seats were the best in the house they were more expensive. The bemused Rogers also noticed that Mohun and Hill had switched coats. There was no question about the identity of the two interlopers; both of them were familiar figures at the theater, and Rogers probably did not relish a confrontation with these two wild boys. But his job was to collect admission, and if they wanted to sit on the stage they were going to have to pay extra, and he told them so. Their response was hardly calculated to divert attention from themselves. Keyed up even more than usual, they loudly refused to pay and threatened to slit Roger's nose if he did not disappear. In this case, their threats of violence might have reflected their disappointment, for Mrs. Bracegirdle was nowhere to be found.

The whereabouts of Hill's ladylove remained a mystery for several hours. Dixon the coachman waited uneasily at the White Horse Tavern in Drury Lane, near the theater, along with six or seven soldiers. All of the two adventurers' confederates but Dixon, who must have been something of a freak among London coachmen, were in the tavern drinking and smoking. By about 9 p.m., having heard that Anne was supping with friends, Mr. and Mrs.

Page, near the theater, Mohun and Hill went to Mr. Page's house in Drury Lane, hoping to waylay her as she entered or left. After lurking outside for a few minutes, they hurried off to the house on Howard Street where Anne lived, thinking that perhaps they had missed her. Still no luck. By now the youths were in a state of considerable agitation; Hill, convinced that somehow Mountford had gotten wind of the attempt and warned Bracegirdle off, strode up and down nearby streets swearing vengeance, as Mohun kept pace in the cold night air. Finally, at about 10 p.m., after the boys had searched in vain for nearly four hours, the door of the house in Drury Lane opened and out came Anne, her mother, brother, and host, Gawen Page. Hill and Mohun were ready. At Hill's signal, the coach rattled forward and the soldiers came running from the shadows.

Hill and his soldiers descended on them so fast that Anne and her companions were taken completely by surprise. The soldiers shoved Page and her brother aside, and Hill threw open the coach door, revealing Lord Mohun, still wearing his friend's coat, awash in pistols. With the soldiers pushing from behind and Mohun and Hill pulling from the front, it seemed inevitable that Anne, who was now crying loudly for help, would be whisked into the coach and away to Hill's love nest in the country. That this did not happen was due almost entirely to the determination of old Mrs. Bracegirdle. Despite the soldiers, she put her arms around her daughter's waist and dug in her heels. At the same time she and Anne set up such a commotion that Hill and his men feared that the watch might soon come to the rescue.

Not desperate enough to engage in a pitched battle in the street, Hill desisted. He ordered the coach and his men to leave, and he and Mohun tried to make their apologies for their extraordinary behavior, like little boys caught in some petty infraction. Not surprisingly, the Bracegirdles wanted nothing but to get away from these young lunatics and safely behind their own door, and so they hurried toward their home, only a short walk away. Hill could not bring himself to admit failure. He and Mohun followed the party all the way home, Hill violently protesting his affections for Anne and Mohun swearing that he would be true to his friend. It was with considerable relief that the women arrived home and rushed in, the youths close on their heels. As the big door to the house slammed, Hill must have realized that his chance for happiness was dashed. Undoubtedly his ruin was the fault of William Mountford. That seemed clear to Hill, if to no one else.

Still, he was not ready to give up his cause. He and Mohun, their swords drawn, paced up and down the cobbled street in front of the house, shouting for Mrs. Bracegirdle to come out, begging her forgiveness, and swearing that Mountford would pay for his meddling. This show went on for almost two hours. Neighbors watched from their windows, a few came out to see what the noise was about, and one enterprising tavern keeper a few doors away sold the youths several bottles of wine. These they drank, getting ever louder and refusing to go away until Anne spoke to them. Old Mrs. Bracegirdle, who emerged pleading for them to go home, also sent a servant to warn Mrs. Mountford about the threats against her husband. She then dispatched another to find a constable to rescue her daughter from this unpleasant siege.

At about eleven forty-five the local constable, William Merry, appeared. Constables were badly paid, armed with only a short truncheon, and usually interested in nothing more than a quiet life. Mr. Merry must surely have cursed his luck when he beheld the two boys stalking up and down the street, full of wine and rage, both brandishing drawn swords. No fool, the constable decided that tact was the most appropriate way to deal with the situation, and he approached Mohun, presumably the more rational of the two. Asking what was the meaning of this display, he elicited the sobering comment, "I am a peer of the realm! Meddle with me if you dare!" This was very bad news. Not only was Mr. Merry dealing with maniacs but at least one of them was a titled maniac. Visions of the wrath of the House of Lords, notoriously touchy where the dignity of even its most undignified members was concerned, probably flashed before the constable's eyes.

After his initial outburst, Mohun seemed ready to cooperate. He sheathed his sword and explained that Hill could not stow his blade because he had no scabbard. The additional explanation from a neighbor standing nearby that the two boys were toasting the health of a sweetheart eased the constable's mind. He urged them to behave more civilly and then went to one of the nearby houses to ask what the fuss was about. It seems the incident was rapidly losing the high drama of its conception and threatened to end in farce. Those involved could imagine how the newsletter writers would enjoy the story and how Captain Hill and Lord Mohun would figure as objects of fun for a few days.

The night was not yet over, however. William Mountford lived nearby in Norfolk Street, and at just about midnight he came home. His house was visible to Hill and Mohun as they stood in Howard Street, yards away. Mountford had not received his wife's warnings. He was entering Howard Street when he saw the two boys and ventured toward them. Mrs. Browne, the Bracegirdles' landlady, spotted him coming and rushed out to head him off, but he brushed past her and addressed a friendly greeting to Mohun. Mohun replied in kind. "I hope," Mountford said, "that you aren't involved in anything dishonorable with such a fellow as Richard Hill." At this point, Hill stepped up to Mountford and replied, "I'll answer for myself! Draw!" With his left hand Hill boxed Mountford hard on the ear, and simultaneously, with his right, he plunged his sword into Mountford's chest. The blade entered just above the actor's right nipple and struck completely through his body, emerging from his back. Mrs. Browne and several others cried "Murder!" while the neighbors' maid, watching from an upstairs window, shrieked and very nearly toppled to the ground. Despite his wound, Mountford managed to unsheathe his weapon, but it was too late; he parried one blow, which broke his sword, and the fight was over. Hill, his bravado gone, took to his heels, while Mountford, desperately wounded, struggled for home. He got as far as his front hall, where he collapsed in a growing puddle of blood. He died the next day at 1 p.m.

By that time, after Hill's flight, only Mohun was in the custody of the authorities. He stood transfixed by the sight of Hill and Mountford fighting a few feet away, and seemed unable to move even after both had left the scene. Several times he called people to witness that he had not fought, that he had no hand in what had happened. Within a very few minutes after Hill vanished, a watchman appeared and took Mohun by the sleeve— of Richard Hill's coat. Mohun was so shaken that the constable later testified that the young lord trembled violently when he touched him.

His sword surrendered, Mohun was taken to jail and held overnight. Here some of the youthful arrogance that had put him in this predicament returned to him. Captain Hill, he was told, had escaped—and his response was "Goddamme I am glad he's not taken, but I am sorry he has no more money about him, I wish he had some of mine. I do not care a farthing if I am hang'd for him." The next day, after Mountford's death, Mohun appeared before the Middlesex justices of the peace charged with murder.* His guardian's titled relative Lord Gerard put up his bail, and the authorities released him.

Mohun's respite was only temporary, however. Mrs. Mountford evidently appealed the magistrate's decision and persuaded Lord Chief Justice Holt to order Mohun's capture. The judge issued a warrant for Mohun's arrest, but before it was served he fled. This was only a temporary solution for the fugitive, however, because Mrs. Mountford might have him declared an outlaw. As an outlaw, Mohun could have his property forfeit to the Crown, and he

---

* With the exception of the square mile at the center of London called the City, which governed itself, all of the urban area north of the river Thames was part of the county of Middlesex. Mountford was murdered near Covent Garden, west of the City, and therefore Middlesex magistrates oversaw the initial stages of the case.

himself put beyond the protection of the law, a man who might be murdered with impunity. The only solution, apart from ruin and exile, was to face a trial. As a lord of Parliament—although a minor who had never taken his seat in the House of Lords—Mohun was entitled to a trial by his peers. On January 12, 1693, he emerged from hiding and presented a petition to the House, asking for bail and a speedy trial.

Two days later, on the fourteenth, Mohun paced outside the door of the House, waiting for an answer to his request. Their lordships' response to the petition was not entirely satisfactory: preparations for a trial would begin immediately, but because of Mohun's propensity to flight, bail was denied. The House's principal usher, Black Rod, carried his masters' answer to Mohun and took the boy into custody.

So it was that Charles, Lord Mohun, arrived before the massive gates of the Tower of London a prisoner, not long after the Earl of Arran had left it. For both peers, time in the Tower was a prelude to an uncertain future; Arran, charged with treasonable practices, and Mohun, with murder, stood to lose everything—even their lives. Arran had been released, though perhaps only temporarily; his commitment to James II remained strong. For Mohun the situation was very different. Though his youth might save him from the consequences of his actions, he could not count on mercy. Unlike Arran, he had no powerful father whose political importance caused kings to tread warily. He had no great estate. He already had a reputation for violence; no doubt his duel with Lord Kennedy was not forgotten. His brief life was a pattern of riotous scandal; he had no education to speak of; he had done nothing of service for the government. His pious grandmother Catherine was finally gone, dead less than a year, and his mother was now an aging harridan, recently remarried to a rapacious lawyer and living in the west of England. He could expect no help from that quarter. All Charles had to rely upon was the discernment and mercy of his peers.

Trials by the House of Lords were rare, eagerly anticipated, and staged with the utmost care. The House appointed a committee to investigate precedents and ordered preparations for transforming Westminster Hall into a court. The hall was part of the ancient complex of buildings that made up the Palace of Westminster, Parliament's home. It was the only venue large enough to accommodate such a trial, and had traditionally been used whenever a noble was judged by his peers. Rebuilt in the fourteenth century, it was a great barn of a room, roofed over with a magnificent hammer-beam ceiling. It could accommodate a multitude of peers and common spectators, unlike either of the two House chambers, which could barely hold their own members. But creating the proper atmosphere for a trial was always difficult, and those responsible found the job maddening. The palace had not served

5. Westminster Hall, home of the law courts
and venue of Mohun's murder trials

as a royal residence for centuries, and had in the meantime been given over to Parliaments and the courts. Like the King's nearby residence of Whitehall, it was a jumble of buildings, all in various stages of decay. The place was notable chiefly for the discomfort of conducting business there. It was frigid in the winter, and in the summer the stench of the Thames, not a stone's throw away, appalled even members used to strong smells. It was damp in every season of the year. But, remarkably enough, a great deal of business was conducted there. Apart from the Houses of Commons and Lords, the King's principal courts of law—King's Bench, Common Pleas, and Chancery—met at Westminster. They were housed in jerry-built spaces at either end of Westminster Hall, separated by wooden partitions. The palace hummed with commerce—and not simply the trade of law and legislation. Between the courts located at either end, both sides of the hall were lined with bookstalls. Their proprietors did a brisk trade in pamphlets, prints, and lawbooks. Political gossip or intrigue could be discussed in the coffeehouse or in one of the two taverns on the premises. Like the courts themselves, these businesses were usually badly built and had a temporary look about them, but they were certainly profitable. This was one of the Surveyor General's biggest headaches in preparing for a trial: the bookstalls had to go for the duration, and their owners were not pleased about the lost trade.

The two men charged with the preparations for Mohun's trial were Sir Christopher Wren, the Surveyor General, and Sir Thomas Duppa. Wren's brilliant architectural skills had done much to make the Great Fire of London nearly thirty years before a blessing in disguise. His masterpiece, St. Paul's Cathedral, was slowly rising over the city even as he transferred his skills to the smaller task of stage-managing a murder trial. The more practical details were left to Duppa, Black Rod, whose days became a weary round of squabbling with workmen and other officers of the Crown. Persuading turf-conscious officials in the King's Wardrobe to cooperate and provide furniture and tapestries to decorate the hall proved to be one of his most frustrating tasks.

A noble's trial was designed to combine the maximum of dignity with the most expansive public accommodation. No one wanted to miss the trial of a peer of the realm for murder, and providing enough space for spectators without turning the occasion into a raucous Roman-style circus was no easy task. The peers themselves insisted upon their privileges, and required that their families and guests have first crack at the limited seating. Each lord—there were nearly two hundred, counting the bishops—received eight tickets, which instantly became the most sought-after scraps of paper in town. The remaining seats, perhaps a few hundred, were filled on a first-come, first-served basis. By the end of January the booksellers had made their grumbling exit, benches for the peers and spectators were installed, tapestries hung along the stone walls, and a throne erected for the Lord High Steward, who would preside over the trial. Their lordships were ready.

Lord Mohun was probably ready himself, despite the fact that he was about to be tried for his life under adverse circumstances. He well knew that the law was not the friend of the accused. In ordinary courts—the sort in which Captain Hill would be tried if he was ever captured—the accused labored under a distinct disadvantage. Juries were chosen not of impartial, or ignorant, men (for of course women did not serve) but, if possible, of men with particular knowledge of the case, especially those who knew the accused and were familiar with his life and background. For someone with an evil reputation this often spelled death; juries sometimes convicted with the idea that the accused was surely guilty of something, if not the particular crime with which he was charged. First offenders, on the other hand, or people whose desperation might be a mitigating factor, sometimes benefited from this rough-and-ready calculus; juries were occasionally willing to acquit someone they thought redeemable despite the evidence.

Most other aspects of contemporary legal practice worked against the accused. They were not allowed legal counsel, except

upon points of law. No lawyer was allowed to intervene and confuse the facts of a case on the prisoner's behalf. Counsel's only
function was to advise about the legal details of a prisoner's case;
he could not cross-examine witnesses or offer any other assistance. In any event, only a rich defendant could afford an attorney, because the state did not pay defense lawyers. Even more
crippling for the defense was its inability to force witnesses to testify. The Crown could subpoena witnesses, whose attendance
and testimony were mandatory. The defendant, however, could
only request a witness's appearance: no one could be forced to
testify against the King. Moreover, witnesses for the defense were
not allowed to testify under oath, unlike the King's witnesses,
who swore to the truth of their testimony: no one could swear
against the King. All these disabilities applied to Lord Mohun as
well as to any common defendant. The fact that his jury was
much larger than the standard dozen—the 180-odd temporal
peers—only ensured that more men familiar with his background
would be included. A bare majority was required to convict.

Proceedings began on Tuesday, January 31. Westminster Hall
was jammed with eager, shivering spectators pressed together on
the simple benches Wren had provided. King William was present, "incognito," though everyone knew he sat in a discreetly
screened chair not far from the throne. Mohun himself stood outside a wooden railing that separated the peers' seats from the
spectators'. There was a table for the King's counsel: the Attorney General, the Solicitor General, and their assistant. Mohun's
counsel—an able group of lawyers whose services must have
come very dear—sat nearby at another table. In front of them was
the woolsack, a rather formless couch upholstered in scarlet cloth,
which provided seating for the judges, who were present to advise
the lords on points of law as they arose.

The shuffling and murmuring in the galleries grew and were
amplified by the hall's bad acoustics as the crowd awaited the
peers' arrival. Many spectators had been in their places for hours
and had brought food and extra blankets to sustain them over a

long stay. Their lordships, after some bustle and confusion while they donned their scarlet, ermine-trimmed robes outside the hall, formed up into a solemn procession. Silence fell in Westminster Hall as the double file of men came in, first officials, then the eldest sons of peers, then the lords themselves, in strict order of rank, the junior baron (Lord Leinster) to the senior duke (the Duke of Norfolk). Finally, Thomas Osborne, Marquess of Carmarthen, the Lord High Steward, walked slowly toward the throne, preceded by Sir Thomas Duppa, who carried the symbol of the steward's office, a long thin wooden wand painted white. The trial of the fourth Baron Mohun for the murder of William Mountford was under way.

Carmarthen could hardly have missed the irony of his situation, for fourteen years before, he had stood precisely where Mohun was, impeached for treason by the House of Commons and a resident of the Tower. Carmarthen escaped the ax, though it had been a very near thing. Mohun would not remember that trial, but he must have fervently hoped that he, too, could avoid execution, as the clerk read out the King's commission for the proceedings. Carmarthen's opening statement gave Mohun little reason to hope. "The case against you is, for the murther of one of the King's subjects, which is a crime the King will at no time pass over . . . This my Lord is charged upon you, not by any slight information, but by the Grand Inquest of this county, made up of Gentlemen of good worth and fortune." The Lord High Steward's age and dignity, combined with the gravity of his words, portended serious trouble. Then the standard forms for the start of a criminal trial began, no less chilling for their regularity. The Clerk of the Crown read the indictment: by "aiding, abetting, comforting and assisting" Richard Hill in the murder of William Mountford, "you the said Charles Lord Mohun, and the said Richard Hill . . . William Mountford feloniously, willfully, and of your malice aforethought, did kill and murder, against the Peace of our said sovereign lord and lady the King and Queen, their crown and dignity."

The clerk then turned to Mohun. "How say you, Charles Lord Mohun, are you guilty of this felony and murder, or not guilty?"

"Not guilty, my lords."

"How will your lordship be tried?"

"By God and my peers."

"God send your lordship a good deliverance."[27]

The Attorney General began his case with an account of Hill's obsession with Mrs. Bracegirdle and his conviction that Mountford was to blame for Anne's coldness toward him. There was malice between Hill and Mountford, the prosecutor said, and it was malice that Mohun knew well. Mohun's friendship with Hill was close enough for him to participate wholeheartedly in the kidnapping scheme on December 9, and his presence outside Mrs. Bracegirdle's house when Mountford was murdered involved him in that crime, as well. Though he made no claim that Charles did anything but stand passively by while Hill murdered the actor, that, he claimed, was no defense. Mohun had aided and abetted Hill in his crime and was therefore as guilty as if he had wielded the sword himself.

The Crown's first witness was John Hudson, who testified that he ate with Mohun and Hill at the Rose Tavern in Covent Garden shortly before the murder, where Hill made repeated threats against Mountford. Another gentleman, George Powell, a friend of Mountford's, told a similar tale. Hudson would not swear that Mohun had heard Hill's threats, but Powell added a potentially damaging detail. He swore that when he spoke to Mountford on his deathbed, the actor told him that Hill had stabbed him "whilst my Lord Mohun talked to me," hinting that Mohun might have been deliberately distracting his victim.

There followed a parade of witnesses who told about the events of December 9: John Rogers, the ticket taker at the Theatre Royal; William Dixon, the coachman; William Merry, the constable; Mr. and Mrs. Page, in whose house Bracegirdle dined; and Anne Bracegirdle herself. The story that emerged left no room for doubt about Richard Hill's culpability, but the issue was whether Mohun's assistance made him guilty of Mountford's death. After some three hours of testimony the King left the lords to their labors, and a rapt audience of spectators to their court-room drama. The sun began to fade shortly afterward, but the peers called for candles and the trial continued as the hall subsided into the murky gloom of a long winter's evening.

Keeping order amid such a large crowd of people strained the court's abilities, and Lord Carmarthen grew increasingly testy when witnesses, some of whom were obviously badly frightened by the majesty of the occasion, spoke in tremulous whispers. Criers called several times for silence, but eventually Carmarthen left his chair next to the throne and squeezed himself onto the woolsack with the judges, to hear better. The star witness, at least as far as the spectators were concerned, was Elizabeth Walker. She was the senior Mrs. Bracegirdle's maid, and an eyewitness to what happened in Howard Street. She eagerly answered every question, and did so in prolix, if somewhat confused, detail. Her description of Hill and Mountford's struggle delighted the court: "I saw them fighting, making passes at one another, I saw them engaged, I never saw men naked fighting so in my life." The image tickled the crowd, which roared with laughter, leaving a rather wounded Mistress Walker to continue, "My lord, I do not understand these matters, I tell you as well as I can, they were fighting with naked swords."[28] The only other diversion in the proceedings came toward the end of the day, when a woman in the public gallery had a seizure in the middle of the Attorney General's summation for the King. It was fifteen minutes before calm was restored in the hall, but at last the prosecution's case was over.

Mohun's cross-examination of the King's witnesses, and the testimony of his own, was intended to persuade the lords that he was no more than an innocent bystander. Hill's extraordinary conduct could not be his fault; the murder was done while Mohun stood on the pavement several feet away, his sword sheathed. One witness told the court about Mohun's regard for Mountford;

he and Charles had recently shared a meal and Mohun had expressed his admiration for Mountford's performance in *Alexander the Great*. Elizabeth Walker, with her gaudy tale of naked swords, was careful to make it seem that the fight took place beyond Mohun's control. Additionally, the defendant quizzed the constables about his arrest. They agreed that he, unlike Hill, made no effort to run from the scene, and offered no resistance when he was taken into custody.

By 6 p.m., when it was quite dark, the evidence had been heard, and Carmarthen took the opportunity to adjourn. The House would begin its deliberations in the morning. Spectators hurried home to their firesides, and Mohun was rowed down the Thames to the Tower, pondering the day's events. Opinion about the weight of the evidence varied. Some of the newsletters predicted an acquittal, but there were more than a few people who expected a guilty verdict—not least Queen Mary, who had been a particular fan of Mountford's.[29]

But the issue remained the same at the end of the day as at the beginning: Was Mohun criminally liable for what his friend had done? He had been an enthusiastic participant in the kidnapping attempt, but how did the murder fit? The case turned upon that issue.

Having a night to sleep on the evidence made reaching a decision no easier. The House met in its own chamber on Wednesday morning, while Mohun, the judges, and the spectators waited in the hall for their return. And waited. What was said in the House that day? No record was made, but a great deal must have been said, because time wore on, the sun began to set, candles were called for, and finally, at 8 p.m., word came that the House had reached no decision and would meet again on Friday to continue its deliberations. Again Mohun was loaded into a barge and rowed back down the dark river to his prison.

On Friday afternoon, once again before a room full of spectators, the lords returned to the hall. They had already puzzled over the case in their own chamber since the morning, and now, at four o'clock in the afternoon, they came to seek enlightenment from the judges, perching wearily on their woolsack after so many hours. The lords propounded a series of questions to the judges in an effort to clarify their thinking about Mohun's particular case. Most questions, such as that asked by the Earl of Monmouth, were favorable to the accused: "'A' conscious of an animosity between 'B' and 'C' accompanieth 'B' where 'C' happen to come, and 'B' killeth him, whether 'A' without any malice to 'C' or any actual hand in his death, be guilty of murder?" No, the judges answered. Some questions were not so benign, as in the Earl of Nottingham's query, "Whether a person knowing of a design of another to lie in wait to assault a third man, and accompanying him in that design, if it shall happen that the third person be killed at the time in the presence of him who knew of that design, and accompanied the other in it, be guilty in law of the same crime with the party who had the design, and killed him, though he had no actual hand in his death?" Yes, said the judges, such a man would be guilty.[30] Mohun, listening at the bar, must have realized what Nottingham was getting at. It was probably not a comforting thought. Their questions put, once again the peers filed out to debate the answers in their own House.

It was late by the time the lords finished their work for the evening and adjourned until Saturday. By now everyone knew a judgment was near, and most people confidently expected Lord Mohun's fate to be determined on the morrow. At four o'clock Saturday afternoon, after another long deliberation, the peers were at last ready. Still in their robes, they returned to Westminster Hall, where the crowd—and the prisoner—waited expectantly. According to custom, each lord stood, placed a hand upon his breast, and answered the question put by Carmarthen, "Whether my Lord Mohun be guilty of the murder of William Mountford, whereof he stands indicted, or not guilty?"[31] Lord Leinster, the junior peer, rose, removed his hat, and, with his right hand held over his heart, said, "Not guilty, upon mine honor."

Lord Capel was next: "Guilty, upon mine honor." And so it went, through the roll, ascending the peerage in rank. It was quickly apparent that Mohun's lawyers had done their work, for the "not guiltys" outnumbered the "guiltys" from the start. When the voting was done, sixty-nine lords voted to acquit and fourteen to convict. The Lord High Steward then broke his wand of office, becoming once more only the Marquess of Carmarthen, and the House of Lords was again merely a legislative body.

Lord Mohun was not in the court when his peers voted; custom forbade the presence of the prisoner. But he was released immediately and was now free to think about his experience. One point that must have been obvious to him was contained in the list of those who voted to deprive him of his life. Conservative Church of England men were definitely not his friends; the vote was admittedly not uniformly split between Whigs and Tories, but it is instructive that the leaders of the most extreme High Church—Tory—faction, Nottingham and Queen Mary's maternal uncle the Earl of Rochester, voted to convict. Mohun's supporters, those prepared to excuse him on the grounds of youth or because his involvement in the murder was peripheral, included many of his father's surviving friends and the leaders of the Whig party. It was a lesson the fourth Lord Mohun never forgot.

Confident in his notoriety, Charles continued to lead the life of a rake. In October 1694, when engaged in a contretemps with one of London's notoriously feisty hackney coachmen, Mohun drew his sword and would have stabbed the man had not a member of Parliament, Francis Scobell, intervened. Scobell received a cut on the head from Mohun's sword for his pains, followed by a challenge from the outraged peer. As far as we know, the duel was never fought. Early in 1695 Mohun cornered and beat a newsletter writer in a coffeehouse, apparently for some slighting reference in print. In the spring of 1697 Mohun and an army officer fought a duel in St. James's Park. Park keepers broke up the swordplay before anyone was killed, but Mohun was wounded in the hand. In September of the same year, after a typically drunken evening spent with army officers and men-about-town, Mohun quarreled with yet another gentleman, ironically named Captain Hill. This officer in the Coldstream Guards, William Hill, somehow or other offended Mohun. He left Hill stabbed and bleeding on the floor of the Rummer Tavern in Charing Cross, and the captain later died. Interestingly, although this was the second murder with which the noble lord had been involved, and despite his incorrigible behavior since his trial, Mohun suffered hardly more than an inconvenience in this case, though he had indisputably killed Captain Hill.

After some time on the run, Mohun was captured by constables at the London home of another of his rakehell friends, the young Earl of Warwick. He was released on bail, and the lords once again prepared to try one of their own. On this occasion, however, there was no trial. Preparations went very slowly, and just before proceedings were to get under way in April 1698 Mohun appeared before the House with a royal pardon from King William that made a trial moot. The fact that Lord Mohun was now only days beyond his twenty-first birthday might have had something to do with the King's mercy. The day after his pardon he took his seat in the House of Lords, another reliable vote for the Crown. William's lengthy wars with France had sapped his popularity: taxes and the national debt staggered the nation, and he found himself relying more and more heavily upon the narrow majority of the Whigs in Parliament—especially those in the Lords, where they were strongest. Hanging a Whig peer who had done nothing more than murder a drunken officer was not good politics. Barely a month later William bestowed a present of £300 in cash upon his new supporter, no doubt confirming Mohun's devotion to the Crown.[32]

Nor was this the end of Mohun's violent career: he faced his peers once again, this time accused of assisting his friend Warwick in the murder of Captain Richard Coote in Leicester Square in the wee hours of Sunday, October 30, 1698. The fight was, as such fights always seemed to be, the result of a drinking party gone bad. Words were exchanged among a group of reeling, heavily armed men, and the result was inevitable: curses, drawn swords, and a blade struck into the vitals of an unlucky gentleman. For once, Mohun really was no more than an innocent bystander, one who had made a genuine effort to soothe the ruffled feelings of some of the quarreling gentlemen. Both he and his friend Warwick were tried separately in Westminster Hall, despite the fact that no one knew for sure who among the five men present had actually stabbed Coote. Amid complaints about the expense Christopher Wren caused the state with his lavish decorations of the hall—he borrowed luxurious tapestries illustrating the stories of Caesar and Pompey, as well as those of Hannibal and Scipio—the House modeled its proceedings on Mohun's first trial. Warwick was convicted of manslaughter. The earl pleaded benefit of clergy, which in the case of a first offense assured him of no more than a symbolic punishment.* Warwick was "burned with a cold iron"; that is, the executioner touched his hand with a cold branding iron, which, had it been hot, would have seared the letter "F" for "felon" into his flesh forever. Mohun was acquitted unanimously, though it seems clear that some peers, despite the weak case, at least contemplated putting a final conclusion to the obnoxious young man's career. The Lord Chancellor, Lord Somers, presided over the trial and at its conclusion warned Mohun that his calamitous life could not continue as it had—the patience of his brother peers, he hinted, was wearing dangerously thin. But only the most optimistic among

* "Benefit of clergy" was a peculiar survival of medieval practice, when clerics were supposed to be tried only by church and not by secular courts. A clerical defendant proved his status by demonstrating his literacy, a skill in those days largely confined to his order. By the late seventeenth century, however, the privilege applied to any one who could pass a literacy test, usually based upon the ability to read a verse from the Bible, the "hanging verse." Since courts often chose the same verse, even the illiterate could escape punishment, though (in theory at least) the privilege could be invoked only once: a second conviction would result in the full punishment of the law.

the onlookers could have imagined that Somers's words would have any impact.[33]

The principal characters of this story were hardly known to each other by the time of Lord Mohun's second trial. Almost twenty years separated Charles, Lord Mohun, and James, Earl of Arran, but they shared much more than a birthday—April 11. They were both fatherless—James emotionally, and Charles literally. They had both experienced life in the Tower of London as state prisoners. They led lives of violence and improvidence that typified an age that had seen much of both. The pulpits rang with denunciations of drinking, fighting, debt, and sexual immorality, but complaining parsons seemed only to encourage new outrages, and these two nobles seemed always among the most notorious sinners. Neither lord had yet encountered the other, except perhaps in the most superficial way—seen across a crowded tavern perhaps, or at some overfilled ceremony at court. But for their politics—one a devoted Whig, the other a barely disguised Jacobite—one can readily imagine them stumbling out of a bout of late-night drinking arm in arm. Politics was more than enough to divide men (and women, too) when political defeat easily led to exile, jail, or even death, but soon these two lords would clash over an even more fundamental cause of rancor: money. Though neither man had ever visited a valuable Cheshire estate called Gawsworth, and neither knew the gentlemen who began a feud over possession of that property over fifty years before, time and chance would make their names all too familiar. The roots of their fatal conflict lay in events that had unfolded long before either was born.

TWO

Evil Inheritance

SIR Edward Fitton's luck ran out at Bristol. Until August 1643 fortune smiled upon the forty-year-old Royalist colonel, never more so than when he survived the storming of England's second city a month earlier. On July 26, 1643, King Charles I's nephew, Prince Rupert of the Rhine, had ordered a direct assault against the heavily fortified city, ignoring the advice of many of his officers. Apart from its port, vital for trade and naval operations, Bristol housed tons of gunpowder, dozens of badly needed cannon, and, better still, a group of merchants whose fat purses could be squeezed to yield a steady stream of gold to finance Charles's war effort. Rupert's plan was costly—the result was carnage on a large scale; Royalist levies were mown down as they rushed the defenses, easy targets for the garrison shielded by its earthen walls. But the general was successful. The King's forces swarmed over the ramparts by virtue of their numbers, forcing the defenders to surrender the city.

Fortune's approval of the officer from an obscure corner of Cheshire continued even after Bristol's capitulation. King Charles arrived to inspect his newly won port city, and Fitton, who had lived a quiet life in the country before the war, found himself at the center of affairs. Never even a member of Parliament before the wars, he saw his King every day, and Charles, impressed by his abilities, appointed him governor of the town. The King's favor demonstrated that Fitton would be a man of importance; the civil war had raised a whole generation of new leaders out of obscurity: why not Sir Edward Fitton? Opportunity beckoned: Charles had already rewarded many with knighthoods and even peerages—perhaps in time there would be a new Lord Fitton.* Edward's estate at Gawsworth, Cheshire, was large enough to support a peerage, and his devotion to the King's cause was unquestionable. But this run of good fortune came to an abrupt end just as Sir Edward began to enjoy it. In August, not even a month after the capture of Bristol, he fell ill.

Fitton had cheated death before the fortifications of Bristol, but now that he had settled into the comfortable quarters assigned to the garrison's commander, mortality would not be denied. The doctors called his illness "consumption," a vague term that covered a wide range of illnesses; and in this case it was very probably pneumonia. The typical remedies of the day served no purpose beyond further weakening the patient, and soon Fitton's case was desperate. Word of the colonel's illness spread, and a ghoulish scramble for his worldly goods began.

Edward Fitton was a rich but childless man. In the previous two centuries his family, through shrewd dealing and lucky marriages, had built an estate in Cheshire and Lancashire that brought in more than £2,000 a year. Fitton's old-fashioned half-timbered manor house at Gawsworth had an air of fusty decay about it; in fact, one wing of the U-shaped structure teetered on the verge of collapse. Yet the beauty of its situation, with a

---

* Sir Edward was a baronet, an ancient title revived by James I and used as a device to raise money (many baronetcies were sold) or reward service. A baronet was a commoner, but he had precedence over other knights (distinguished by the title "Sir") and had the advantage of being able to pass his title to his eldest son, a privilege not granted to ordinary knights.

6. The Old Hall at Gawsworth, Cheshire,
home of the Fitton family, inherited by the Earls of Macclesfield,
and disputed by Mohun and Hamilton

medieval church a stone's throw from the hall and well-stocked fishponds at the door, made the estate as attractive to live in as it was profitable. The family's conservatism probably added to the value of the land. Despite the hall's unfashionable antiquity, the family never undertook any elaborate rebuilding, thus saving considerable expense. Many gentlemen found themselves in financial trouble as a result of their building projects; the Fittons preferred to invest in more land, enhancing the value of their property for future generations.

But in 1643 the problem facing a dying Edward Fitton was the future generation itself, not his provision for it. Producing heirs was the first duty of a gentry family, and the Fittons had excelled at this for over two hundred years. The ladies Fitton, like many gentlewomen, routinely spent much of their married life pregnant. Infants came and, unfortunately, went in startling numbers, thanks to the high rate of infant mortality. Sir Edward's parents, for example, produced a dozen children: four boys and eight girls. Edward was the only male alive by 1643, although seven of his sisters survived. But Sir Edward failed to live up to his family's tradition. His first wife, Jane, bore him a daughter who died when she was seven, but no other children. His second wife, Felicia, had no children. The prospect of an end to the family line loomed.

Fitton conservatism balked at the family's disappearance from Cheshire, and Sir Edward had thought seriously about how to resolve his dilemma, a problem that grew more pressing as the kingdom spiraled toward civil war in November 1641. How to keep Gawsworth in Fitton hands? His seven sisters were all married—at a cost to himself of some £11,000 in dowries—so none still bore the Fitton name. One solution offered itself in the person of a kinsman, William Fitton. As an heir William left much to be desired; he was only a cousin and his estate was none too large. Worst of all, he was an Irishman. Only the most acute family crisis would force an English gentleman to look across the Irish Sea for rescue, but Sir Edward's situation seemed desperate. It might have been a comfort that William's Irish roots were relatively shallow; his father, Sir Edward Fitton, had left Cheshire and gone to Ireland in the 1570s to make his fortune. Queen Elizabeth's determination to stamp out resistance to English rule there led many ambitious gentlemen to Ireland, where they prospered, provided they were ruthless enough. Evidently the Elizabethan Sir Edward Fitton had been well suited to the task. After overseeing the devastation of Connaught in the west of the island, he settled into the more comfortable and profitable post of Lord Treasurer. Secure in his high office, the Treasurer was never tempted to return to his home; he focused his attentions upon founding a new, Anglo-Irish, Fitton dynasty. When he died he was buried in St. Patrick's Cathedral in Dublin, leaving his son William as head of the family.

Anglo-Irish society, built upon conquest and the brutal suppression of the native majority, often produced grasping men skilled in the arts of self-aggrandizement. The Irish Fittons were no exception, and no doubt the English Sir Edward embraced his cousin with considerable wariness. Whatever his doubts, however, on November 9, 1641, Fitton made a new will, leaving his estate to his cousin. Aside from a few legacies to his sisters' children, nothing descended to the rest of the family. This new settlement, for obvious reasons, provoked bad feelings. Lady Fitton would be provided for; if she outlived her husband she would hold Gawsworth until her death. But his sisters did not appreciate Sir Edward's devotion to the family name, and pressed him repeatedly to change his mind. On this score the last of the Gawsworth Fittons was adamant: "I would rather settle my estate on Ned Fitton the bonny beggar than on any of my sisters or their children."[1] Handing the property over to Ned—who was not of the family at all—would have been even more extreme than giving it to the Irish Fittons. Ned was "a poor man who kept idle vagrants from Sir Edward's gates" in return for the occasional penny tossed at him by the lord of the manor.

In the midst of his family's importunities, civil war broke out between the King and his Parliament, and Sir Edward marched away to his destiny in the governor's house at Bristol. But the family did not allow minor details like war and near anarchy in the countryside to divert their attention from their own interests. Charles Gerard, son of Edward's sister Penelope, became the family's point man in the harassment of his uncle. Charles was the connection that would ultimately draw Mohun and Hamilton together—as a kinsman and potential benefactor to both. Gerard could talk to his uncle; he, too, was a colonel in the King's service. The two men were linked by blood and as comrade-in-arms, and Charles was determined to persuade his uncle to reverse his will—especially once illness struck.

A city in the midst of war is no place to lie deathly ill, and Sir Edward's sufferings were made even more excruciating by the demands of a battalion of expectant relatives. Upon hearing the news of his cousin's plight, William Fitton set out immediately from Ireland, despite the chaos prevailing on both sides of the Irish Sea. His rivals, closer to the scene, arrived even faster. Colonel Charles Gerard's uncle, Ratcliffe Gerard, persuaded one of Fitton's closest friends, Captain John Davenport, to press his nephew's case. Charles Gerard, he argued, was a sound Royalist, obviously the man to carry on the Fitton traditions. The Irish Fittons had done nothing to advance the King's cause; in fact, the Gerards claimed that they were in arms against the King.[2] This pressure did nothing but irritate the dying man: though weak and barely able to move in his bed, Sir Edward summoned up enough energy to reprove his friend sharply, "Well, Jack, I smell a *Rat;* they that put thee on this, shall never be the better for troubling me, I have already settled my estate, and thou knowest on whom. I neither will nor can alter it."[3] Sir Edward's punning reference to Ratcliffe Gerard put his friend on notice that he was well aware of the machinations of his heirs.

Not long afterward Sir Edward Fitton died, leaving a raft of angry, quarreling relatives to accompany his corpse to the King's civil war capital at Oxford, where it was buried. The Fitton sisters saw no reason to give up their claims simply because of their brother's unnatural mulishness. They took advantage of the disorder of the times and seized part of the property. The widowed Lady Fitton continued, as was her right, to live in the manor house at Gawsworth. William Fitton, determined to make good his claim, worked assiduously to succeed her. He produced Sir Edward's will, confirming his right to the property. More important, Fitton kept a weather eye on the political situation. No one knew better than an Anglo-Irishman that the law served those who made it; after all, English rule in Ireland was based in part upon the manipulation of the common law. The indigenous Irish had lost their land not through a simple process of military conquest (though there was that, too) but by more subtle means: lawsuits and legal judgments issued in behalf of an alien legal system. The King's capture of Bristol marked a high point in the

Royalist war effort, and by 1645 Parliament stood poised to triumph. The crushing Parliamentarian victory at Naseby in the summer of 1645 made Fitton's course obvious: rely upon Parliament and Parliament's law to dislodge the other heirs from Gawsworth.

Several lawsuits ensured the ejection of the sisters from the lands they seized after Edward's death, and finally, after the death of Lady Fitton in 1654, the Irish Fittons took full control of the entire estate. Sir Edward Fitton's will was finally fulfilled. Or was it? The vanquished, including Charles Gerard, were still unsatisfied, but Gerard was, in the 1650s, hardly in a position to vindicate his own right. If the Fittons had adroitly attached themselves to the winning side in the war, Gerard was inextricably bound up with the losers. Finally a general in Charles I's service, he was rewarded with a peerage in 1645. He had no choice but exile after the war, and was helpless as the Fittons took control of Gawsworth.

Gerard did not, however, waste his years of exile. He made many enemies among Charles II's devoted band of followers, but the new King himself became a close friend. Charles was attracted by Gerard's decisive nature; Gerard was a man for whom action, even ruthless action, was natural. When not quarreling with the more moderate members of the exiled court, he plotted the assassination of Lord Protector Oliver Cromwell and intrigued, fruitlessly, against the usurper's government. When in 1660 the revolutionary government in England collapsed, no thanks to Gerard's schemes, he entered the promised land. And Gawsworth, as far as Lord Gerard was concerned, was the capital of this new Canaan. The Irish Fittons, opportunists who had battened onto Cromwell and emerged with an estate of over £2,000 a year, found too late that they had placed their fortune in the hands of an unreliable god.

William, now old and in declining health, had no stomach for the upcoming struggle, and left the work of defending the family's position to his son Alexander. Alexander was himself no mean opponent. Unlike most gentlemen of his day, he had a thorough knowledge of the law, having been trained as a barrister in London. He was well respected and, as events would show, a dogged combatant, even when all the odds were against him. He married an Englishwoman, and determined to follow his fortune in England rather than return to Ireland, where the rest of the family lands lay.

For a year after the Restoration, the two sides gathered their forces, watching and waiting for an opportunity to act. Alexander, probably aware of his own weakness in a contest with one so close to the King, made the first move, a conciliatory one. Traveling the abysmal roads between Cheshire and the capital, he paid Gerard a visit. Worrying rumors were circulating that his rival would soon lay claim to the property, and he thought a meeting with Gerard might settle matters. The interview, according to Alexander, went well. He found a jovial Lord Gerard ensconced in pleasant lodgings close to Whitehall, basking in his own newly acquired eminence. Gerard's demeanor was friendly, but his questions about the estate seemed ominous: Did Alexander have much trouble about his estate? Did he think that anyone might try to challenge his possession? Obviously concerned about his title, Alexander suggested an amicable settlement, an offer that Gerard ignored.[4] Returning to Gawsworth, Alexander Fitton could have had little doubt that an attack would soon be launched from London.

He did not have to wait long. Soon after the London trip, Gerard began undermining Fitton's claim to the estate. He filed lawsuits challenging Sir Edward Fitton's disposition of his property and asserted his own right to the land. He produced, for the first time, a document he claimed was a will, written when Sir Edward lay dying. This document, dated August 16, 1643, gave the whole Gawsworth estate to Charles Gerard, a reward from one devoted Royalist to another. True, it appeared as though Fitton had not sealed the will as the law required, but the clerk who registered the document years before claimed that an unnamed "interested party" had torn the seals off the will. It was also true that nearly all the witnesses were long dead, but Gerard could get some of their friends and relatives to confirm that the signatures were genuine. And it was also true that this document remained unknown and unheard of from the time of Sir Edward's death until Lord Gerard miraculously produced it, but this, too, could be explained; after all, he had been in exile for most of the time since his uncle's death, and he certainly would never have received justice at the hands of Oliver Cromwell's judges.

Now the issue was joined. Each side rested its claim upon the late Sir Edward's wishes and had documents to prove its case. Lord Gerard had a will. Alexander Fitton had a will. The King's judges would decide who would prevail, relying upon principles of common law and equity. The courts existed to search to the bottom of such cases and give redress to those who had been wronged—that, at any rate, was the theory, and sometimes even the reality, of the legal process. But no lawsuit was conducted in a vacuum, and no litigant could safely assume that the truth would inevitably triumph. As one of Lord Gerard's henchmen said, "Do you not know that truth is a naked and weak thing of itself?"[5] The art of successful litigation lay in clothing naked truth in plausible raiment. This Lord Gerard was well equipped to do.

In keeping with his piratical nature, Gerard did not simply leave matters to the courts. His first ploy was to make life at Gawsworth as uncomfortable as possible for his opponent, and at the same time weaken Fitton's ability to fight back. The efficacy of a well-timed dirty trick was something the King's friend had learned long ago; years of plotting against Cromwell gave him experience in these matters, and he never forgot those lessons. Two of Gerard's servants appeared in Cheshire with a sheaf of papers freshly printed in London. These documents simulated official parliamentary orders, and were even signed by the clerk of

Parliament. The papers proclaimed that after a careful search the clerk of Parliament had found no order of the House of Commons instructing the tenants at Gawsworth to pay their rents to the Fittons or forbidding Lord Gerard from suing to gain possession of the estate. This pseudo-proclamation was a clever idea, for there never had been such an order made by the House of Commons, nor had the Fittons claimed that one existed. Gerard's ploy served his cause by raising questions among the tenants in Cheshire about their landlord's rights to the property. Tenants would often seize upon such excuses to avoid paying their rents. Any ambiguity about the estate's title was an open invitation for wily occupants to avoid their obligations. Even conscientious tenants might be dissuaded from paying by the fear that a new landlord might demand that they pay their rents all over again. Gerard's trick would not win the case, but by sowing uncertainty among Fitton's tenants he could enhance his prospects of success. More important, by impeding the collection of rents, Gerard could make it harder for Fitton to pay his legal bills. Nor could Fitton easily borrow money if he had to offer as security an estate with a disputed title. Such troubles usually sent lenders scurrying back to their ledgers, fearful of risking their money.

In 1661 Fitton returned to London, hoping to restore confidence in his position and to challenge Gerard's tactics. Fitton found his opponent swaggering through the New Palace Yard just outside Parliament, followed by a train of heavily armed lackeys. A belligerent Gerard inquired if Fitton dared charge him with forging Acts of Parliament. He threatened to accuse Fitton of defamation and to haul him before the House of Lords. Gerard then blustered his way back to the House, trailing bloodcurdling promises to cut off several noses. Fitton, intimidated by Gerard's rhetoric, stood aghast outside Westminster Palace, stunned by the force of the peer's hostility.

The pressure on Fitton continued; Gerard had notices read in Gawsworth parish church warning tenants not to pay their rents and threatening further retribution. Yet Fitton was not a negligible figure in Cheshire, nor was he prepared to withdraw from the field. The Cheshire Grand Jury denounced Gerard's phony proclamation as false and scandalous, giving Fitton a victory where it counted most, at home among his tenants. Nevertheless these minor exchanges were merely a prelude to Gerard's most determined assault on Fitton. He set his sights on the all-important will executed by Sir Edward in 1641. This document confirmed the Irish Fittons as his heirs should there be no son from Sir Edward's second marriage. Somehow the courts must be persuaded that Fitton's will was invalid if Gerard was to win his case. Charles, Lord Gerard, had a plan.

London, Britain's largest city and the political and social center of the realm, was also the kingdom's crime capital. Its wealth attracted unscrupulous men and women searching for easy money, as well as the unemployed and desperate struggling to survive. The dingy alleys and side streets of the city abounded with criminals: pickpockets, sneak thieves, burglars, and con artists of all sorts. These people managed to secure a precarious living by preying upon the careless or vulnerable. As James, Earl of Arran, would later discover when he was assaulted in his chair, the streets harbored many dangerous predators. The criminal underworld flourished despite the harsh penalties of the law: hanging was often the first resort of the state. Many Londoners, however, knew no other way to make a living, and some would choose no other.

One of these desperate characters was Abraham Granger. A shifty crook with an evil reputation, Granger lived by his highly regarded skills as a forger.[6] In London, where the opportunities in his trade were widest, he was known for his ability to counterfeit nearly any style of handwriting. In early 1662 he was making his living forging a newly invented type of security: naval tickets. These documents were issued by the Admiralty to unpaid sailors, acknowledging the amount of the King's debt to them. When money was available from the Treasury, the tickets could be exchanged for coin. The Crown's chronic lack of cash made such royal IOUs necessary, and soon there was a market for them. Sailors could not eat IOUs, and they sold the tickets for cash—at a discount—in order to feed hungry families or fund long-awaited binges in taverns and brothels. At some later date the buyers redeemed the tickets for money, often turning a handsome profit. Abraham Granger manufactured his own naval tickets, swindling the government in the process. The crime was a felony; possibly even treason (counterfeiting the King's coin was treason; no one knew about the recently invented tickets). If convicted, Granger would, at a minimum, be hanged. If he was unlucky he might also be drawn and quartered, the grisly punishment reserved for traitors.

Riding into town one day in March—probably pleased with a business that put him on the back of a horse, while so many other common fellows trudged through the mire of London's streets— Granger entered Gray's Inn Lane, a crowded thoroughfare leading to the heart of the city. Suddenly he found himself surrounded by strangers who pulled him from his horse and dragged him to the Gate House, a city prison. Granger recognized some of the men who seized him as professional "thief takers," unsavory bounty hunters who worked for anyone who would hire them. The men rifled his pockets, stealing thirty gold coins and some valuable lace. When Granger protested, they threatened him with hanging if he made any more trouble: "They had one of the biggest at the Court would justifie them in whatever they did against me . . ."[7]

A week passed before Granger began to understand what was in store. Late in the evening the turnkey, Sergeant Rowe, "a murderous villain," burst into his prisoner's cell and asked whether Granger had counterfeited a will for Mr. Alexander Fitton. Lord Gerard wanted most particularly to know the answer. Startled, Granger said he had never heard of Alexander Fitton, nor did he know Gerard. Disgruntled, Rowe left. Over the next several days

Rowe returned repeatedly, disturbing Granger's sleep, to put the same question. The turnkey told the bewildered Granger that Lord Gerard was determined to prove Fitton's will a forgery. Unless Granger confessed, there was more than enough evidence to hang him on other charges. Abraham faced a dilemma: forging a will was no less a hanging offense than forging naval tickets, but on the other hand Lord Gerard was a powerful man, a friend of the King, and His Majesty could pardon a convicted felon. What to do?

Rowe's brutal treatment of Granger continued, but Mr. Dobson, Gerard's secretary, soon appeared to give the frightened prisoner hope. Testify against Fitton, and not only would the forged tickets be forgotten, but Gerard would pay him an annual pension of £100 for life. This was a great deal of money, the gallows were uncomfortably near, and Granger had no reason to help the mysterious Alexander Fitton. So with a show of reluctance—possibly even with genuine reluctance—Abraham gave in and promised to testify. He was immediately moved to more comfortable quarters, paid for by Dobson, and rehearsals for his role in the trial began.

Learning his part was hard work. Understandably wary, Abraham hoped to avoid incriminating himself as far as possible, but this would not do. Temporizing only enraged Gerard, who swore that he would have Granger's "fingers and arms cut off" and see to it that the forger spent the rest of his life in a dungeon.[8] Mr. Dobson brought a variety of disreputable characters to Granger's cell, where they concocted the story of Fitton's alleged misdeed. Granger would testify that Alexander paid him forty pounds for the forgery; one of Fitton's old servants would tell how he saw Fitton and Granger together, and a troop of soldiers and thief takers would provide corroborating evidence. Several weeks of labor produced a story that Dobson judged fit for the court, and by the time the case was scheduled, Gerard's preparations were made.

The trial unfolded in the Court of King's Bench in November 1662. Granger's mentor Dobson took his pupil to Westminster

Hall before proceedings began; Abraham had never seen Alexander Fitton, and there could be no slipups when the two men met in court. Whether inspired by fear of Gerard's wrath, the prospect of a comfortable £100 a year, or both, Granger performed flawlessly. He identified Fitton in court as the man who paid him to produce a forged document, and was supported by "a regiment of witnesses" who all testified to the truth of the story, though some were such poor actors that they required the assistance of a script, held furtively in their hands. The tableau convinced the jury, which declared Fitton's evidence a forgery: his property was lost.

Alexander was beaten, but he refused to give in. He continued his struggle in the courts—unsuccessfully—and then foolishly turned to the court of popular opinion. A lively market for gossip and scandal flourished in an increasingly literate England, especially in London and the larger cities. Fitton chose to take his case directly to the public: a dangerous course, for the press was hardly "free" in the modern sense. Theoretically, all books and pamphlets had to be licensed before they were printed, but an author with a dodgy work might have it published in Holland and smuggled into England—or printed in England with a false imprint. The law punished violators severely, and attacking powerful men in print, particularly nobles, was especially risky business. Fitton, denied legal redress, sought revenge. No pamphlet, however hard-hitting, could reverse a judgment of the King's Bench, but Alexander went ahead anyway.

Abraham Granger suffered a fit of conscience after the verdict— or so he claimed. We might suspect that his real grievance against Gerard was the disappearance of his promised £100 annuity, but in any event, he offered his story to his victim. The result was *A True Narrative of the Proceedings in the Severall Suits in Law That Have Been Between the Right Honourable Charles Lord Gerard of Brandon, and Alexander Fitton, Esq.* Granger told his tale, presenting himself as the innocent victim. Lord Gerard, not surprisingly, emerged as a grotesque bully and villain. The title page of the pamphlet said

that it was published at The Hague—it was certainly unlicensed—
and when the injured peer presented the work to his colleagues in
the House of Lords, they were outraged. *Scandalatum magnatum*—
libeling a peer—was a serious offense, and though Granger was
nowhere to be found, Fitton was available, because he had only just
been released from jail, where Gerard had sent him on a perjury
charge.* The Lords hauled Fitton before the House and accused
him of insulting one of their own, obliged him to apologize on
bended knee, fined him £500, and denounced the pamphlet as
false and scandalous. The hangman publicly burned two copies of
the work in a solemn ceremony, but there is no doubt that quite a
few survived to indict Lord Gerard to his contemporaries. Unable
to raise the money for his fine, or to find anyone willing to stand as
sureties, Fitton remained in jail for over twenty years.

Gerard's victory over Fitton seemed complete; his vindication
in the Lords confirmed his good fortune, and soon he took up residence in Gawsworth Hall. The new lord of the manor took his
place among his servants and tenants, who well knew the power
he wielded. Alexander Fitton had gone back to jail, while his
enemy enjoyed the rents and profits of an estate worth at least
£40,000. In 1665 the King awarded Gerard an annual pension of
£1,000, and three years later Gerard sold his command of the royal
guard for £12,000 more. Gerard's fortune financed a new house in
London as well as a life of noble extravagance. His children married well. But success did nothing to limit Gerard's greed or temper his ruthlessness.

Gerard's star rose to its loftiest height in the spring of 1679, when
King Charles promoted him to the rank of earl. He took the title of
Macclesfield, a market town about three miles from Gawsworth.
That the people of Macclesfield felt flattered by this choice seems
doubtful. For some time, with his usual brutal methods, he had

---

* Except in rare cases, criminal charges in the seventeenth century were privately
prosecuted.

worked to dictate their choices for members of Parliament. Further attentions from the Gerard family could hardly be welcomed.[9] But Gerard's promotion was an impressive achievement: from his beginnings as a poorly endowed nephew of Sir Edward Fitton, he was now an earl and wielded great power. Success came at a price, but the heaviest costs were borne by those who stood in his way. To the new earl, Gawsworth more than repaid him for the broken lives, the lies, and the deceit it took to secure it.

Macclesfield, like some others among his acquaintance, including the third Lord Mohun, never appreciated the virtues of moderation. One successful intrigue encouraged another, and even as he reached the pinnacle of his career he searched for new opportunities to exercise his talents. But in 1679 Macclesfield at last overreached himself, for this time he chose King Charles as his opponent. Destroying a half-Irish country squire was one thing, but now the stakes were far higher. Macclesfield, perhaps envisioning himself as a kingmaker, espoused the cause of the Duke of Monmouth. The King's bastard son was handsome, charming, and popular, as was his father. But unlike King Charles, Monmouth lacked political skill, and ambitious characters like Shaftesbury and Macclesfield wanted to use him for their own ends. The goal was to force the King to abandon his brother the Duke of York's claim to the throne, and replace him with the Protestant, and incidentally much more pliable, Monmouth.

Charles II was himself a practiced political infighter, and was, moreover, the King. In 1680 Macclesfield supported York's exclusion from the succession: his vote was tantamount to a declaration of political war against Charles. The Crown's retribution was swift: Charles deprived Macclesfield of all of his offices, and the steady stream of royal gold that once poured into the family coffers ceased abruptly. Eventually, someone remembered that a broken gentleman named Alexander Fitton lay in prison nursing a hatred for the Gerard family. Fitton might prove useful, and in 1684 the government released him. The title to Gawsworth was again in dispute.

This was a stunning reversal of fortune. Now Macclesfield was naked to his enemies. The King and his allies had already broken the back of the Exclusion movement; Shaftesbury lived in exile; Exclusionist friends like the third Lord Mohun were dead or had been hounded into submission. A determined government sent several peers to the block on dubious evidence, and one of the accused traitors claimed that Macclesfield had encouraged the assassination of the Duke of York. The earl faced enemies on all fronts, and Fitton, anxious for revenge, intended to make the most of his opportunity.

Macclesfield's situation was grim. As he knew very well, the courts could be subjected to pressure. The King appointed his judges; juries could be manipulated; evidence could be manufactured and witnesses intimidated. Fitton surely approached his new trial before Lord Keeper Guilford, a loyal anti-Exclusionist, with confidence.* It was now Fitton's turn to attack the Gerard claim to Gawsworth. Macclesfield, he maintained, held the estate on the basis of a phony will. Now Fitton accused the earl of forgery. To Alexander's shock, however, Guilford defied expectations: Fitton had waited too long to challenge Macclesfield's title. The courts had handed down their last verdict twenty-two years earlier, and Macclesfield's possession was sanctioned by the passage of time. Guilford dismissed Fitton's claim, and the Gerards retained possession of Gawsworth.[10]

Macclesfield's escape was a narrow one, however, and he had little time to savor his victory. James II's accession in February 1685 made him a marked man, and in the aftermath of Monmouth's abortive rebellion the earl fled to the Continent with a charge of treason hanging over his head. Fitton was in high favor at the new King's court: he pleased James by declaring himself a Catholic, and in reward the King granted him a knighthood and

---

* As Lord Keeper, Guilford's task was to preside over the Court of Chancery in the absence of a Chancellor; kings sometimes chose not to appoint the latter officer.

appointed him Lord Chancellor of Ireland. Now Alexander experienced another dizzying turn of fortune's wheel, as Gerard had done. From imprisoned forger and perjurer, he now held the highest office in his native land. Though still denied his estate at Gawsworth, with Macclesfield in exile it seemed only a matter of time before a Fitton once again resided in Cheshire.

But like his father and Sir Edward Fitton before him, Alexander had backed the wrong horse. Before the slow-moving machinery of the law could pry the Gerard family out of Gawsworth, James II's government was no more. In 1688 Fitton followed his master into exile, losing forever not only Gawsworth but his family's Irish lands as well. Parliament declared him a traitor, and his loyalty to James was hardly compensated when the exiled monarch granted him a meaningless title. But Alexander, defiant to the end, offered a final calculated insult to Macclesfield, the man who had ruined him, and chose to be Baron Fitton of Gawsworth. He died without seeing the Old Hall again, but the memory of the estate for which he had fought so tenaciously never faded.

The Earl of Macclesfield returned from his exile in the train of William of Orange in an ironic replay of his role in Charles II's Restoration. King William's need for loyal support among the peerage overcame the old villain's reputation, and Macclesfield soon found himself back at Gawsworth, a Privy Councilor and Lord President of the Council of Wales. Admittedly, the earl now had less scope for his talents as a licensed buccaneer, but both posts were highly honorable ones. He would spend his latter years boasting of his crucial part in the overthrow of James II and complaining about the state of his house.

Unlike Sir Edward Fitton, the first Earl of Macclesfield had at least prepared for posterity: he had five children, two boys and three girls. His daughter Charlotte married Sir Thomas Orby, a gentleman closely connected with the Mohun family. Those ties became closer still when Thomas's father, Charles, married off his ward, the fourth Lord Mohun, to his own granddaughter, also named Charlotte. Another Macclesfield daughter, Elizabeth, married a distant cousin, Lord Gerard of Bromley. Elizabeth and her husband produced only one child, a daughter named for her mother. Thanks to the vagaries of inheritance, the younger Elizabeth Gerard would in time be a great heiress: just the sort of woman a young peer with money troubles dreamed of. In this case the dreamer was James Douglas-Hamilton, Earl of Arran and the Duke of Hamilton's heir. But daughters were less important than sons to seventeenth-century noblemen, and Macclesfield's three girls, though all of them married well, had little chance of inheriting their father's estate.

Gawsworth might have been an evil inheritance, destroying those who failed to obtain it and making miserable those who succeeded, but that made it no less attractive to prospective heirs. The Old Hall was uncomfortable and unfashionable; the tenants, encouraged by two generations of disputes, were recalcitrant and disloyal. But the land yielded a steady profit, and it gave its owner political and social importance. Thanks to the first earl's never-ending efforts, his eldest son, Charles, would one day take his place among the great men of the kingdom.

The young lord was unquestionably his father's son. He first appeared on the national scene in 1676. At the age of sixteen or seventeen he killed a servant in St. James's Park with an overenthusiastic blow to the head. But the death was unintentional, Gerard was drunk, and the victim, by contemporary standards, was of no account. After a short spell in hiding, Gerard emerged to resume his career, unpunished. Family ties and political affinity made him one of the fourth Lord Mohun's staunch friends: he would later stand bail for the young man after Mountford's murder and support his acquittals in the House of Lords.

Like his father, the younger Gerard was closely bound to the cause of Exclusion in the 1680s. He was twice imprisoned in the Tower on treason charges, and in November 1685 convicted and sentenced to death. King James, perhaps hoping to secure a convert to his regime, pardoned him. While his father the earl was in exile, young Gerard remained behind, looking after the estate, flirting with the government's policies.[11] The Revolution enabled him to ignore his obligation to King James, however, and from the first Gerard was a strong supporter of William III's new government.

Gerard's politics brought him in contact with the hard-drinking rakes of the capital, and the pleasures of the flesh attracted him from his earliest days. While his father schemed to advance the family fortune and annihilate his enemies, Gerard made the rounds of the London taverns and theaters, swilling wine, chasing barmaids, and gambling. But as the heir to a great estate, Charles knew that there was a future to provide for. As he entered his twenties, in the early 1680s, the necessity of marriage and an heir loomed larger. From the old earl's point of view, the ideal would be a wealthy, healthy young woman who would add large amounts of cash to the Gawsworth treasury. If his son found the girl attractive, and if the couple were compatible, so much the better. If not, then Charles would have to be reminded of all the sacrifices his father once made to build an estate: exile, legal struggles, and years of vigilance made Gawsworth a prize worth having. No one knew better than young Charles the consequences of crossing his father. Bachelor life had attractions, but the Earl of Macclesfield's revenge could ruin them for his son.

There was no particular reason why marriage should end Gerard's pleasures; many of his married friends conducted themselves as they pleased without much regard for their wives. Many couples lived almost as strangers, but it could not be denied that a wife could, if she was determined enough, turn her husband's pleasures to ashes. As a friend of the Mohun family, Charles would have known this for years. Lady Phillippa Mohun was an object lesson in the perils of matrimony. Nevertheless, family pressures demanded action by the time Gerard entered his early twenties.

The earl and his son winnowed the list of candidates for the position of future Countess of Macclesfield until one eligible woman remained: Anne Mason. Anne's father, Sir Richard, was a rich Londoner, the kind of man who would happily sacrifice a substantial sum to establish his daughter as a peeress. Lawyers for both sides hammered out an agreement, filling sheet after sheet of parchment with the details. The vows exchanged at the marriage ceremony were as nothing compared to the byzantine complexity of a nobleman's marriage settlement. To secure its interests, each family employed a team of highly paid lawyers who made the agreement as ironclad as they could. Creating settlements always brought tension, because harmonizing competing interests was difficult. The bride had an interest, for example, in obtaining as large a jointure as possible. Should she outlive her husband—a distinct possibility, assuming she did not die in childbirth—no sensible gentlewoman wanted to depend upon the generosity of her son for a living. Many heirs were dutiful and never begrudged their mothers a penny, but many others, like Lord Mohun, would cheerfully have starved their aged relatives if given control of the estate's entire revenue. There were even competing interests within families. The groom's father, whose goal was the preservation of his estate over the long term, often wanted to prevent his son from wasting his inheritance or ignoring the claims of younger siblings. The heir wanted as much flexibility in his stewardship of the property as possible, lest he find himself staked down like Gulliver, needled and prodded by niggling restraints imposed upon him by a now-dead parent. Not all heirs—indeed not many of them—had any desire to abandon their trust, but circumstances, combined with their own improvidence, could make a settlement a straitjacket. Through this thicket the Gerards and the Masons managed eventually to reach a satisfactory end. The couple married in June 1683.[12]

Within a month of the marriage, Gerard's politics landed him in the Tower, accused of treason. Anne left London, most unwillingly, for Gawsworth, where she would have to stay under her father-in-law's crumbling roof. She did not long for the quiet of the country: Anne was a headstrong woman who evidently had difficulty accepting her place as obedient wife and humble daughter-in-law. Spending her days isolated in the countryside with an ill-tempered old man was hardly agreeable. She complained that Macclesfield mistreated her, and by the time Gerard was released from prison, in November 1683, she despised the whole Gerard clan. The earl was no less fed up with his daughter-in-law, whom he turned out of the hall.

Relations between Gerard and his wife worsened steadily. Charles, Anne claimed, had married her for money and cared nothing for her. He was unfaithful. He was reckless. He was cruel, and threatened to strike her—a threat she later claimed he carried out. Charles had his own grievances. Anne was disrespectful. She belittled his family. She was disobedient. She entertained company sitting in front of a smelly coal fire, "as if I refused you wood." She was unfaithful. By March 1685 the marriage was effectively finished. After Anne fled to her parents and refused to return home, Charles wrote her a long, accusatory letter, putting a formal end to their relationship: "I now resolve to ease both you and myself of so unpleasing a conversation."[13]

In the later seventeenth century, men and women trapped in broken marriages had few choices. A couple was bound not only by the law of God, which commanded a permanent relationship, but by their marriage settlement. When husband and wife could no longer bear the sight of each other, they lived apart. For a husband, such a state of affairs might be bearable, even convenient. His children remained in his control; in fact, a father could, if he chose, deny his wife all contact with their children. Under the law, all his wife's property was in his power; if she left him he could use its income as he pleased, and though he was required to abide by his marriage settlement and pay for his wife's maintenance, an importunate woman might be intimidated by threats to deny her access to her children. A determined husband could even force her to return to the family home against her will. For an estranged wife, the freedom from her husband's immediate presence could be an expensive luxury. Moreover, the prevailing moral double standard accepted a man's decision to keep mistresses, while it discouraged women from searching for other partners. Only a very determined woman defied society's rules.

Henry VIII notwithstanding, the option of divorce was hardly feasible. The Church of England oversaw what we would now describe as family law; husbands and wives could, by suing in an ecclesiastical court, obtain legal separations. Within a patriarchal system, the courts did try to protect wives, whose position was so much weaker than that of their husbands. The courts ordered maintenance allowances and could decree permanent separations. What they never did, however, was grant divorces that left the couple free to marry again. Additionally, church courts worked very slowly and could involve considerable expense—they charged substantial fees, as did the lawyers who represented litigants.

Most people, including Charles and Anne, opted to live separately without recourse to the law. This state of affairs continued for a decade, even after the old earl died and Gerard became the second Earl of Macclesfield in 1694. By 1695 this solution was unsatisfactory. The countess's life had for a decade been of no concern to her husband, whose political career and private pursuits kept him too busy to worry much about a woman he despised. But suddenly Macclesfield found himself very interested in her. After a decade of solitude, Anne found a companion: Richard Savage, fourth Earl Rivers. Rivers was estranged from his own wife and had garnered a formidable reputation as a seducer of women. The Countess of Macclesfield became one of his trophies.

A dalliance on the countess's part might not have bothered her husband. His own life had certainly not been free from such affairs, and celibacy, though often admired from the pulpit, was a virtue of limited attraction for many aristocrats of the day. Anne lived in London, where temptation was omnipresent; aristocratic society, with its balls, bawdy plays, and heavy drinking, encouraged sexual license. Not every fashionable woman succumbed, but social pressures encouraged illicit sexuality. The Countess of Macclesfield, separated from her husband for a decade, did not resist those pressures forever.

The crisis came with Anne's pregnancy. In her brief life with Charles there had been no children, although they shared a bedroom at least occasionally. The countess did her best to hide her predicament. She probably consummated her affair with Rivers in the spring of 1693, when he was quietly admitted into Anne's bedroom by her maid. Pregnant by November 1694, Anne managed to keep her secret for several months, until at last she took her servant Diana Allsup into her confidence. There may even have been an earlier pregnancy that ended in miscarriage. If Anne had wanted to end her pregnancy, she could have done so, for miscarriages could be induced, and abortifacients were available to women who wanted them. But a termination was dangerous—as dangerous as a normal delivery, if not more so. Moreover, it was illegal. The law considered abortion murder and some women were hanged for it. If Anne considered any of these options, she rejected them. With Diana's help, she organized what she hoped would be a secret delivery. In June 1695, Sarah Richardson, a midwife who lived in Queen Street, Soho, received a visit from a well-dressed woman, whose face was hidden by a mask. This woman engaged Sarah's services and also sought a nursemaid for the coming infant. Richardson, a rather seedy character, provided the house in which Anne began her labor on about the tenth or eleventh of July.

Anne's first labor was excruciating, an experience she had in common with every other mother of her day. There were, of course, no anesthetics, and the circumstances made her situation all the more difficult, as Diana hustled Anne, disguised with a mask, through the streets to the midwife's house. She kept her mask to her face for most of the labor, until finally, in agony, she let it fall. Sarah may not have known the countess's face, but she must have known that she was not dealing with just another lady's maid in trouble. Anne's obvious prosperity tempted Sarah. When in her pain Anne cried out that she was sure that she would die, Richardson said, "I hope not, but if you do, give me your petti-coat." Anne cheated Sarah of her fancy undergarment, because she survived, and gave birth to a girl. Servants hurried the baby off to the nearest church and christened her the same day: Anne Savage. Mary Mountaine, who sold her services as a nursemaid for six shillings a week, then took over from the midwife. Little Anne went to Chelsea, on the outskirts of London, while her mother, feigning illness, went to take the waters at Bath.

Nursing infants led risky lives. Their maids were all too often unhealthy or undernourished, conditions frequently passed on to their charges. Anne Savage had not been in Mary's care long before she became very ill. Only recently returned from Bath, the countess received word that her daughter was sick, after which she paid a visit to Chelsea. It was the last time she saw her infant daughter. The arrival of an apothecary did no good, and the child died, only a few weeks old. The nursemaid placed her charge in a tiny coffin and arranged for her burial; "I was told I might swear the name was Anne Smith or Savage, which I pleased." Diana appeared before the funeral for a lock of the baby's hair, which she passed on to the grieving mother.[14]

The infant's death, sorrowful though it was, must have been a relief for Anne, who was now free to forget her own folly. But her passion for Rivers still lived, despite his increasing indifference. By mid-April 1696 she was again pregnant. By the time Anne began to show her condition, rumor had given Macclesfield a hint of something seriously amiss. In November he sent his sister Charlotte Orby to see his wife, but it seems likely that she was denied entrance to the countess's lodgings.

Once again Anne tried to conceal the birth. Another discreet midwife, Elizabeth Wright, organized Anne's secret lying-in. A heavily pregnant Countess of Macclesfield appeared at Mrs. Wright's narrow home in Fox Court, calling herself Mary Smith, and on January 16, 1697, she gave birth to a son, named Richard for his father. This birth was not as traumatic as her first and was even attended by what the midwife knew was an omen of good fortune: a caul over the baby's face. The caul was a sign of second sight; an infant born with one grew up seeing ghosts and enjoying especially good fortune, or so people had believed for centuries. Two days after Richard's birth, his father brought the minister of St. Andrew's, Holborn, to Mrs. Wright's house. She led the clergyman and his sexton up two narrow flights of stairs, emerging in a small room where "Mary Smith" lay with her newborn son. The fortunate child, his caul removed, was then baptized Richard, son of John and Mary Smith. But Richard was different from others born with a caul; the secret of his birth was too scandalous even to a society accustomed to scandal. He was an embarrassment; a living example of the disgrace brought upon one noble family by the head of another. But there were many in London, who for a price—and not a particularly large one—would look after an unwanted child. Anne put her son in the hands of a Covent Garden baker's wife named Anne Portlock and did her best to forget about him.*

The Earl of Macclesfield, now well aware of his wife's illicit behavior, did not forget. Apart from feeling the humiliation of a cuckold, he worried about the succession to his title and estate. By law, children born to his wife—even those given false names and raised in obscurity—were presumed to be his. The prospect of Richard Smith-Savage-Portlock demanding a seat at Gawsworth's table was intolerable. Even worse was the image of this bastard seated in the House of Lords, wrapped in the Gerard ermine and calling himself the third Earl of Macclesfield. In the summer of 1697 the earl sued his wife for adultery in ecclesiastical court.

---

* Richard's ultimate fate is at the heart of a fascinating story. In 1718 a young man calling himself Richard Savage appeared; Anne claimed he was an impostor and that the real Richard Savage had died young. But he found many supporters, among them Dr. Samuel Johnson. A dispute ran on for years in which Savage, an accomplished poet, tried to claim his rightful inheritance, though in the end he failed. Most scholars now believe that he was in fact a fraud.[15]

To Charles's amazement and mounting frustration, Anne fought back vigorously. The case dragged on for months, the countess's lawyers delaying proceedings when they could. When they could not, they obscured the points at issue with absurd or irrelevant argument. The children born to the countess were in fact the earl's, who tricked her into sex by means of a mask and a wicked servant—a contention so ridiculous that it was trotted out only once. The countess had saved her husband's life when he was in the Tower, they argued irrelevantly. Anne might not win, but she intended to make it a long fight.

But like his father, Macclesfield was a formidable adversary. Church courts, with their grindingly slow procedure and niggling demands to hear all sides, made his task difficult, but he had another option: Parliament. The earl, a devoted Whig, a personal friend of King William, and a man of considerable influence in both Houses, thought he could outwit his wife by an appeal to a higher authority. Parliament had granted very few divorces in the past, apart from Henry VIII's.[16] Yet Macclesfield wanted an unprecedented divorce, one without a prior verdict in a church court. Other cases had involved marriages in which the court had already determined a wife's guilt. What Macclesfield asked was for Parliament to act *before* the spiritual court rendered a verdict, when his wife was, in theory, at least, still innocent. The idea shocked many members and sparked heated debates in both chambers, but especially in the Lords, where the business of government stood still while their lordships pondered the issue.

As the Lords remained bitterly divided between Whig and Tory, it is hardly surprising that their debates generally followed party lines. High Churchmen like the Earl of Rochester strenuously opposed the bill, and strong Whigs, even bishops like Gilbert Burnet, spoke in favor of the divorce. For almost four months, from December 1697 to March 1698, the House of Lords struggled with the bill, examining witnesses and debating the divorce's implications. In a chamber too small to house all its members, the case drew a large attendance, despite the discomfort of squeezing into a crowded and poorly heated room. The salacious details of Anne's secret deliveries kept the house enthralled, and the overwhelming case presented against her ensured that Macclesfield had its sympathy. Ever sensitive to the reputations of its own members, the Lords studiously avoided considering who the father of Anne's children might be, though the evidence was clear.

Finally, after a last protest against the divorce from the arch-Tory Rochester, the bill passed and the King signed it in April 1698. Parliament declared Anne's two children bastards. Both she and Charles were allowed to remarry, and, to Macclesfield's chagrin, the act required him to refund his wife's £12,000 dowry. The divorce became an important precedent. By undermining the role of the spiritual courts, it marked an increase in Parliament's power in matrimonial cases. For the moment, at least, the implications of this new power were limited, because only the wealthiest and most powerful people in the kingdom could consider a resort to Parliament. Nevertheless, the state, rather than the Church, would have the last word about divorce in the future.[17]

For Macclesfield personally, the act was of tremendous importance. It freed him from the specter of a supposititious heir, but it also created a new problem. The earl, nearly forty, had no son. Gawsworth might be left as it had been in Sir Edward Fitton's time: with no direct heir but a crowd of greedy relatives determined to grab a piece of the estate. Charles's marriage settlement with Anne had set forth a strict line of succession: failing any children of his own, the property would go to the earl's younger brother, Fitton Gerard. If Fitton did not survive, or had no heirs, then his sisters and their children would divide the estate among themselves. But the dissolution of Charles's marriage rendered the settlement null and void. Unlike most owners of a large estate, the Earl of Macclesfield was free in 1698 to dispose of his property in whatever way he chose.

Fitton Gerard, a member of the House of Commons for the city of Lancaster, was the obvious person to succeed his brother. He would, assuming Charles had no son, become the third Earl of Macclesfield in due course, for the descent of his title was out of Charles's hands. Gawsworth would, presumably, go along with the title. But all was not well between Charles and his brother. Their relationship had been friendly enough for years. The earl had sponsored his brother's political career, and they have left no evidence of difficulties before the divorce. But the divorce caused a rift between the two men. Fitton presumably had no sympathy for his sister-in-law, but the dissolution of her marriage bore on his rights as Charles's heir. If Gawsworth was solely in his brother's hands, what could stop Fitton from being disinherited? It was a troubling prospect. In March 1698, as the divorce proceedings wound to a conclusion, Fitton petitioned the House of Lords to consider his rights. Macclesfield apparently took his brother's intervention very badly. Fitton thought better of what he had done, and later withdrew his request. But bad feeling remained.

Macclesfield's most devoted supporter, Charles, fourth Lord Mohun, just missed his chance to vote for the divorce. King William gave the royal assent to the bill only days before Mohun took his seat in the House, having just presented his pardon for the murder of William Hill. Mohun was Macclesfield's protégé; perhaps, as a man who had also killed as a teenager, the earl saw something of himself in the wild young baron. Their relationship was cemented by Mohun's marriage into the Gerard clan. Charlotte, Lady Mohun, was Macclesfield's niece, the daughter of his sister Charlotte Orby.

The story of Mohun's first marriage has a familiar ring. The circumstances of the match remain obscure. Sir Charles Orby was Mohun's guardian. His son Thomas was Macclesfield's sister Charlotte's second husband. Lady Charlotte had a daughter, also named Charlotte, and it was this young woman whom the fourteen-year-old Lord Mohun married in 1691. The Orbys probably took advantage of Mohun; no record of a marriage settlement survives, and Charlotte apparently brought no dowry. The embarrassed condition of Mohun's estate might not have rated a very large sum, but some money should have come from the bride's family. If Charlotte received no settlement and Mohun no dowry, Sir Charles put his family's interests above his ward's.

In November 1692 the new Lady Mohun gave birth to a boy, who was baptized, and very shortly afterward buried, in the parish of St. James, Westminster.[18] The death of a newborn infant was by no means unusual; weak babies often died. Yet despite the relative frequency of such bereavements, many parents were deeply touched by their loss, especially if the child was the first. This could hardly have been the case with little Charles; his body had barely come to rest under the church floor before his father began helping plan the abduction of Anne Bracegirdle.

Charlotte's marriage, perhaps never strong, fell apart quickly. Opinions about what went wrong varied. Mohun's mother-in-law later claimed that the wedding only took place because Mohun and her brother "overpersuaded" her. The Orbys charged that from the first Mohun mistreated his wife, and that his immoral lifestyle made him a very bad husband. Given what we know about the way Mohun lived, such an argument seems eminently believable. Furthermore, the Orbys claimed that they supported Charles and Charlotte, gave them a regular allowance for their living expenses, paid their servants' wages, and even contracted a loan of £5,500 to pay Mohun's personal debts. All these charges ring true. That Charles might already have run up thousands in debt would shock no one who knew him. He was already notorious for his drinking and carousing, and of course the murder of Mountford spoke for itself.

Yet it is hard to put all of the blame on Mohun. The Orbys probably pretended to be more innocent than they were. The circumstances around the marriage encourage the suspicion that they saw Mohun as a potentially valuable commodity to be secured in their own interest. Nor did the young Lady Charlotte inspire flattering reports. Mohun later claimed that he abandoned her bed soon after their wedding, for "just cause." He implied that Charlotte was unfaithful. Later, he denied that his wife's daughter, Elizabeth, born about 1693, was his. And a story went abroad, bolstering the rumors about Charlotte's waywardness.

Soon after the wedding, Mohun and his bride made the long trip west from London to Cornwall. Her husband's county was almost as far from metropolitan life as Charlotte could go and still remain in England. The sight of Boconnoc, set on its hill in central Cornwall, could hardly have cheered her. Charlotte must have felt very much as Anne Mason did when introduced to Gawsworth for the first time, although Gawsworth at least stood in a beautiful setting. Like the house in Cheshire, Boconnoc was old and dilapidated, thanks to the sorry state of the Mohun family finances. Charlotte found herself surrounded by clannish family retainers who spoke a dialect virtually unintelligible to a girl who had spent her life in Cheshire and London. Her husband, too, obviously preferred his bachelor's life in the city. After a short stay in Cornwall, Mohun rushed back to the capital, leaving his wife in the hands of an uncle—probably James Mohun—who lived nearby. Apparently, Uncle James seduced Charlotte. The most malicious gossip of the age, Mrs. Manley, said that Mohun actually caught his wife in James's bed. Even if this unlikely scene did not occur, Mohun and his wife separated and lived apart from at least 1694.[19]

The real mystery of the story was Charlotte's fate. After the separation, she becomes a shadowy figure. She did not return to her parents' house, as one would expect of an innocent and badly used young wife. Did Mrs. Manley tell the truth? Charlotte's mother asserted that she gave her daughter twenty pounds a year for three years—a sum that would have been inadequate to support a gentlewoman even in modest circumstances. Unless Mohun subsidized his wife—an unlikely prospect—she must have had other means. The gossip in later years was that she found support as a genteel mistress. There were many women in similar situations at the time; well born but of slender means, they sometimes arrived in London as companions for more prominent ladies. Once in the city, the vagaries of fortune turned them into "kept women." An affair with a gentleman, or even a rape, could render a woman unmarriageable. Relationships formed in these circumstances could be stable and long-lasting; in later years, Mohun himself had such a long-standing affair. In this era a woman in Charlotte's position had considerable autonomy: she was under the thumb of neither husband nor father and might do more or less as she pleased. But these relationships were also precarious, for a lover might tire of his mistress at any time and refuse to pay for her expenses or lodgings. Moreover, as a woman aged she found it more difficult to hold her protector's attention. Almost every public coach that rumbled into London carried some hopeful girl who might become a successful rival.

Charlotte seems to have suffered this fate: she lived in a twilight between prostitution and marriage, dependent upon lovers who might or might not support her. Though the details remain obscure, the life she led after 1694 was wholly unlike the one she expected when she married. She was in London as late as 1702, when she paid a visit to the Earl of Macclesfield's house, probably in an attempt to wrest some money out of the Gerard family. After this fleeting glimpse, however, Charlotte vanishes. Her parents had no idea where she was in 1704, and most people (including Mohun) presumed her dead. Mrs. Manley's story has her sailing away with a lover and drowning picturesquely in a storm at sea. She might have been cast away on a passage to Ireland.[20] The fate of Charlotte, Lady Mohun, was grim. Yet drowning in one of the howling storms that sometimes plagued the Irish Sea might have been preferable to the gradual immiserization endured by those who lived a hand-to-mouth existence as glorified concubines.

Charlotte did leave something of herself behind, however. Her daughter Elizabeth, "my pretended daughter," as Mohun always described her, remained his responsibility, although in fact her Orby grandparents seem to have raised her. She, too, lived an obscure youth, largely ignored. Mohun fixed his interest more intensely upon his wife's maternal relatives, the Gerards, than on any of his own people. The second Earl of Macclesfield was very fond of his young nephew-in-law, and the two were virtually inseparable. They had much in common: loose women, alcohol, and Whig politics being the most notable. They also shared the experience of disastrous marriages, and knew what it was like to be denied an heir. In fact, the lack of an heir interested everyone connected with the Gerard family.

The group of people interested in the Earl of Macclesfield's family life grew more exalted in 1698. On July 17, James, fourth Duke of Hamilton, took another of the earl's nieces as his wife. The negotiations that led to the marriage had lasted for almost three years. Each side haggled enthusiastically over what turned into an extravagantly complex settlement.[21] Elizabeth Gerard, daughter of Macclesfield's sister Elizabeth, was young, attractive, and immensely rich. She was her parents' only child, and her father, a distant cousin of Macclesfield's, had left an estate worth some £70,000. Elizabeth's inheritance of the real portion of the estate would come to her husband on their marriage. Apart from his fortune, Lord Gerard of Bromley had never been an especially attractive man. In life he had few talents, but in 1698 he was dead. He had met his end while drinking heroically in one of Lord Mohun's favorite haunts, the Rose Tavern near Covent Garden, dropping dead of an apoplectic stroke. When Elizabeth's mother, Lady Gerard, died, Elizabeth— or rather her husband—would inherit the entire estate, as well as any property of her mother's. Moreover, as the niece of the childless Earl of Macclesfield, Elizabeth could hope to inherit a large part of the Gawsworth property as well. The prospect of such a fortune, and the desperate nature of his own finances, made James lower his demands for a £20,000 dowry by half, and even sign an agreement, insisted upon by his prospective mother-in-law, that he would never sue her over his wife's inheritance.[22]

Despite his serious financial troubles, James had been very reluctant to marry. Elizabeth would be his second wife, for he

7. A scene from Hogarth's *Rake's Progress*,
set in a private room at the Rose Tavern in London, c. 1730s

had been happily married to Lady Anne Spencer, the second Earl of Sunderland's daughter, from 1689 until her death in childbirth in 1690.

Although James and Anne had little time together, his confinement in the Tower during much of this period was no bar to cohabitation, and they must at least have seen each other regularly, if they did not actually share quarters there. Their marriage had been a refuge from the storm that had enveloped James's life as a result of the Revolution. Hamilton resisted another match for years afterward, despite constant pressure from his family. He was happier with his mistress, Barbara Fitzroy. Barbara was the daughter of Barbara, Duchess of Cleveland, though there is some ambiguity about who her father was. Cleveland was one of Charles II's mistresses, and Barbara was her youngest child, born as the King's passion was waning and the duchess's eye was wandering. The girl's father might have been John Churchill, the great commander soon to become Duke of Marlborough. King Charles was skeptical about his own responsibility, but nevertheless acknowledged the little girl as his. She was about eighteen or nineteen when her affair with James, then still Earl of Arran, began. Their son, Charles, was born while James was still confined in the Tower at William III's orders—in fact, he might even have been conceived there. Eventually, Barbara left England and settled in France, where she became a nun and the head of the priory of St. Nicholas in Pontoise.[23]

The delights Barbara provided, without the fuss and bother of negotiations, marriage settlements, and expensive legal fees, attracted Hamilton, but finances ultimately made the single life impossible. Marriage brought compensations. Elizabeth was beautiful, though temperamental. As Swift described her in 1712, she "talks too much, is a plaguy detractor, and I believe I shall not much like her."[24] She seems to have been used to getting her own way, a characteristic she did not abandon merely because society gave her husband the right to order her around. But for James, the cash from his new wife's dowry reduced the clamor of tradesmen and other creditors. And he expected that part of the Gerard fortune would swell his own after Lady Gerard and her brother Macclesfield died. Nor did all illicit pleasure have to be forgone. In December 1698, a London newsmonger heard that James, less than six months after his marriage, had been "much bruised" by a London mob. He visited one of the city's many alleys where streetwalkers plied their trade for a few pennies a time, and an altercation arose. Perhaps there was an attempt to pick his pocket. In any case, a crowd quickly gathered and gave the discomfited duke a sound drubbing.[25] James's parents had often complained about his fondness for low company, and in this case they were right. Of course, James was by no means unusual in seeking his pleasure so publicly; men of all ranks frequented the alleys in search of cheap sex, and more than a few found themselves the victims of thieves and cutthroats. Even more common were men who spent a little on cut-rate intercourse, then far more on the wide array of cures for venereal disease advertised in the newly founded daily press.

Perhaps his brush with an enraged mob made James more circumspect, for he was never caught in such an awkward situation again. He had more serious concerns: Jacobite politics, his burden of debt, and, more important in the long run, the Gerard family death watch. His mother-in-law was frail and in poor health, and Hamilton, as a potential heir to Gawsworth, took a keen interest in Macclesfield's divorce. He could not vote on the case himself, because he was a peer of Scotland rather than of England, but he followed the proceedings carefully.

Hamilton must have been aware of the developing relationship between Macclesfield and Lord Mohun, and he, too, attempted to cultivate the earl. He badgered his wife to name their son and heir Gerard, a request that she adamantly refused.[26] The Hamiltons kept a house in Lancashire, a ride of a day or two from the Cheshire estate. There they could keep an eye on what happened at Gawsworth. In his fancy the duke must have seen the beginnings of a great English estate, after the two Gerard properties in Lancashire and Cheshire were united in his hands.

Keeping Macclesfield friendly was not easy. Politically, the two peers were poles apart, one Jacobite Tory, the other Whig. At least they could not clash on the floor of the House of Lords. Hamilton played out his political life north of the border in Edinburgh, where a separate Scottish Parliament met until 1707. But James could hardly have ingratiated himself with his rich relations. He sued his mother-in-law within weeks of his marriage. He had refused to keep his promise, made before the wedding, not to question Lady Gerard's stewardship of her daughter's estate. According to their agreement, Lady Gerard did not have to account for income and expenditures collected from the estate. Hamilton, however, insisted upon a full audit. The courts sided with the duke, ruling that to secure a wife no one could be forced to sign an agreement so potentially damaging to his own interests.[27] Some said that the shock of her son-in-law's betrayal hastened her death. In any case, she named her brother Macclesfield her executor, and the legal wrangling fell to him when she died in 1700.

Following these matters became extremely difficult for Macclesfield, because the King required the earl's services. In 1701 William III sent his old friend on a crucial mission to the Continent. The Whig Parliament, in an attempt to prevent the restoration of the exiled James II, had just passed the Act of Settlement. The law settled the crown upon the House of Hanover, should William and his successor, his sister-in-law, Princess Anne, die childless. Sophia, Electress of Hanover, was a granddaughter of King James I and the nearest Protestant heir to the throne. William chose Macclesfield to take her his best wishes and a ceremonial copy of the act. Legal matters between the earl and the duke would have to be postponed for a more convenient time.

Macclesfield's embassy succeeded. He arrived in August with a train of lords and gentlemen—including Lord Mohun—who took over the sleepy city of Hanover. They filled every available inn and public house, crowding out the usual clientele. The diplomatic style of the day required that ambassadors put on as lavish a show as possible—often funded with their own money. A vigorous round of feasting and drinking honored the Electress and her oldest son, George, who responded in kind with valuable gifts for the ambassador, and feasts of their own. The Hanoverian court was no less sophisticated than William III's, but communication problems (most of Sophia's courtiers spoke French or German; few had English) ensured that apart from official events there was relatively little contact between the English visitors and their hosts. It is doubtful that Mohun knew more French than was required to buy a bottle of brandy or negotiate a price with a prostitute, and he almost certainly knew no German. Yet Mohun avoided serious trouble. Was he learning to control himself? In later years, one of the earl's companions went to inordinate lengths to deny that the English had in any way misbehaved while doing the King's business. Some more jaundiced observers, however, maintained that few English embassies could match the bad reputation Macclesfield left behind when he finally left Germany, with its legacy of broken crockery, hymens, and heads.[28]

The ambassador's return to London on October 30, 1701, marked the peak of his political career. Despite his personal woes, Macclesfield supported the Whig administration with unwavering fervor even though he always stood outside the first rank of politicians. But being named to an important embassy was a step toward higher things, and there is little doubt that he made his report to the King confident that his political career was on the rise. His personal life was also recovering its equilibrium after the trauma of the divorce and the feud with his brother. He was negotiating a new marriage—a circumstance that displeased the expectant mob of Gerards and other relatives who hoped to share out the spoils of Gawsworth someday. The second Earl of Macclesfield was about to enjoy a new run of luck as the leaves turned in London's parks. At forty-two years of age, standing at the threshold of a revived career and a new and successful marriage, the earl had every reason for satisfaction.

Charles contemplated this latest turn of fortune's wheel from Macclesfield House, located on prime London real estate between the City on the east and the court on the west. The front of the house looked down on Gerard (now Gerrard) Street, and Macclesfield owned most of the property in the neighborhood. It had once been vacant land, used for training the militia and a dumping ground for the trash Londoners produced. Dead dogs and cats, broken glass, and empty space had given way in his father's time to substantial houses, shops, and cobbled streets, bustling with life and commerce. Many of the gentlemen and ladies living in the fashionable brick homes that lined his street were also his tenants—no different from the simple farmers and laborers back in Cheshire, except that their rents were far higher. Conscience might have warned him, as he prepared to resume his London life, that his wealth and power were based upon an injustice. James II's Baron Fitton of Gawsworth—Sir Alexander as he once was—had only recently died in his miserable French exile. More probably, however, the earl congratulated himself upon his father's ruthlessness and thought only of how to extend what he had inherited. Life was good for the second Earl of Macclesfield.

The earl's self-satisfaction did not last long. Within hours of taking up residence in Gerard Street once again, he felt feverish. He retired to his bedroom, and the fever worsened quickly. News of Macclesfield's illness spread among the expectant heirs—some must have felt triumph that there might not be a second marriage and a new heir after all. Mohun, already in London, hustled to Gerard Street to see his friend and patron. Fitton Gerard was also in town, serving as Lancaster's member of Parliament. The Orbys and Hamiltons waited tensely for word from the sickroom, for if the earl should die they anticipated a substantial inheritance, even though they did not know precisely what their relative's will contained. By November 4 the doctors despaired, and soon afterward Charles Gerard died. The Earl of Macclesfield's luck had run out.[29]

THREE

Lawyers and Politicians

THERE was no formal reading of the will. Nevertheless, the contents of Macclesfield's testament became public knowledge almost before his body was cold, for the earl had done a very extraordinary thing: he disinherited his family. The earl enjoyed unlimited freedom; he left no dowager to support and no children to establish in the world. There were, of course, potential heirs—anxious ones, whose expectations were high. Fitton Gerard, now the third Earl of Macclesfield, had the best claim. As he was the only surviving male bearing the Gerard name, and the successor to the title, most people believed that he would take over the bulk of the property. An earl required a great estate, and Fitton, although he possessed a small property in his own right, could not support his new rank without his paternal inheritance. Apart from the new earl, the most important heirs were the second earl's surviving sister, Charlotte, Lady Orby, and his niece Elizabeth Gerard, now the Duchess of Hamilton. There were others, nephews and cousins, who also hoped for their share, but their limited resources kept them on the margins in the war over the estate.

To the shock of contemporaries and the outrage of the family, Macclesfield chose his young friend Lord Mohun as his heir. There was, of course, a family connection, for the disgraced Lady Mohun was one of the earl's nieces. But as the rest of the family repeatedly asserted, Mohun had no blood ties to the Gerards. His emergence as heir to the estate was, they claimed, wholly unnatural and probably the result of a dastardly imposition upon the earl's weak mind. Making Mohun his executor, all the second earl gave the third was the right to live at Gawsworth for the rest of his life. When Fitton Gerard died, the property would go to Mohun. The earl left diamond jewelry worth several thousand pounds to the Duchess of Hamilton—but only on the condition that she and her husband would "give no trouble to my executor." Several of the earl's faithful servants received rewards from their master; his steward, Richard Whitworth, found himself £300 richer. True to his own beliefs even in death, Macclesfield ordered his heir to follow the Whig path in the future: "my desire is that in what relates to the publick he will take the advice of the Earl of Orford and the lord Sommers." Both of these peers led what came to be called the Whig "Junto,"* an aristocratic alliance whose ruthless efficiency in the pursuit of its political goals made it the ultimate Tory bugbear.[1]

As executor of the will, Mohun organized his benefactor's funeral. What happened to the corpse before its burial? The earl no doubt lay in state at Macclesfield House for several days before the undertakers prepared him for his final journey. As a man of rank and fortune, he might have been embalmed, but Mohun could have dispensed with this expensive extra. Local shopkeepers provided favors—gloves or simple gold rings—for Mohun to distribute to the mourners. If he complied with the law, he had the body wrapped in a woolen shroud before it was placed in the coffin—a Parliamentary gesture toward the wool trade. Finally, on November 14, 1701, a solemn procession, with Mohun as chief mourner, wound through the streets of Westminster. The hearse

---

* Members of the Junto were Charles Montagu, Earl of Halifax (1661–1715), Edward Russell, Earl of Orford (1653–1727), John Somers, Baron Somers (1651–1716), Charles Spencer, Earl of Sunderland (c. 1674–1722), and Thomas Wharton, Earl of Wharton (1648–1715).

would have been decorated with a painted board displaying Macclesfield's coat of arms, but aside from this customary extravagance, the funeral was a simple one, in keeping with the Low Church sympathies of both the deceased and his heir. The service unfolded late in the evening, originally a Puritan custom designed to reduce the showy worldliness of funerals. The dead should be disposed of decently but simply. Yet Mohun's modesty went only so far, for his benefactor's resting place would be in the most magnificent of all English sepulchers: Westminster Abbey.

For centuries the great had chosen the Abbey as their resting place: King Henry VII's extraordinary chapel was only the most spectacular of the monuments to past glory in the building. Queen Elizabeth; Mary, Queen of Scots; and King James I were all buried in the Abbey, and countless lesser folk followed their example: dukes, earls, and even some commoners lay in tombs or under the floor of the great church. By the time of the Earl of Macclesfield's demise, the Abbey had become a veritable warehouse of distinguished bones, and every nook and corner was crammed with elaborate—if grim—monuments. The first Earl of Macclesfield lay beneath the floor, and we can assume that, if space allowed, Mohun chose a spot for the second earl near his father amid the jumble of coffins that filled the vault.[2]

Even before the second Earl of Macclesfield's funeral, London buzzed with rumors about his disposition of the Gerard property. Gossips related many more or less distorted accounts of the will and the heirs. Some claimed that the earl had left jewels worth £2,500 to a woman he courted; another said it was two thousand gold guineas. Some, unable to imagine that Macclesfield could disinherit his brother, said that the will awarded Mohun only the earl's personal estate—his furniture, pictures, cash, and other personal effects. The real property—Gawsworth and the land in London— were to go to Fitton, the third earl. None of these rumors proved correct—Macclesfield left the jewels to the Duchess of Hamilton, conditionally, as we have seen. He made no such lavish provision for the unlucky mistress, and Mohun received the bulk of the entire estate, real and personal.

It was a fortune of admirable proportions. Contemporary observers put its value at anywhere between £40,000 and £100,000, and in fact it was probably closer to the latter than the former. The estate brought in an income of about £5,000, or even £6,000 a year, and in addition there was a considerable fortune in jewels, cash, and plate—perhaps as much as £20,000. The total sum would have sustained a community of ten thousand in relative comfort for an entire year. That the wastrel Mohun—only recently pardoned for murder—had engrossed the whole of their family's property was too much for the Gerards to bear.[3]

The shock hit the Duke of Hamilton hardest. Charlotte, Lady Orby, a convinced Tory, could not have been surprised that her brother ignored her. Moreover, her father, the first earl, had paid her dowry and given her cash from his own estate. Even Fitton, despite the humiliation of the will, had less to complain of. He was well aware of the ill will his brother bore him. He had a life interest in the estate and would live out his days in comfort. Because he had never married, he had no heirs who would be deprived of their birthright by an uncle's whim. And in 1701 he was already sick, not likely to provide an heir, or even to survive much longer. The Duke of Hamilton had expected much from Macclesfield. Once the third earl was gone, he—or rather his wife—would have stood to inherit an even greater share of the estate, possibly even the bulk of it.

Hamilton desperately needed an infusion of property by 1701. Although he was now a duke, outranking most of his peers, and a politician of considerable importance in Scotland, James was in financial trouble. His mother stubbornly lived on. Although he respected Duchess Anne, whom he had tried and failed to please, to take his rightful place in the world he needed independence—especially financial independence. His mother controlled the family property, an arrangement all the more galling because it was unusual. Dowagers were troublesome enough, as Lord Mohun knew, but ordinarily their demands on the property were limited. But Anne, Duchess of Hamilton in her own right, wielded more power than the typical aristocratic widow. She did not intend to surrender it to a son who had shown an aptitude for nothing but improvidence. She rarely agreed to lend her son money, and harried him to repay the money she did lend. Anne's tight fist was understandable: she saw her responsibility as stewardship. The Hamilton property must survive into future generations, and James's recklessness threatened to ruin the family.

But this attitude, if farsighted, did nothing to make her son's life easier. Nor did it take into account the social and political pressures the duke faced. Status and political power required wealth. The duchess commanded an income of around £9,000 a year; her son, much less. A duke could not be a pauper; though the family income was very handsome, in comparison to that of people of similar rank the Hamilton fortune was quite small. Already James had garnered a reputation as grasping, a serious fault in a gentleman, but unforgivable in a duke. He could hardly be blamed for his obsession with money; maintaining his standing on a slender income would have broken many others. Debts mounted, tradesmen charged higher and higher prices for their credit, and some refused to do business with such a poor risk.

Gerard money could rescue James from impecunity. James's marriage to Elizabeth Gerard had brought him £10,000, enough to clear many debts, and his mother-in-law's death in 1700 brought with it land in Lancashire and Cheshire. These English lands provided a steady income, and a measure of independence from his mother. But it was not enough. Consequently, he squeezed his English tenants for their rents, and in the process reinforced his reputation as a pitiless landlord. A landowner took a considerable risk if he pressed his tenants too hard. Apart from the damage he did to his reputation among his neighbors, he opened himself up to his tenants' malice. They were not utterly defenseless, even before a powerful lord like Hamilton. Livestock on the duke's

property was attacked and mutilated by unknown assailants—
digruntled men crept into the pastures at night and cut the ten-
dons of cattle in the fields.[4] There was no police force to search
out the criminals, and none were ever apprehended. The protest
put Hamilton on notice that maintaining a good reputation
required some consideration for people further down the social
ladder. The duke was not deliberately harsh; those who knew
him frequently commented on his generosity. But he was under
great financial pressure. Money was always in such short supply
that he felt forced to stoop below the level thought suitable for a
man of his rank.

Although his wife's estate brought some relief from the most
pressing of his woes, it also created new difficulties. Now that he
owned property south of the border he not only competed with
Scottish peers, but also faced the daunting prospect of cutting a
figure among the English. His income was ludicrously small compared to that of other English dukes, but his ambitions were at
least as extravagant as his debts. The bills continued to pour in;
but his mother became even less sympathetic than she had been
before his marriage. Her reply to a plea for a loan reminded him
that he had a rich wife: "I am sorie for the difficulties that you
mentione, that you are under for the want of money but I hope
the creaditt of your wife's estate will supply that want."[5] Such
advice was cold comfort. In September 1703 Hamilton wrote
plaintively to his mother from Edinburgh, desperate for a loan.
The Scottish Parliament had just finished its session, and the
duke was now confined to the palace of Holyroodhouse, too straitened even to leave the city. Holyroodhouse was his only sanc-
tuary. Although it was officially a royal residence, the palace's
hereditary keeper was Duchess Anne, who had apartments there,
which her son could use rent-free. Without them James faced the
intolerable prospect of what amounted to ducal homelessness,
wandering the famously noisome streets of Scotland's capital with
a mob of creditors following him. How was he to survive as a political force in such circumstances?[6]

Not surprisingly, Hamilton led the attack upon Mohun's good fortune. Using his own Tory bona fides with Charlotte, Lady Orby, he quickly enlisted her in his cause, and secured the allegiance of the Whig third Earl, Fitton, through the judicious use of his wife's charms. He ordered Elizabeth down to London, where he learned with great satisfaction that the new earl had "resolved to be wholly governed" by his niece. Fitton remains something of an enigma; no doubt he deeply resented his brother's affection for Mohun, but it evidently took some effort to talk him over. Gavin Mason, Hamilton's man of business in London, gloomily complained in January 1702 that Fitton was unreliable. He was practically a recluse by this time, he rarely appeared in public, and his health was failing.[7] Mason predicted that in a legal struggle Mohun probably would win—a verdict that Hamilton was by no means prepared to accept.

Fitton eventually resolved to contest Mohun's good fortune. But Fitton was dying. On Christmas Eve 1702, with Hamilton directing the proceedings, the feeble earl signed several long-term leases, renting Gawsworth and other property to Charlotte, Lady Orby, at favorable rates. Mohun would have to wait ninety-nine years before the leases expired and he could take possession of the land. The duke took care to work behind the scenes, ensuring that his name appeared nowhere in the formal documents. He nevertheless engineered the coup and intended to benefit handsomely from it. His stalking-horse, Charlotte Orby, would take possession of Gawsworth as soon as Fitton died, and then some more equitable arrangement might be worked out. The earl died almost immediately after executing the leases, on December 26, leaving Hamilton gloating about the success of his scheme: Fitton had "done all he could doe to dissapoint my Lord Mohune and I fancy his Lordship will find itt most effectuall."[8]

No sooner had Fitton signed his leases and passed on than Hamilton dispatched his servants to take control of the property. The duke, like many people in the early eighteenth century, believed that possession was nine-tenths of the law. Dislodging an occupant could require months or years of expensive, complex legal effort. Battles for ownership could take place in a wide variety of venues ranging from the humble—manorial courts and the county sheriff's court—all the way up to the House of Lords. In the meanwhile the occupant collected the estate's rents and plotted his next move. His case might be thrown out, and the court might even require him to account for the rents he had received while in possession—but that merely opened new vistas for delay and obfuscation, as the parties wrangled over the accounts. The process could take years, and Hamilton intended to pursue his every advantage. Having orchestrated Mohun's discomfiture, Hamilton could congratulate himself on a successful bit of legal legerdemain.

Something went wrong. Lord Mohun naturally launched his own campaign to recover the estate, and soon Hamilton must have realized that he had underestimated the opposition. Mohun was reputed to be a lazy, debauched, and irredeemable young man. In his mid-twenties, he was already running to fat and displayed little self-control: his life was an endless round of drunken evenings and smirking assaults on female virtue. And yet a close observer would have noticed something more: a man of no mean ability. However raucous the previous night's party had been, Lord Mohun was always on the floor of the House of Lords the next day. As long as the House was in session—generally from the autumn until late spring—Mohun attended. He took his work seriously, sitting on many tedious committees, voting whenever there was a division, and speaking from time to time, always on behalf of his patrons in the Whig Junto. Mohun's final brush with the law, the death of Captain Coote, seemed to have taught him a lesson: usefulness in the House outweighed many another sin. It is true that he continued to live a disreputable life, but moralists would have been distressed to acknowledge that drink and loose women seemed to make Mohun a more, rather than less, competent peer.

The duke's servants ensconced themselves temporarily on Fitton's property, claiming to represent Lady Charlotte. Almost immediately, Mohun struck back with eviction notices from the county court. These were secured, most likely, with the assistance of friends in Cheshire. Mohun had the advantage of local ties. He had been to Gawsworth and knew how to get things done quickly. Hamilton, on the other hand, was a stranger—a foreigner, in fact. If known at all, it was as a harsh landlord in neighboring Lancashire. Hamilton's men were dismayed to find that Lord Mohun served his evictions quickly. Before anyone could stop him, he had made himself the new master of Gawsworth Hall. Mohun had the assistance of the household servants. A few smaller properties remained in the duke's control, but the big prize, the rich Cheshire property, had fallen to the enemy.

Hamilton was furious. His servants struggled to defend themselves against his charges of negligence; they maintained that they had been betrayed. Who had betrayed whom? Some blamed the duke's allies, the Orbys, and some their fellow servants. Fingers pointed in every direction. Lord Mohun had, they said, subverted the old Gerard servants with promises of money and continued employment—a charge made as one of Hamilton's agents was attempting to subvert them for the duke. Another Hamilton servant stayed near Gawsworth for days in January 1703, hoping to enlist some of the servants in a scheme to open the gate some night and let in a group of the duke's partisans. Neither side spared any effort to win the allegiance of the hall's inhabitants—Mohun promised gold to those who remained true, and threatened those who wavered with dismissal. Few servants made more than a few guineas in the course of a whole year, and everyone knew what poverty might befall an unemployed servant. The choice was not very difficult.

Still, Hamilton's agents tried their best—sending commands to various members of the staff to travel the three miles from Gawsworth to Macclesfield, where they would meet Lady Charlotte and the duke himself. No one but Hall, the groom, showed any interest. Unfortunately, he turned up for his appointment drunk. The two most important servants, the gardener and the housekeeper, avoided the duke. The only good news came in a conversation with John Hamond, the rector of Gawsworth's parish church. Hamond, "a man of sense and resolution," spoke disparagingly of Mohun and promised his support for Hamilton. In fact, the rector showed his "sense and resolution" in a disappointing fashion. Lord Mohun lived next door to his church. The patron of the living, Mohun had the right to appoint Hamond's successor. The young baron could make his local clergyman's life difficult with harassment over pews, tithes, poor rates, and perhaps many other things a peaceable rector might not have imagined. Hamond, indeed a man of sense, went over to Mohun's side. One of Mohun's first acts was to build a school for the parish children—whose master was almost certainly appointed by Mr. Hamond. Mohun was a shrewd opponent.[9]

Hamilton launched suits against Mohun at every opportunity; one of the first had been over the jewels Macclesfield left Hamilton's wife. Hamilton ignored the earl's demand that Mohun not be troubled in administering the estate. In August 1702 Hamilton's lawyers presented a large parchment before the Court of Chancery, accusing Lord Mohun of unlawfully withholding valuable jewels. Mohun responded with an equally impressive document denying the duke's claims. From this point, the production of documents to feed the Chancellor's legal machine became relentless. Formal complaints to Chancery, or bills, as they were called, and the answers defendants made to them, marked the beginning of a process whose complexity almost defies description, and in which the opportunity for delay was virtually limitless.

The court, housed in its jerry-built corner of Westminster Hall, was in theory, at least, an attractive recourse for litigants. Presided over by the Lord Chancellor, the highest legal officer of the realm, it was, according to the lawbooks, the "King's conscience," empowered to set aside the common law when its rigidity threatened injustice. Not bound by precedent, as the common law was, it could be more flexible. In a court of equity, the Chancellor could cut through the thickets of the law in pursuit of justice. By the beginning of the eighteenth century, however, practice and theory had grown far apart. The expense and delay involved in Chancery suits were a byword: as Jonathan Swift wrote in *Gulliver's Travels:* "it will take thirty years to decide whether the field left me by my ancestors for six generations belongs to me or a stranger 300 miles off."[10]

The languid pace of justice in this era was in part due to the court's heavy burden. Thousands of suits were filed every year and were handled by a pitifully small staff. There were six clerks, assisted by a few dozen more menial servants—copyists, writers, and underclerks, who handled the parchments lawyers brought into court. In the 1650s, reformers claimed the court had a backlog of over twenty thousand cases, many of which had gone unresolved for decades.[11] This press of business did not trouble the staff, whose income depended upon the fees they charged for their services. Those who ran the court thrived upon delay and prolixity: men who received a fee for every page they wrote had every incentive to write as many pages as possible, spinning out the life of a case as long as the litigants' energy and money held out.

The same held true for lawyers who practiced in Chancery. Some lawsuits became hardly less than a lifetime endowment, bringing in for decades substantial fees for briefs, exceptions, answers, depositions, and every other ingenuity a legal mind could invent. Lawyers, for example, did their best to add as many defendants to a suit as possible—partly to ensure that no one with any resources might escape a judgment. This tendency was further encouraged by the clerks and writers, who received fees for every Chancery bill they wrote; every person named as a defendant needed a copy of the charge filed against him. Therefore, the more defendants, the higher the fees. In 1682 a litigant filed a suit in Chancery naming five hundred defendants in a document some three thousand pages long. Every defendant would have been forced to spend over one hundred pounds to obtain a copy of this legal monstrosity. Fortunately for them, the obvious absurdity of the case did not escape the Lord Chancellor, who threw it out of court.[12]

Practicing in the Court of Chancery was lucrative, and as a result lawyers proliferated, hurling writs and lawsuits with ever-greater abandon; on his famous "incognito" visit to England in 1697, Russia's Czar Peter the Great was astonished when he visited Westminster Hall. The place buzzed with lawyers and their clients, preparing for their cases or plotting a new sortie against their opponents. "Lawyers!" exclaimed the Czar. "Why I have but two in my whole dominion, and I believe I shall hang one of them the moment I get home."[13] Many English litigants, trapped in the toils of the law, would have cried a fervent amen to the Czar's sentiment.

Hamilton's first Chancery suit against Mohun—there would be others—was typical of the sort of business done in that court. Most cases revolved around land or inheritances, the cynosure of a gentleman's family interest. Here, it was jewels—diamonds worth over two thousand pounds, the duke claimed, and by rights the duchess's property. They had once belonged to her mother, Lady Gerard, and Lord Mohun, who inherited the executorship of the Gerard estate from Macclesfield, was obliged to hand them over. By no means, said Mohun. The jewels were not the duchess's. But if they were, they were forfeit because the duke, contrary to the will, had disputed Mohun's executorship. Anyway, they were not worth two thousand pounds. What followed was a classic example of Chancery procedure. Instead of deciding the main point at issue—to whom did the jewels belong?—Mohun's lawyers chose to fight on different ground—how much were they worth? The lawyers knew that merely deciding this matter could take months; once that issue was settled, there would be many more to raise, thus holding off the duke longer.

Delay and obfuscation remained a key element in legal strategy on both sides throughout their battles. Sometimes both parties

pushed for delay for no apparent reason. In this case, the reason
was obvious: if Mohun could hold out until the fall of 1703 (the
case was apparently first heard in the winter of 1702), he could
claim privilege of Parliament. As a member of the House of Lords,
he would have all legal proceedings against him automatically
stopped until the annual session was over. It gave Mohun a great
advantage, and virtual immunity from the duke's actions for the
better part of eight months in every year. This was an advantage
that Hamilton did not enjoy. Because he was a peer of Scotland,
rather than England, he had no seat at Westminster and so had to
live with Mohun's evasions.

The process was frustratingly slow. Once the plaintiff—Hamilton—had filed his bill, Mohun was granted time to reply. Then
followed a time-consuming exchange of exceptions, in which
each side objected to the points made by the other. Eventually
the court appointed a master, or arbitrator, to establish the jewels'
value. A master in Chancery was a lawyer who practiced in the
court, appointed by the Lord Chancellor to inquire into the facts
of a case. His report formed the basis of the court's later judgment. But complications often ensued. Plaintiff and defendants
had the right to reply to the master's report. Some masters were
notorious for squeezing the last penny out of their assignments—
they charged both sides for their expenses and fees. They sometimes wrote deliberately inadequate reports, knowing that another,
follow-up, report would double their profit.[14] Some deliberately
included errors in their reports, knowing that one side or the other
would raise objections, which would require yet another report—
and more fees. Skilled lawyers could manipulate the system with
ease. Mohun's lawyers were among the best. They kept the
duke's attorneys waiting for weeks. Gavin Mason, who handled
the matter for Hamilton, wrote a series of increasingly frustrated
letters describing the endless delays he endured. It took some
ten months simply to get a master appointed to value the diamonds, and all through the summer of 1703 Mason struggled to

get Mohun to hand them over for an appraisal. He made appointments with Mohun's lawyers, who failed to turn up, or who came, but without the jewels. The duke's man found himself sending sharp reminders two or three times a day to his opposite number. Finally, a servant did arrive with the jewelry, but refused to leave it with the master—making a valuation impossible. At last a compromise was reached: each side would have its own jeweler appraise the diamonds, and the master would arrive at some figure based on their judgment. The jewelers came up with similar figures: £921 and £1,105, far from the duke's original claim that they were worth over £2,000. By November 1703 the arguments had made their way to the House of Lords, which reviewed Chancery's actions in the suit and sided with Mohun—not surprisingly, given his political views and the Whig majority in the House. And this quarrel was only the run-up to the main event, for the diamonds were, after all, only a small part of the Macclesfield inheritance.[15]

The tedium and the expense of these cases in Chancery (and other venues, too, for suits were also filed against Mohun in the common law courts) encouraged Hamilton to seek victory through other means. Always hopeful, he now believed he had a new advantage over his adversary: political influence. War against Lord Mohun in the days of William III would have been extremely risky; after all, Mohun had literally gotten away with murder under the King. Moreover, William harbored a personal dislike for Hamilton. Additionally, Mohun's ties to Whig grandees—such as the Lord Chancellor, Lord Somers—made action either in the courts or at court a very difficult proposition. But times were changing, and by 1703 Hamilton thought they had changed dramatically. William III was no more: in early 1702 his horse stumbled over a mole hole, hurling the wizened little King from the saddle and fracturing his collarbone. The injury, superficially not very serious, triggered his final illness and death. For years afterward supporters of the exiled King James (including the Duke of Hamilton) raised their glasses in honor of the "gentleman in black velvet"—the mole—who had done them such a favor by removing their nemesis from the scene.

There was now a new monarch: William's sister-in-law, Queen Anne. From Mohun's point of view her accession, in March 1702, was potentially disastrous. She had despised her brother-in-law and the Whigs who had so avidly supported him and his protracted wars against France. She hated most of the members of the Junto, whom she saw as irreligious libertines. Their disreputable lives were all the worse for their presumptuous belief that they could order their sovereign about. She was devoutly religious herself and led an impeccable private life. She and her husband, the amiable but useless Prince George of Denmark, lived peacefully together, regularly conceiving children. Despite her relative youth when she inherited the crown—she was not yet forty—Anne's struggle with fecundity had undermined her health. She had endured over a dozen pregnancies, but none of her children had survived. Only one, the Duke of Gloucester, made it past swaddling clothes, and he died at age eleven in 1700. The Queen's disappointments and constant sickness made her all the more religious. She was determined that her regime would set England back upon the right path. Anne intended to chart this new course with the assistance of moderate Tories, in particular the Earl of Marlborough (soon to be a duke) and the Lord High Treasurer, Sidney, Earl of Godolphin. There was no room in her plans for Whig rakes like Lord Mohun.

The Queen's subjects knew her political opinions. Hamilton, himself a Tory, expected to benefit under the new regime. Undermining Mohun's claims through the normal course of the law was slow and uncertain, but perhaps royal favor would succeed; the days when a sovereign smiled upon him seemed near at hand once again. The Queen would surely rally to the assistance of a loyal Tory like himself. In May 1703 he wrote her a fulsome letter proclaiming his devotion, and incidentally asking for her intervention. He hoped that "your majesty's goodness and justice would not prefer Lord Mohun" and that she would agree that the second Earl of Macclesfield "had itt not in his powr by the unaturall will he made of robing his family of what they have a just tytle to."[16] This letter came on top of an attempt to lobby the Queen personally only a few days before, and although Hamilton did not realize it, Anne had already begun to find his constant pressure annoying.

The duke thought it only natural that he should seek the Queen's help. He learned the value of royal patronage in his youth, and although he might have realized that the postrevolutionary monarchy wielded less power, he would not neglect any potential ally. Even with the limitations 1688 imposed upon the Crown, no one, least of all James, doubted Queen Anne's power. And as we have seen, the search for favor was absolutely necessary. Mohun was growing fat on the revenues of Gawsworth—at least a third of which, the duke figured, were rightfully his. Hamilton's status depended upon securing his financial independence; he could never hope to acquire political eminence on a few thousand pounds a year. He had to dislodge Mohun or accustom himself to insignificance. Hamilton's position was in many respects pitiable. His ancestors had for generations been figures of great importance, both in Scotland and in England. His parents had hectored him throughout his life about the place he would one day occupy in the world, even as they denied him the means of attaining that place. Scots looked to him for leadership—but it was very difficult to lead when hiding out in Holyroodhouse, evading creditors. Even worse, as a Scottish peer, Hamilton enjoyed no immunity from arrest for debt in England. His marriage to Elizabeth Gerard had added new pressures. She was herself a woman of spirit and ambition, who could not get along with her in-laws, and she especially disliked her rigid mother-in-law, the Duchess Anne. The stage upon which she wanted her husband to strut was not the poverty-stricken one in Edinburgh but the real world: London, where important things happened, and where no one in the best houses had lice. But playing an important role in the south meant added expense—a house in London, extra servants, more coaches, clothes, and furniture. And all of this was to be provided upon an income far smaller than that enjoyed by the upstart Mohun. All these factors combined to make the possession of the Gerard fortune a matter of supreme importance for the duke, and helps explain why he became so obsessed with winning it.

The stakes were no less important for Lord Mohun. Without his Macclesfield windfall, he would have been one of the rather pathetic figures who skulked about the House of Lords cadging free meals and small loans from their peers—the "poor lords" who were prepared to sell their votes to survive. Mohun's paternal estate in Cornwall was actually worth a considerable amount of money—forty or fifty thousand pounds—but it was so heavily mortgaged that paying the interest on these loans swallowed its income. Forcing Mohun to return to Cornwall would be sending him to the poorhouse, as Boconnoc continued to molder. And Gawsworth ensured that Mohun, too, could pursue his ambitions. Already, in his mid-twenties, he was a man of some importance in the House of Lords. He had shown his diplomatic talents in Hanover with Macclesfield. Now war with France over the succession to the Spanish throne gave him a chance to demonstrate his military prowess. For all these he needed the revenue and prestige of a great landed estate. Gawsworth was all he had.

The duke's ham-fisted attempts to sway the Queen had less success than he had hoped. Hamilton was not the resolute supporter of the Queen's government he claimed to be, and Anne knew it. Since the third duke's death he had been more of a troublemaker for the government than a loyal ally. King William, goaded nearly to distraction by the importunities and bad temper of his Scottish subjects, derisively called Hamilton "the little Scotch prince," and said that he wished that Scotland were a thousand miles farther away—and that Hamilton were its king.[17]

Anne's experience was not much different—the duke, whatever his hopes from the new regime, was prepared to obstruct the Queen's government until, at the very least, it recognized his importance.

Scotland was an unruly and difficult place to govern in the best of times, and the two decades from about 1690 on were bad ones. Poor harvests, economic depression, and the indifference of William III heightened the natural tensions of the Anglo-Scottish relationship. William III, as later Queen Anne, preferred to leave Scottish affairs in the hands of a clique of powerful aristocrats—a group that did not include the Duke of Hamilton. Otherwise, the King looked upon his northern dominion as a whiny annoyance whose only value was as a nursery for soldiers who would later be hurled against the French. Scottish complaints about English neglect and oppression grew louder and more insistent in the 1690s. Discontent grew rapidly after London merchants success-fully lobbied the King to snuff out the feeble life of the Darien Company, a Scottish adventure many north of the border expected to bring the wealth of the Indies, hitherto monopolized by the hated English, into their pockets. Many investors lost a great deal of money in this fiasco; one of them was Hamilton, for whom the loss of a single pound was a matter of some importance. Scottish national feeling was, then, very high when William III had his appointment with the gentleman in black velvet. And the gener-ally recognized leader of Scots nationalism, standing against the English and their Scottish lackeys, was Hamilton.

The de facto head of Scotland's government at Anne's acces-sion was the Duke of Queensberry: an affable man, and a shrewd politician. He brooked no rivals, dominating patronage and ensur-ing that the fruits of office were denied to his enemies. Foremost among his foes was Hamilton, who made it his goal to thwart Queensberry—an attitude that would never endear him to the Queen. Despite his protestations, James's loyalty was suspect. For his part, Queensberry distrusted and disliked Hamilton and he repeatedly warned London that his rival should remain firmly out of favor because "I am not persuaded of his integrity."[18] After 1702 Scottish politics was shaping up as a struggle between Queensberry, leading a court party, and Hamilton, the chief of a country, or nationalist, force.

The death of William III offered new opportunities to rout Queensberry, but it also was a potentially risky moment. The duke's battles with Lord Mohun were just beginning, and alienating powerful people at court in London could do him no good. But the potential prize—the overthrow of his Scottish rival—was tantalizing enough to encourage an effort. So at the same time Hamilton was writing letters of congratulations to the new Queen and her closest advisers, Lords Marlborough and Godolphin, he laid his plan of attack against Anne's Scottish administration.[19]

The principal battleground for this campaign was Edinburgh. This was where Queen Anne's first Scottish Parliament would meet, presided over by Queensberry. A personal appearance by the Queen was unthinkable. Her health was far too fragile. Many courtiers considered a trip across a Kensington Palace drawing room a minor victory for the Queen; jolting hundreds of miles north to Edinburgh would have been quite foolhardy. Nor was it likely that Anne or any of her English ministers would have gone north in any case, for they liked neither Scotland nor the Scots. No small part of Scottish resentment of the English originated in the sneering condescension of their neighbors. Englishmen believed that Scots could easily be recognized, for they were "a kind of lean Carrionly Creatures, with reddish hair and freckly faces, being very much given to scratching and shrugging, as if they held lousiness no shame, and the itch no scandal." Jonathan Swift was even less kind: "Scottish scoundrels," "Scotch dogs," "Cursed Scottish Hell Hounds," "Cursed Hellish Scots," "Greedy Scotch Rebellious Dogs," "Deceitful Scots," "Diabolical Scots," "Impudent Scottish Scoundrels," "Rank Scottish Thieves," "Abominable, Damnable, Scotch Hellish Dogs Forever," he called them.[20] It was no wonder that Queensberry found managing Scotland at London's command a difficult task.

In June 1702 Edinburgh bulged with gentlemen and nobles from all over Scotland, waiting for the start of the Parliament. The city was at the best of times one of Britain's most crowded, but Parliament inevitably worsened a bad situation. As the capital of an ancient kingdom, Edinburgh left much to be desired. Its poverty and general state of dilapidation excited the derision of the more sophisticated Londoner, and its unhealthiness and squalor made even Scots reluctant to spend much time there. Apart from what Englishmen would have identified as the habitual slovenliness of the Scots, the city's main problem was lack of space. Edinburgh writhed along the top of a steep ridge that stretched from the formidable castle on its highest end to the palace of Holyroodhouse at its lowest. On one side of the ridge was the Nor' Loch, as polluted a body of water as any in the British Isles—it served as Edinburgh's cesspool, receiving the contents of every chamberpot in town and whatever else wanted quick disposal. Water circumscribed the city's growth on the opposite side of the ridge as well, and so Edinburghers built up, rather than out. The contrasts with fashionable sections of London was extreme: there were no elegant squares, and very few of the sort of town houses Lord Mohun now owned in Gerard Street. The Royal Mile, the main street that made its way from the castle to the palace along the crest of the ridge, was lined with tall, narrow buildings—five and six stories were not uncommon. Branching off the main street were narrow alleys, or wynds, with still more tall narrow structures. Residents were packed together in great discomfort, enduring the stench of the town and its loch, and paying the additional tariff of climbing flights of badly lighted stairs whenever they sought an escape from the rest of the city. The atmosphere was claustrophobic as well as unhygienic.

Near St. Giles Cathedral, the austere, rather pokey center of Scottish Presbyterianism, stood the Parliament House, one of the few buildings in town with pretensions to style. Here, on June 9, 1702, Edinburghers waited for the opening of Queen Anne's first Parliament north of the border. Everyone knew that there would be a showdown between Hamilton and Queensberry, and the sympathies of the mob were decidedly with the former and not the latter. When word came that Hamilton had left his quarters at Holyroodhouse for the short drive to the Parliament, a crowd boiled out of the wynds, surrounding the duke's coach, shouting acclamations and good wishes for the man they expected to stand against the English ministry. It was a heady moment. This was the kind of role James had always wanted to play, and it was a vindication. Neither his father nor his grandfather had ever had such a reception among the people; every shout set up by the adoring multitude was further confirmation that his parents had been wrong to underestimate their son. He would be a success; a man to be reckoned with.

James was certainly important on that June day. Surrounded by his cheering supporters, he made a stately progress to the Parliament—making a far more showy entrance than Queensberry. Entering the House to the acclamation of many of its members, Hamilton took his place, and everyone waited the inevitable confrontation.

Unlike its English counterpart, the Scottish Parliament was not bicameral. Lords and Commons sat under the same roof, making it easier for Hamilton, an effective speaker, to reach all of the kingdom's political class. Though some of his enemies sneered at his "bawling" style, he could hold an audience spellbound. Unfortunately for his cause, the government side almost invariably held the trump cards. Scots Parliaments had never been as powerful as those in Westminster, and were frequently manipulated into quiescence. The ministry's partisans dominated the Parliament whose session was about to open. Dependents of the government, most had been elected in King William's day and owed their places to Queensberry. This, in fact, would be the point at issue: traditionally the death of the sovereign automatically caused a dissolution of a sitting Parliament, requiring new elections. But Queensberry and the English ministers advised Queen Anne not to dissolve; given the state of public opinion in Scotland, Queensberry had no desire to risk an election that would almost certainly weaken his faction.

When the House was called to order, Hamilton leaped to his feet, and demanded to be heard. He denounced the recalling of the old Parliament as illegal, and argued that elections must be called. Having electrified his audience with what amounted to a direct challenge to the Queen's authority in Edinburgh, the duke left the building, leading seventy-nine members in a boycott. They emerged to a tumultuous reception from a crowd of thousands in the street. With much ado, and accompanied by an enormous crowd of well-wishers, Hamilton returned to Holyroodhouse, the most popular man in Scotland. He left behind him an enraged and embarrassed ministry. The rump, composed of those who would not question the official line, resolved that anyone who challenged the legality of their body was a traitor. It was an empty gesture. Any attempt to arrest Hamilton would have led to violence. Queensberry and his supporters would simply have to move ahead and urge the London government to take steps to shore up their authority.

After the cheers of the crowds died away, Hamilton wrote London, explaining his conduct to the Queen and her favorites. Although his adversaries portrayed his obstructive actions as inimical to Anne's government, he assured them that he acted out of devotion to the Crown. If only Her Majesty would heed his advice, not the slanders of the Queensberry clique in Edinburgh, he could promise a smooth-running administration. It is doubtful that the Queen credited these protestations. Neither Marlborough nor Godolphin found them convincing. They refused to allow Hamilton to present a petition requesting new elections, and they advised him to prove his loyalty by cooperating with the Queen's chosen servant, Queensberry.[21]

The year 1702 must have been an optimistic one for Hamilton: his popularity in Scotland had never been greater, and his legal contest with Mohun looked promising. Debts still plagued him, but the Gerard estates would end those troubles. This optimism probably encouraged the duke's obstructionist tactics in Edinburgh, but by the beginning of 1703 it seems that James's outlook on life was growing more somber. Legal setbacks in the Mohun case may have played a part, as did the refusal of the ministry to budge from its defense of Queensberry. Relations with his wife, Elizabeth, were also tense: in the summer she refused to visit Hamilton Palace, where their children were staying with their grandmother: "To my sorrow I think she cares but litle for them. I cant tell you all my woes but they are yett greater than you can imagen," he wrote his mother.[22] Whatever her feelings about her children, it is clear that Elizabeth would pay almost any price to avoid being locked up with her formidable mother-in-law in her vast damp palace in the wilds of Clydesdale. New financial worries piled up: pressure from English creditors increased. Some shopkeepers pursued their client through the courts and won judgments against him—the amounts were petty, less than one hundred pounds. But the threat that all credit might be withdrawn was real. That fate would be catastrophic. Bankruptcy loomed, and it would wreak havoc upon his political standing.

In 1703 some of those who had seen the duke as Scotland's savior only a year before began to suspect him of treachery to the cause. His legal worries kept him in London, fretting over Mohun's next move and his own growing legal bills. James was seen more and more frequently at court, probably hoping to placate the Queen after his rash actions. The Earl of Kincardine, a staunch Scottish nationalist temporarily marooned in London, wrote a friend that "he decays dayly in esteeme here, whereas formerly the world was disposed to consider him a generous lustie spirited man, they nowe incline to consider him a meane spirited creature sneaking here to gett some mark of favour or benefite, for they can putt no other construction upon his hanging about a Court."[23] Such gossips did James an injustice—or at least failed to recognize that opposition politics required a great deal more financial independence than he could muster.

Kincardine was at least correct about one thing: Hamilton was engaged in shady business, but of a different—and far more dangerous—variety. The duke had never broken his ties with the exiled court of James II. Even though the former King died in 1701, his claim to the throne passed to his son, James Edward Stuart, who called himself James III but was best known in Britain as "the Pretender." The possibility of a restoration waxed and waned, but no one considered it impossible. A fortuitous English naval victory foiled an invasion from France in 1692, and Jacobites hatched further plans in subsequent years. The accession of Queen Anne, who many believed felt sympathy for her exiled half brother, boosted the hopes of Jacobites on both sides of the Channel.

Contact with the exile's court at Saint-Germain was treason: the law was clear. Nevertheless, many prominent politicians, especially Tories, kept surreptitious lines of communication open with the Pretender's camp. Very few of these dalliances blossomed into action, and they were often simply insurance against the future. Both Marlborough and Godolphin at times paid court to the "King over the water," though by the time Anne became Queen, their sincerity was doubtful. The Pretender had great difficulty finding genuine support in England, but it was quite natural for him to put his faith in the Duke of Hamilton, and to expect results.

Hamilton's difficulties with William III and his repeated protestations of support for James II made the exiled court confident in his reliability. Lord Middleton, James II's secretary, believed that Hamilton was the key to his master's restoration, and by 1700 the duke was universally considered the leader of the Jacobite cause in Scotland. James II and his son depended upon

8. The château at Saint-Germain,
home of Hamilton's mentor, the exiled James II

him to represent their interests in the Scottish Parliament, a role
that Hamilton found congenial. He had no connections at court,
having earned the enmity of King William. Before 1702 he had
little to lose. Hamilton also funneled Jacobite money into Scotland. The Pretender hoped to maintain his cause through the
judicious distribution of gold to important but impecunious Scots.
The money—thousands of pounds—did not all come from the
Stuart purse. James Edward Stuart lived almost entirely upon
the largesse of Louis XIV. Most of the money Hamilton received came from the same source. The French even persuaded
Pope Clement XI to invest £25,000 in the Jacobite cause in Scotland. Hamilton, said the French King, was "a most trustworthy
man," who had "given time after time assurances of his zeal, and
of his fidelity to the King his master."[24] What happened to this
money, brought over in small amounts by agents sent from
France? Gold coins in false-bottomed trunks, sewn into coats, and

concealed in hatbands trickled into Hamilton's coffers for years. He almost certainly used some, if not all, of it to bolster his fellow conspirators, despite the temptation to direct some of it to relieve his own desperate financial situation.[25]

The duke's situation grew far more complicated after Queen Anne's accession. She might show the Pretender favor and be sympathetic to her exiled half brother's plight. She would not, however, abandon her throne to salve her conscience. Hamilton, beset by financial and legal woes, needed a friend at Westminster more than ever. But his relationship with the Pretender was his oldest political commitment; the Stuart cause had defined his career. James was obliged to play a double game, assuring Saint-Germain of his fundamental loyalty, while at the same time persuading St. James's of his reliability. This political dilemma led Hamilton into a series of dangerous contradictions and ambiguities.

In time, his efforts to succeed on both sides of the English Channel would prove costly. William III had never trusted the "little Scotch prince," and there is evidence that he used information about his Jacobite intrigues gathered by government spies as blackmail. Hamilton received subtle hints of the extent of the government's knowledge of his affairs, along with the suggestion that good behavior in Parliament might be wise. William's agents infiltrated the Jacobite network. Despite every effort to maintain secrecy through coded letters and opaque messages, the King knew more about what went on at Saint-Germain than did the most fanatical Jacobites in Britain.[26] Nor did Anne's accession reduce official suspicion. The post office routinely opened the duke's letters, and spies followed him everywhere.[27]

A few at Saint-Germain began to doubt Hamilton's reliability. As early as 1700 one English spy suggested that James II had his doubts. Someone heard the duke remark that he, too, had royal blood in his veins. Indeed, he claimed to be the Protestant closest in line of succession to the Scottish throne. Might he not abandon his old patron and establish a new Scottish dynasty?[28] These questions could not have helped the duke's credit in France. Nevertheless, he continued to insist upon his loyalty to the Pretender and kept up his secret correspondence. In 1702 he dispatched a cousin to France, with a plea for a quick invasion—which went unheeded. By 1704, when Anglo-Scots relations had reached their most critical phase in a generation, he was still considered the Pretender's most reliable man in Scotland.

England had ignored or dismissed Scottish complaints and grievances for years, but the accession of Queen Anne gave Scotland leverage. Though it was the fondest wish of many, William III's death had not established a permanent peace in Europe. His wars against France were unpopular, and the burdens they imposed upon his kingdoms were heavy: high taxes, high casualties, and reduced trade all combined to teach the lesson that war had its costs. But Louis XIV's imposition of his grandson upon the Spanish throne was too much even for a peace-loving Queen Anne, and in 1702 Britain again found itself fighting a massively expensive and difficult war. Opposing France on battlefields ranging from Canada to Bavaria absorbed most of the energies of the Queen's government. In these circumstances, the succession to the Scottish throne threatened unrest and instability in the north, which would weaken the war effort, as the opposition in Edinburgh, now dominated by Hamilton, knew.

Legally, Scotland was an independent state. Its union with England was coincidental: Anne Stuart happened to be Queen of both nations. Accidents of inheritance and royal marriages had combined to unite the two thrones in 1603, when the last of the Tudors, Elizabeth I, died unmarried. Queen Anne, childless despite her excruciating pregnancies, threatened to be the last of the Stuarts. The English solved the problem of an heir in 1701, when they passed the Act of Settlement, which decreed that the crown would pass to Sophia, Electress of Hanover. Sophia, a woman of wit and considerable intelligence, seemed the perfect bar to a return of the Pretender, even if her son and heir Prince

George inspired less confidence. Although some in England hoped that the Pretender might abandon his strongly held Roman Catholicism and regain his father's throne after Anne's death, the Hanoverian solution at least temporarily put an end to much of the uncertainty surrounding the future—in England.

For Anne's opponents north of the border, however, the revival of the succession issue was a godsend. The Parliament in Westminster could dispose of the English crown however it pleased. What it could not do was award Scotland's crown to some German as if it were simply an additional bauble in its gift. The power to confer a crown north of the river Tweed belonged to the Parliament in Edinburgh, and there was nothing to prevent it from choosing someone else. Perhaps, as Jacobites most fervently hoped, the crown would go to James III. Or it might be offered to someone closer to home.

In 1704, with the enthusiastic leadership of Hamilton, the Scottish Parliament passed the Act of Security, badly frightening the Queen's ministers in England. The act did not settle the crown on anyone but made plain the Scots' position that they could not be bound by the acts of a legislature that had for years ignored—or harassed—the Scots nation. Should England refuse to treat Scotland as an equal, the Scots would reserve the right to sever their connections and go their own way. Here was a challenge of the most dangerous sort: in essence, Hamilton and his supporters threatened to open another front in the war, turning Scotland into an independent base from which the enemy might launch an assault on England's rear.

The English responded furiously. Parliament declared that if the Scottish act was not repealed, all Scots would be treated as aliens in England and throughout its overseas possessions. This portended devastation for the Scottish economy, but many Scots argued that they had been at the mercy of English merchants for too long anyway. They were still counting their losses in the Darien disaster, and the threat of an English embargo seemed hollow by comparison. An independent Scotland, relieved of taxes required to support English adventures in Europe and beyond, might even compete more successfully.

Now at last Scotland made itself noticed. The Queen's advisers faced a very unpalatable choice: either come to some kind of arrangement or resign themselves to the probability that at some point in the not-too-distant future (given the Queen's fragile health) Scotland would have to be conquered by force: a fully independent state north of the Tweed was unthinkable. This dilemma led Anne's government to press for a complete Union between the two British kingdoms, an event that would change Hamilton's life.

Union was hardly a new idea; James VI and I, the first Stuart king of England, had pushed for one a century earlier. Cromwell had actually created one, by force of arms, but it did not survive his regime. William III toyed with the idea, but English self-interest stymied him. Most of the English people saw nothing advantageous in a merger of the two kingdoms. The popular mind envisioned hordes of poverty-stricken scarecrows surging south in pursuit of England's plenty. Keeping Scots out of England and out of the English colonies was good business; inviting them to share in the profits of empire foolish. Only the threat of Scottish independence coerced a very reluctant nation into considering a treaty.

The government's decision to press for a treaty with the Scottish Parliament led to anxious political maneuvers, with the Duke of Hamilton at the center of everyone's calculations. In this potentially rewarding but dangerous situation, the pressures and inducements Hamilton faced were mutually contradictory. Scottish Jacobites fervently opposed a Union, but the Queen wanted one just as much. The duke could not hope to satisfy both sides, but he did his best to parlay his opportunity into an important position.

From the first, Hamilton appeared to be the Union's strongest opponent. The Edinburghers worshipped him as the great defender of Scotland's independence, and his reception in the capital for the beginning of the 1705 session of Parliament illustrated his popularity. A large deputation of gentlemen and nobles met him on the road into town, and he entered the city surrounded by a cheering multitude. A sour English spy noted that the duke's arrival was the excuse for a binge that carried on till daybreak in the streets.[29] Throughout the session the duke proved himself to be the government's principal opponent. The ministry's agents sent reports to London, describing his "bawling" speeches and swaggering demeanor on the floor of Parliament. Less jaundiced reporters commented upon the skill with which James spoke and controlled the opposition. His attacks on government policy kept the Queen's commissioner, Queensberry, on the defensive. The adulation of the crowd, together with the discomfort he inflicted upon his political foes, made the session memorable for the duke.

Despite his successes, Hamilton faced considerable pressure from every side. Before the session began, the English Secretary of State, Sir Robert Harley, had sent an emissary to Hamilton's Lancashire retreat to put the government's case. Colonel James Graham no doubt offered both threats and promises to induce the duke's cooperation. The Queen would not take him into favor until he "would be pleased to make the first step towards Her Majesty."[30] Not much later James received a visit from Colonel Nathaniel Hooke, bearing promises from Saint-Germain. The duke met him less openly than Graham. If one of London's spies had detected the arrival of a Jacobite agent, Hamilton might have been imprisoned for treason. Nevertheless, he had to maintain his ties to the Pretender. In the early morning hours, servants cautiously ushered Hooke into the duke's bedroom. These meetings impressed Hooke with the duke's resolution and sincerity, but precautions went further than even he, a professional spy, was used to. Hamilton refused to light a candle or a fire in the grate so that, he said, he could swear that he had "never seen" Hooke if he were questioned. On one occasion, noticing that the dawn was

breaking, the duke jumped up and climbed into his bed, from
where he continued the conversation, a muffled voice, unseen
from behind the curtains.[31]

The crucial moment of the Parliament's session came in September, with the appointment of commissioners to negotiate a
treaty of Union. Jacobites wanted to ensure that Parliament
would elect the commissioners, but London wanted them named
by the Queen. The difference was important: Jacobites, a strong
presence in Parliament, wanted to be able to wreck the treaty
(or, as they would have put it, protect Scotland's interests). The
Queen, on the other hand, would name dependents who could be
relied upon to negotiate a treaty acceptable to the many people in
England already skeptical of a united kingdom.

Hamilton championed the nationalist cause, and the Parliament heard his arguments against the ministry's plans. Late in
August he delivered a speech that electrified the House. "I am for
an honorable treaty," he said, "but to be thus cudgeled into one
was below the courage of our ancestors, and I hope that it shall
never be said that their descendants had grown so degenerate as
to lie down groveling in the dust, and patiently receive the stripes
and lashes that should be laid upon their backs without repining.
No!" he thundered.[32] Such rhetoric was popular in Edinburgh,
evoking ancient Scottish battles against English domination.
Hamilton seemed to be taking on the mantle of William Wallace
or Robert the Bruce in his effort to prevent the final eclipse of
Scotland's independence.

Hamilton's unparalleled standing as Scotland's defender made
his next move incomprehensible. On September 1, when many
members were absent, the duke rose in his place and moved that
the treaty commissioners be nominated by the Queen. The government's allies seized their opportunity, and in a snap vote the
motion carried by four votes. Scots nationalists were devastated:
the anti-Union cause was lost: "From this day may we date the
commencement of Scotland's ruine," wrote the Jacobite George

Lockhart.[33] Now the terms of the treaty would be dictated by the English and their Scottish subalterns.

The duke's betrayal of the cause seemed unaccountable. Lockhart was especially puzzled, for only a few hours earlier James had informed the anxious Jacobite that the issue would not come up that day. In hindsight, Lockhart thought that he should have been more aware of rumors circulating about Hamilton's contacts with London. The duke negotiated with both sides. In May he had invited one of the government's principal supporters, the Earl of Seafield, to dine at his country house outside Edinburgh, where the earl was "verie weal receaved." The duke hinted at a possible accommodation, though Seafield stalled for time.[34]

Had Hamilton come to an arrangement with London? More likely, the contradictions inherent in his position finally compelled him to make an unambiguous choice. His legal struggle with Lord Mohun, in which lay his hopes for financial security, was sinking into the morass of Chancery. He incurred new expenses as a popular hero, and his family's lack of sympathy made matters worse. His wife sulked at Kinneil, their house outside Edinburgh, hating Scotland and everything Scottish, especially her husband's family. His mother blamed James for bringing his money troubles upon himself. She wrote to one of her younger sons, "your brother Hamilton is always right in his own eyes; I wishe he may prove so in others."[35]

The duke's difficult relations with Saint-Germain might also have inclined him to take the court's part. His meetings with Colonel Hooke had led nowhere, and the Pretender's promises of a fresh infusion of gold had remained unfulfilled. By late August, only days before his motion, £10,000 due from France had not yet appeared, to Hamilton's great distress. He gave a Jacobite agent an intemperate lecture: his enemies at King James's court were undermining him, and without the money he had been promised he could do the Pretender no good in Scotland. He had decided, he said, to quit the exiled King's service.[36]

The duke's own explanation for his action depended upon his audience. In a letter to the Pretender he claimed that he expected to be chosen one of the treaty commissioners, where he could do the exiled court more service than in opposition. He told government agents that his goal was "a good understanding between the two kingdoms," and boasted that he had "done Her Majesty signal service" in Edinburgh.[37] Indeed, James may have believed both statements. He could serve the Pretender as a commissioner, but closer ties to the court might relieve his mounting problems. Here probably lay the reason for the duke's sudden abandonment of the anti-Unionist cause. As the Unionist Sir John Clerk wrote, "I knew that this duke was so unlucky in his private circumstances that he wou'd have complied with anything on a suitable encouragement." In January 1706, Hamilton, in seclusion at his wife's Lancashire estate, wrote a letter to his brother Charles, the Earl of Selkirk, that reveals his state of mind: "I am really soe fatigued with the multiplicity of troublesome affairs one [i.e., "on"] all hands that I am quite worne out and I am sure there are many in the gallies have more satisfaction and less trouble then I have uppon me, this joyned to the narowness of my circumstances everie where makes me quite almost in despairre how to weare it any longer ... I meet with constant reproach and at the same tyme if you'l believe me monie is as scars here as in Scotland. I have non nor can command non but has milliones of demands everie day."[38]

Brooding in his country house about his misfortunes, beset by Elizabeth's shrill demands for a trip to London, and badgered by his lawyers and creditors, James spent a miserable winter. He bitterly noted that his "signal service" in September had gone unnoticed except by those it disobliged most, the Jacobites. An indomitable Scottish Jacobite, the Duchess of Gordon, claimed "he ... has been the ruin of all."[39] The ministry in London was already desperately fending off the assaults made upon it by the Junto, and undoubtedly Godolphin viewed any association with a known Jacobite such as Hamilton to be far more trouble than it was worth. When the commissioners for the Union treaty were named, he was left off the list.

Now that he was banished to the political wilderness, only opposition remained to the duke. So despite his egregious misstep in the last session, Hamilton once again prepared himself to lead the nationalist cause. That he still retained any of the prestige and standing of the previous summer is an indication of both the force of his own personality and the lack of alternative leaders in Scotland. Although he had forfeited the trust of many, opponents of Union knew that the duke was the highest-ranking, and most gifted, of their allies. His personal difficulties had rendered him unreliable in the past, but they hoped that the court's rejection of his services might return him to the anti-Unionist camp.

The treaty negotiations in London yielded a document that appeared, to the English, generous almost beyond reason. Scotland would retain its own established Presbyterian Church and its distinct legal system. Scottish merchants and settlers would stand on an equal footing with the English, not only south of the border but throughout the colonies. The Scottish Parliament would be abolished, but the new British Parliament that would replace it provided for representation from what was now being referred to as "North Britain." The House of Commons would accommodate forty-five representatives from Scottish counties and boroughs, and Scots peers would choose sixteen of their number to sit in the House of Lords. Despite the easy terms offered, Godolphin realized that a permanent solution to the Scottish question was well worth the sacrifice. English merchants would have to bear with more competition and members of Parliament would have to squeeze more tightly together on their benches. But Scotland, smothered in the embrace of her more powerful neighbor, would no longer be a threat.

Feelings in Edinburgh were different. Most Scots declined to be grateful for English condescension, preferring their independence to the mirage of prosperity conjured up by the treaty's advocates. Scottish supporters of Union were far outnumbered —but they were strong in the Parliament, where government patronage and the self-interest of merchants had done much to build a pro-English bloc. And this Parliament would have the final word on the treaty: ratification would mean that the Scottish nation had voted itself out of existence.

The Scottish Parliament began its annual session in the fall of 1706 as usual. But this time its only business was the Union treaty. Before the session began, the government had sounded Hamilton out on his intentions. Despite receiving vague assurances that he would be rewarded if he followed the Unionist line, James made clear that he would stand against it, "For this nation will never swallow it, and force can only keep it."[40] Excited crowds, unanimously anti-Union, filled the streets daily to demonstrate contempt for the treaty and those who supported it. Despite his disappointing performance in the previous year, Hamilton was still their darling, and they followed his coach "from the House through most part of the city crying Huzzas, casting up their hats and blessing him as the protector of the nation."[41]

The treaty progressed through Parliament much as London had hoped, and each article was methodically ratified by the Unionist majority. Hamilton spoke eloquently against every clause, turning in the most impressive forensic performance of his career. His speech attacking the first article of the treaty was so effective that observers noted that even many of the Union's supporters had tears in their eyes.[42] Committed Unionists were impressed but not swayed by Hamilton's tactics. "The Duke of Hamilton spoke too with a good deal of force (I mean loud speaking)," said Lord Mar, a court pensioner. Two days later, Daniel Defoe, in Edinburgh serving as Secretary Harley's eyes and ears, reported that Hamilton had "raved" in that day's debates.[43] The majority ignored the duke's pleas and advanced steadily toward Scotland's eclipse as a separate country.

The frustrated nationalist majority outside the doors of Parliament watched the process with mounting rage. Crowds marched up and down the High Street, following a booming drum, shouting "No Union! No Union!" The appearance of an Englishman or a Unionist triggered violent reactions: "English dogs!" and other epithets pursued them through the streets. Often volleys of stones hurried them along. Hamilton did nothing to discourage these demonstrations—the government suspected that he encouraged them. The biggest riot of the session took place one night just after Hamilton had paraded through the streets in a sedan chair, waving and smiling to a frenzied crowd. After the duke had been borne to his lodgings, the mob took control of the streets. They extinguished the wavering light shed by Edinburgh's streetlamps, plunging the town into a mischief-sheltering darkness. Householders quickly put out their own lamps, as stones shattered any window that showed a light. The small town guard declined to intervene as rioters assaulted the home of Sir Patrick Johnston, a prominent Unionist. The crowd surrounded the house, shouting curses and throwing stones, while some people hammered on the doors. Inside, Johnston waited grimly with his servants and friends, prepared to shoot the first to break through. Upstairs, Lady Johnston wailed for help as stones came flying up from below. Only the timely arrival of troops prevented the mob from tearing the house down.

Hamilton denied any connection with the violence. Nevertheless, his frustration at being again on the losing side had led him to flirt with popular discontent. At one point in the session he was said to have invited a group of boys into the Parliament House to have a look at the royal regalia stored there, "for perhaps they would never see it more," and "That night he told the mob as they went home that he wisht they had evry one a vote in the House, for they wou'd vote like honest men."[44] In the cool light of day, Hamilton would hardly have been enthusiastic about a democratic order in which men in the street were as good as members of Parliament. But the emotions surrounding the Union's ratification were high enough that such sentiments seemed warranted.

With the Union treaty inevitable—the Act of Union became effective May 1, 1707—Hamilton's dealings with the Pretender became still more ambivalent. The adulation he garnered as leader of the anti-Unionist cause was gratifying, but potential advantages lay in acquiescing in the Queen's plans. His family, especially thanks to his Gerard marriage, held lands on both sides of the border, and the duke was in some respects more "British" than Scots. Union would help him in his disputes with Lord Mohun, for he could now compete in the English courts on a more nearly equal footing. He would probably be one of the sixteen representative Scottish peers in the first Union Parliament. He could fight his legal battles using the same weapons Mohun had employed so skillfully: parliamentary immunity and the partisan support of fellow peers. Financed by the Macclesfield estate, buttressed by royal favor, and assisted by his rhetorical skills in the House of Lords, James could at last hope that in the new united kingdom he would to prove his parents wrong for dismissing him as a hopeless failure.

The Pretender's agents reported the duke's new reluctance back to Saint-Germain. James Edward and his advisers saw great opportunity in the aftermath of Union. Scottish discontent with the treaty was at its height in 1707 and 1708, and many in the exiled court argued that there would never be a better time for the long-awaited invasion. The Pretender obtained French promises of troops and money. Again Jacobite agents made their shadowy way into Britain to organize support. This time James was even more cautious than he had been two years earlier. Nathaniel Hooke, whose difficult task it was to treat with Hamilton, found that on this occasion he was not even admitted into the duke's presence for one of his nocturnal conferences. Hooke visited nearly thirty times, but each time Hamilton suffered a mysterious "fever." Finally, furious at the duke's "shuffling evasions," Hooke abandoned his efforts, convinced that Hamilton was insincere in his professions of loyalty.

Hooke's pessimistic judgment was not shared by his masters on the Continent. The Pretender, his mother, Queen Mary of Modena, and Louis XIV all clung to their confidence in Hamilton, and they continued their planning. Hamilton encouraged their belief, writing Saint-Germain that he supported an invasion, but repeating his advice that it must be a strong one, involving at least fifteen thousand troops. Whatever his assurances to the Pretender, however, Hamilton intended to act cautiously.

Nor was he wrong to behave circumspectly: London knew a great deal more about Jacobite plans than many at Saint-Germain realized. Isolated in the big gray château that had been the home of the exiled Stuarts since 1688, the court seemed to be losing touch with reality. Secretary Harley received regular reports about the Pretender's plans, and he knew that Hooke was stirring up trouble in Britain. The perennial disappointments Jacobites endured had much to do with their consistently overoptimistic view of their support in Britain as well as the efficiency of English espionage.[45]

The dangers inherent in Hamilton's position became clear in the spring of 1708. With a French invasion force assembling in the Channel ports, the duke found himself once again on his way to the Tower. The Queen's messenger, bearing a warrant from the third Earl of Sunderland (whose intrigues had recently toppled Secretary Harley from office), found James at Elizabeth's Lancashire home, fending off creditors and their writs. An indulgent jailer, the Queen granted his urgent request for time to wrap up some of his most pressing legal affairs, but by the beginning of May, he had taken up residence in his old quarters.[46]

If the duke had forgotten the intricacies of English politics since William III had excluded him from them twenty years before, he was about to receive a forcible reminder. There was more to the government's move than keeping Hamilton away from invaders. Parliamentary elections loomed, and a fierce struggle was under way for power at Westminster. Godolphin, the Queen's most trusted servant, found himself losing political ground. The war with France continued with no end in sight, consuming lives and money at a frightening pace. The victories of the Duke of Marlborough on the Continent made the Lord High Treasurer's job somewhat easier, but the nation was weary of the high taxes and sacrifices war demanded. The war's strongest supporters were the Junto Whigs, upon whom Godolphin found himself more and more dependent, to his great discomfort. Godolphin was caught between Anne, who chafed under the rule of the "five tyrannous lords," as she called them, and the Junto, whose parliamentary influence made them vital for carrying on the war. The price for their cooperation was stiff: they demanded a clean sweep of their political opponents, especially the moderate Tories who had clung to office thanks to Godolphin's protection. He had already been forced to give up Robert Harley, whose lukewarm partisanship made him anathema to men like his replacement, Sunderland, one of the most important members of the Junto. In 1708 the Lord High Treasurer faced the very unpleasant prospect of further inroads on his authority and even the possible loss of Queen Anne's favor.

In this atmosphere, the arrival of sixty-one Scottish peers and commoners as representatives to the first British Parliament offered a considerable opportunity. They could, potentially, be at the heart of the ruling coalition that would emerge after the election. Hamilton's importance in North Britain made him a great prize in the political struggle, because his influence in elections might be vital. His arrest on suspicion of treason might seem a poor way for the government to ingratiate itself with the duke, but there was a crude logic to the act. Locking him up was an unmistakable demonstration of the power of the ministry. No one knew better than Hamilton that the government could prove his dalliance with either the Pretender or the great national enemy, the French. He lived at the sufferance of those who controlled the levers of power, a point that Godolphin must have made clear to him on a visit to the Tower. As the Treasurer wrote to his principal ally, Marlborough, "Mortifications are of some use to some tempers. I found him [the duke] less unreasonable than I expected, but very desirous, however, to be set at liberty."[47] A bargain followed: Hamilton agreed to support the election of government candidates in Scotland; in return,

Godolphin released him, probably adding hints of future royal favor, on condition of good behavior. Not to be outdone, the Treasurer's Junto rivals did their best to woo the duke for themselves. On May 5, 1708, after a relatively brief stay in the Tower, James was released when four Junto Whigs, lords Montagu, Dorchester, Bradford, and Orford, posted bond. The rumor of Hamilton's alleged defection to the Junto spread far and wide: "he has changed his principle as one might see by his bail." It seems obvious, however, that for the duke, the alliance was one of convenience.[48]

After his release, James went north to fulfill his part of his bargain, which he managed with some success. He won election as a representative peer, garnering the largest number of votes, and he persuaded other members to look upon the government with a more benign eye in the coming session.[49] Although the government threatened him with personal and political disaster in the maneuvering over the elections, Hamilton could have concluded that he was indispensable. The lengths to which powerful men went to enroll him in their cause gave him hope for the future.

With a delighted Elizabeth in tow, Hamilton set about establishing himself upon the London scene. His lawsuits with Mohun continued to go badly, and creditors were as pressing as ever, but he rented a large house in London's most fashionable neighborhood: St. James's Square. The square, dominated by expensive red brick houses looking out upon a cobbled street surrounding a gravel court, was widely considered to be the most beautiful in London. From the time it was laid out in the 1660s, the square had been the most desirable address in the city, and it was home to some of the capital's most important people. The duke's archrival, Queensberry, had a house there. Hamilton's choice was obvious. His new abode symbolized his elevation from the backwoods of Scotland to the heart of a world empire. He chose the most exclusive address possible to demonstrate his position in the inner circle of British life.

The duke brought servants from Scotland and Lancashire and no doubt hired some locally as well. He had to keep a coach and horses, and perform the role of hospitable host, keeping an open

9. St. James's Square, Hamilton's London home after 1708

table and dining out frequently. In his first weeks in the square he gave a series of elaborate dinners for his neighbors and political friends, cultivating social bonds that were vital for success.[50] Still deep in debt, he needed even more money. As a member of the House of Lords, he was now immune from arrest for debt, a small consolation, as his mother invariably rejected his pleas for more money. Duchess Anne refused to subsidize her son's political career. She was not convinced that an investment in her son would ever repay itself. After all, she had spent many thousands over the years, and James had always disappointed her. James felt humiliated when untitled but rich English gentlemen sneered at poverty-stricken Scots lords, and moreover such sneers damaged him politically. Hamilton must defy the stereotypes that hampered most of his countrymen. Success among English politicians, most of whom were far richer than he, depended upon making a show of prosperity and generosity.

Securing a long-coveted position in the first rank of British politics required a victory in Hamilton's feud with the usurper of his wife's fortune. Lord Mohun had carried the day in their lawsuits. But this string of victories, gained, Hamilton believed, by underhanded influence in Parliament and the chicanery of lawyers, would soon end. The assembly of the first Parliament of Great Britain would be the first occasion upon which the duke, because of his rank, would have precedence over the English baron. At last James could force Mohun into combat on his terms, and the struggle over the Macclesfield estate might finally take a turn for the better. But Hamilton's arrival on the British scene, ominous though it might have been for Mohun, did not necessarily portend disaster for the younger lord.

Mohun continued to win in the courts. In January 1708 and November 1709 Hamilton lost yet another round when the Lord Chancellor ruled that Mohun was entitled to repayment of £1,500, plus interest, which Duchess Elizabeth's father had borrowed years before from his brother-in-law, the second Earl of Macclesfield. To pay, the duke was forced to turn lands worth some £5,000 over to Mohun, who would collect the rents until the debt was satisfied. In Hamilton's view, his enemy had not only taken his wife's rightful inheritance but now further encroached on an estate already far too small to support a nobleman of his rank.[51]

Charles, Lord Mohun, was a formidable opponent even though the scrapes of his youth had convinced many that he was a worthless degenerate. While he had refrained from murder since his last trial before the Lords, his behavior remained as scandalous as ever. Yet, by the beginning of Queen Anne's reign, his drinking and whoring had become more a hobby rather than the vocation they once had been. When Mohun drifted into the orbit of his benefactor Macclesfield, he found a new purpose. For the first time in his life he had a patron—a replacement for the father he had never known. From that moment his life took a new turn.

Mohun's first real experience in the world of affairs, apart from his theatrical escapades on the streets of London, had come in 1694. At the age of seventeen, he accompanied Macclesfield in an abortive attack upon the French port of Brest. The expedition's goal was to deal a crippling blow to Louis XIV's navy as it rode at anchor. The French easily repulsed the assault, thanks to alert intelligence. Mohun, under fire for the first time as he sailed in an open boat for the beach, behaved bravely, and earned Macclesfield's admiration.[52] More important, Charles earned a commission as a captain in the earl's regiment of horse, a position that eased his then pinched finances.

A military career suited Mohun. Officers led an adventurous, carefree life, as Mohun already had. He enjoyed the company of soldiers, who were not bound by the petty rules of genteel society. As the satirist Ned Ward said, a soldier "is generally beloved of two sorts of companions, viz., whores and lice, for both these vermin are great admirers of a scarlet coat."[53] Moreover, officers were relatively well paid. On campaign, a captain of horse received twenty-one shillings and sixpence a day, and even when he was in London awaiting assignment he collected half pay, or about £175 a year.[54] For a young man who had always faced penury, the prospect of regular income, combined with foreign adventure, promotion, and uninhibited debauchery, made the army an attractive career.

King William's and Queen Anne's wars with France created a much larger and more important military presence in British life. The army had never been larger; no less than one in seven Englishmen shouldered a musket at some point during King William's reign.[55] Regiments, and the officers who commanded them, multiplied rapidly; between 1684 and 1694 the number of officers jumped from around five hundred to five thousand. Success and fortune awaited many officers who found themselves a place in the army. The supreme example of the lucky soldier was the Duke of Marlborough, whom Mohun worshipped, despite his rather suspect political credentials. Marlborough, a mere gentleman of no estate, rose from obscurity under Charles II—in no small part thanks to the favor of the king's brother James—to immense wealth and power under Queen Anne. His success as a general, directing a steady run of victories against the French, as well as his skills as a courtier and politician, made him a model for Mohun to emulate.

Mohun's military career was a success, but not all that he might have hoped for. His Gerard inheritance transformed him from a disreputable young captain into a man of importance, with a large income and considerable ambition. The army rewarded talent, as Marlborough's example illustrates, but it also had a very high regard for social rank, wealth, and political connections. Lord Mohun, at first bereft of all these qualifications, apart from his title, possessed them in abundance after Lord Macclesfield's death. The approach of renewed war against France in 1701 ensured that the army would expand even further than it had under William, and Parliament authorized the enlistment of several new regiments. The Crown appointed Mohun colonel of one of these, which filled with recruits in 1702.[56]

As the commander of a regiment, Mohun left something to be desired. His fondest wish was to serve with Marlborough's army, where he might make a name for himself in battle with the enemy.[57] But his regiment drew the luckless chore of garrison duty in Ireland, a job of such tedium and unpleasantness that Mohun did everything he could to avoid crossing the Irish Sea. Apart from a brief, unhappy stay with his men, highlighted only by quarrels with his subordinate officers, Mohun commanded his regiment entirely by post. The distaste he had for writing anything ensured that he subjected his officers to minimal interference. Abandoned amid the bogs and hostility of the Irish, the regiment decayed. In 1705 the Duke of Ormonde, the commander in chief in Ireland, told Lord Godolphin that Mohun's regiment was a hopeless mess: "I find them in so very ill a condition that I could not answer the sending them where there was like to be action."[58] A year later, Mohun's regimental agent, Captain Harte, died. He had administered pay and supplies in the colonel's behalf and left his accounts so tangled that no one could tell what had happened to large amounts of the Queen's money.[59]

While Mohun's troops shivered in Ireland, with officers who embezzled their pay and supplies, Mohun remained in London, following his lawsuits against the Duke of Hamilton. Neglecting his command caused comment but did not block his promotion, in 1706, to the rank of brigadier general. This entitled him to an extra eight pounds a day, in addition to his profits as colonel, for light service. While his regiment was abroad, "Here is . . . my Lord Mohun," groused Lord Godolphin to Marlborough, "a brigadier walking in St. James's Park and everyday in the chocolate house." The brigadier used his pressing legal affairs as an excuse to avoid taking ship for Ireland—an attitude that Marlborough deplored, but could understand, "it being for his whole estate, it might look hard to punish him for it."[60]

Mohun never became a heroic general, leading British troops in campaigns against the French. Marlborough harbored some sympathy for him, but never suggested giving him a Continental command.[61] Despite his rapid advance in the service he never led troops in combat. His promotion very likely had more to do with his political utility than with his military talents. He supported the war and the army in the House of Lords, and was befriended by powerful Junto lords like Wharton—enough to ensure a successful career. By 1708 Mohun's military career had reached a dead end. The possibility of winning battles in Flanders or Spain faded at the same time that a more crucial front had opened at home: Union with Scotland brought the Duke of Hamilton to London, full of optimism and determined to pursue his destiny. That destiny could not be fulfilled as long as Mohun possessed the Macclesfield estate. Considering the importance of his legal business, expeditions against French armies in Europe would be quixotic. In May 1708 Mohun sold his regiment to a new colonel, pocketing £3,000, a useful addition to his own legal war chest.[62] His later promotion (in 1709) to major general was essentially honorific, giving him neither a regiment to administer nor an army to command.

Mohun was more comfortable fighting in the halls of Westminster. Although only in his early thirties when the Union took effect, he had already spent a decade attending Parliament and had turned himself into a respected politician. Almost every day the House of Lords was in session Mohun was present. The House ordinarily began its business at 9 or 10 a.m., and the clerk of the House would have been surprised if Mohun was not present to answer the roll. There is no doubt that he must have attended many sessions with a headache from the previous night's debauch, but he came, and when in the House, he worked.

Most of the work of the House of Lords in the early eighteenth century was routine, despite the faded elegance of the chamber.[63] The room, crowded when everyone was in attendance—a very rare event—echoed with the drone of daily business: private bills being read or lawsuits being argued. This process bored many members, who avoided hard labor. Mohun, however, assumed far more than his fair share of the work. His peers named him to dozens of legislative committees charged to report to the House on proposed bills. Even if he sat through only a minority of these meetings, he must have endured many tedious hours. He worked on some committees whose reports he delivered to the full House, the responsibility of the committee chairman.[64] The mundane business of settling estates or passing private bills took up most of Mohun's time as a politician, and as his experience increased, so did his standing as a reliable member. This regularity stood him in good stead in those relatively few moments when the House took up matters of national importance.

The House of Lords was the senior chamber in Parliament. Contemporaries valued it above the Commons, as did the peers themselves. Its actions carried more weight and were watched with more interest than those of the Commons. Members of Parliament were often irritated when they were overshadowed by

10. Queen Anne in the House of Lords, 1710

what went on "in another place," as they referred to the Upper House, but society saw them as the junior partner in the legislative process. When matters of great importance came before Parliament, it was the House of Lords that took the lead.

The Lords, like the Commons, were bitterly divided along partisan lines, with High Church Tories and Junto Whigs at the extremes. Moderates such as Godolphin and Marlborough found themselves increasingly ground between these extremists as partisanship grew over the course of Anne's reign. High Tories, epitomized by the Queen's uncle, the Earl of Rochester, demanded a stronger monopoly of faith for the Anglican Church and tended to see the French war as a scheme to enrich Whigs and Dissenters. The Junto, on the other hand, charged their opponents with disloyalty to the Protestant succession and claimed that they harbored a desire to set the Pretender upon the throne. Such positions had virtually no common ground. Mohun weighed in on the Junto's side at every opportunity. He could not have forgotten that Rochester and other High Tories had voted him guilty in the Mountford murder case. Furthermore, nearly all of his connections, friends, and family were Whigs.

Because of his faithful attendance in the House, Mohun became an increasingly important figure in its daily partisan skirmishing. Tories, in the minority throughout most of this period, found to their chagrin that Mohun was always present, with a few other dedicated Whigs, to frustrate the ambushes they laid. Snap votes in a thin House became more difficult with Mohun on guard. He held the proxies of some Whig peers, and in their absence ensured that their votes would be cast on the correct side of every issue.[65] In the chair of numerous committees, he shaped legislation and prevented Tory surprises. Though he was not in the first rank of Whig leaders, when necessary he could deliver an effective speech.

One of Mohun's interventions had come in December 1704. The Tories, attempting to reduce the political strength of Protestant Dissenters, most of whom were dedicated Whigs, tried to pass a bill forbidding the increasingly common practice of occasional conformity. By communing with the established Church of England once or twice a year, Dissenters evaded laws excluding them from political participation. Their legal obligation done, minimal though it was, these people—Baptists, Presbyterians, and others—returned to their chapels. These communicants, argued the Tories, were not true members of the Church and should not be allowed to vote or hold office. A bill forbidding the practice failed thanks to the Whig majority in the Commons, but Rochester and his allies unveiled a shrewd legislative trick: when the vital bill appropriating funds for the French war made its way up from the Lower House, they proposed to add a provision outlawing occasional conformity. The Whig majority, wanting to continue the war, would have to accede to the Tory demand. The amendment first needed to be approved by the full House of Lords. Leaders on both sides spoke at length before a packed house, as each tried to sway the small group of peers in the middle. Rising to his feet before a set of elaborate tapestries that depicted the defeat of the Spanish Armada, Mohun conjured up another foreign invasion. The amendment, he said, would weaken the Protestant interest in Britain, a first step toward a Jacobite restoration. "If they passed this bill, they had as good tack the Pretended Prince of Wales to it," argued Charles.[66] The bill failed, and Mohun's reputation as a man of affairs rose still higher.

The one issue upon which Lord Mohun could not be counted a reliable Whig was the one closest to his heart: the Duke of Hamilton. The single incident in which we know that he strayed from his party's line came shortly after the Union in a parliamentary dispute over the rights of the Duke of Queensberry, Hamilton's archrival. The Junto, intent upon complicating Godolphin's life, challenged Queensberry's right to vote in the election of representative peers from Scotland. In a show of the Queen's confidence, Queensberry had just received a new English title: Duke of Dover. This gave him the right to a seat in the House of Lords without standing for election among his fellow Scottish lords— and without the risk of losing. The Junto's mischievous position was that Queensberry, as a peer of the newly created Great Britain, had no business interfering in what was meant to be an all-Scottish affair.

Mohun, contradicting all of his previous political career, stood against the Junto on this issue and defended the one man whom

Hamilton might have hated even more than the baron himself. Not only did Charles vote against the Whigs but he chaired a committee on the issue. He also acted as teller for the pro-Queensberry side when the House finally voted. Counting votes, the teller's function, was a strong declaration of support. There seems little doubt that in this instance Mohun's actions were driven by his intense dislike for the man who intended to deprive him of his estate.[67]

By the time the first united Parliament of Great Britain met in 1708, Mohun and Hamilton had been at war with each other for six years. Hamilton's arrival in Westminster would heighten the struggle, adding partisan feeling to their bitterness. Both men could exert formidable power in the campaigns that lay ahead, and neither intended to resign the cause. Both needed the Gerard property: for Hamilton it was the key to his advancement into the center of British politics; Mohun's successful political career also depended upon it. The crisis would come now that they shared the same social and political world: the cockpit that was London.

The Revolution

WITHIN the world of aristocratic London, nobles like Mohun and Hamilton counted often on the support of their friends. For Mohun, one friend in particular was to prove central to his social and political life.

Lieutenant General George Maccartney, like his best friend, Lord Mohun, had led a charmed life. He was born about 1660 in Belfast, and it soon became clear that the career of his merchant father held no attraction for young George. Restless and ambitious, he traveled to France for his education, but never abandoned his Scots-Irish prejudices against Catholics or those, like Tories, whom he considered fellow travelers. When James II's policies provoked rebellion in 1688, George returned to Britain, where his enthusiasm for the new regime won him a commission as a captain in the Scots Guards.[1] The army became Maccartney's home: he was a born soldier, and despite his lack of social cachet he moved steadily up through the ranks. He caught Marlborough's eye. The Captain General, impressed by his ability and courage on the battlefield, marked him for high command. Maccartney became a lieutenant colonel in 1691 and colonel of his own regiment of foot in 1704. He fought with Marlborough in three campaigns, and through the duke's influence he won the command of a brigade of troops in the British expeditionary force sent to Spain in 1707. The troops were inadequately supplied and outnumbered, and the brigadier's skills were of no avail in the face of superior forces at the disastrous battle of Almanza; Maccartney was captured and his regiment annihilated. Nevertheless, despite this setback, Marlborough continued to look favorably upon his protégé, arranging for Maccartney's exchange and repatriation. The duke rated the general as a superior soldier and worked to advance his career. Maccartney became a major general in 1709—he received this promotion on the same day that Mohun was promoted to major general.

General Maccartney was a good soldier. His behavior at Almanza, where he fought a brave rear-guard action despite overwhelming odds, might even have entitled him to the status of hero. But the black-haired, saturnine general had a darker side. "Our whole officers and soldiers have such a terror of Colonel Maccartney's coming upon our head," wrote one of his comrades-in-arms in 1705, "that they are all in despair about it, looking upon the regiment as inevitably ruined, for he who has already squandered all his own and his lady's fortune, and I fear her children's also, and has in one year by his gaming and rioting run his own regiment into debt, and is so much himself in debt that he can now neither go to England or Scotland, must by these measures not only oppress but soon utterly ruin any regiment he gets." "He has the character of a man that will get mony at any rate, and will spend it as fast as he get it," wrote the gossipy Peter Wentworth to his brother the Earl of Strafford.[2] And Maccartney's profligacy, so common among his brother officers, at times shaded into brutality.

In April 1709, at the height of his career as one of Marlborough's lieutenants, the heroic general attacked his London landlady, the widow of a clergyman. In a drunken passion, he assaulted the woman, who charged him with rape. At Maccartney's trial, she testified that her resistance enraged her attacker, who "when he could not obtain all his beastly desires of her, . . . swore . . . he wou'd make her unfitt for the use of any other man, and so with his fingers has tore her in those parts past the skill of the ablest surgeons to cure." The news of this vicious behavior spread rapidly, though little information appeared about it in the press, according to Wentworth: "What's now most talk't of in town is the affair of Major General Mackartney, and perhaps wou'd be related in the *Tatler* if they did not fear to have their throats cut by this poor Gentleman whose fortune seems to be in a desperate condition."[3] Luckily for Maccartney, Lord Chief Justice Holt proved sympathetic, declaring the victim's prosecution to be "vexatious." After paying a fine and damages, George was released to wreak further havoc.

The general's defenders played down the incident as the consequence of too much wine and a heroic temperament. "Unhappy George Maccartney! One fatal spark of lust taken in a drunken fit and fir'd at an old woman's face." Despite these rationalizations, when the victim appealed the injustice done her to the Bishop of London, she received a hearing. The bishop, appalled at her suffering, took her case up with Queen Anne, who insisted that Maccartney suffer some penalty for his misbehavior. Against the united appeals of Marlborough and Godolphin, she dismissed him from his command.[4]

By August 1709 the general was in desperate straits. Without his military employment, he lived on the charity of friends like Mohun, who loaned him the money he needed to scrape by. Lord High Treasurer Godolphin wanted at least to appoint him deputy governor of Virginia: "it would be an act of great charity and compassion, for [in spite of] all that the Duke of Somerset and I could say together t'other day on his behalf, we could not get the Queen to say she would ever employ him again . . . the poor man must otherwise starve."[5] Gradually, the combined efforts of the Queen's most trusted advisers weakened her resistance. They persuaded her that "the story had been most maliciously aggravated against him" and she reluctantly allowed him to resume command of a regiment—though she denied him the higher positions he once sought.[6]

While at home awaiting their next assignments, soldiers were invariably unruly. For officers like Maccartney, military discipline extended no further than the limits of the battlefield, and a lifetime spent at war had coarsened him. Widowed landladies, to such gentlemen, looked free for the taking. Civilian standards of behavior were, at least officially, higher; his arrest and trial proved that. But Maccartney's case showed that even brutal crimes could be papered over provided one possessed political influence. This the general had in abundance: his chorus before the Queen could hardly have been more influential, and in the end his supporters overcame both her conscience and justice. Yet the consequences of failure would have been disastrous for the general. Without his rank and military office, George Maccartney, like many other officers in the Queen's swollen army, would have been destitute. He had already frittered away his paternal estate and ruined his wife: only the Queen's gold allowed him to maintain himself as a gentleman. Without it, poverty and obscurity were inevitable.

Yet the general's close dependence on politicians for his good fortune entailed a risk: his security depended upon the survival of the Godolphin-Marlborough ministry. Without his champions, however talented George was in battle, his career was in jeopardy. In the end, a far less serious offense than rape brought the Irishman down. By early 1710, the Queen's faith in her ministers had dwindled alarmingly, and by the autumn they had been replaced by Robert Harley, the bête noire of all Whigs. Harley's pursuit of peace was anathema to officers like Maccartney, whose vocation was war. Peace meant a scaled-down army: disbanded regiments, unemployed colonels, and an end to the regular salary that allowed many officers to live like gentlemen. In December 1710 Maccartney and two of his comrades, Colonels Meredith and Honeywood, contemplated these developments during a typical evening of uninhibited drinking. The party's comments on the new ministry became increasingly disparaging, and soon the officers were roaring out toasts damning Robert Harley and all who supported him. After still more drinking, they dressed a stick in a coat and hat, called it Harley, and used it for a target. Word of these high jinks reached the court, and soon the Queen had once again dismissed Maccartney. This crime was far more grave than his assault upon a defenseless widow. He had attacked the dignity of the Queen's government. And this time there was no one at Anne's side to plead his case. General Maccartney was about to experience what he dreaded most: genteel poverty on the streets of London.[7]

The political revolution of 1710 was played out in the capital; intrigue and courtly machinations took place in drawing rooms, coffeehouses, and taverns across the city, as well as in the Palace of Westminster. The stakes for men like Maccartney, as well as his friend and patron Mohun, were high. A change of ministry could mean the difference between prosperity and ruin for both men, and there were many more in the same situation: peers and gentlemen of slender resources who clung to a ministerial lifeline that threatened to part at any moment. These motives mixed with genuine political convictions: the belief that Tory government was but a halfway house to Jacobite government. In the waning years of Queen Anne's reign, Whigs and Tories struggled ceaselessly for dominance, neither asking for nor giving quarter. London had become a battlefield no less crucial than Blenheim, though the foot soldiers in this war often bore high rank and aristocratic titles.

London was Europe's largest city, a metropolis of over 500,000 souls. Yet the political and social world in which Mohun and Hamilton moved was very small. Members of both Houses of Parliament, judges, and higher-ranking civil servants totaled fewer than one thousand. Many of these preferred life in the country to performing their duties. Politically active society in Queen Anne's Britain amounted to a few hundred gentlemen and nobles, and many of their wives and mistresses, all living within a mile or two of the Palace of Westminster. So restricted a world intensified personal dislikes as men and women intrigued their way through the city.

A century earlier, success for an ambitious gentleman depended upon achieving prominence at court, but by the early eighteenth century the rules had become more ambiguous and complex. The court no longer dominated patronage as it once had. James I, to the disgust of many of his subjects, could—and did—distribute fabulous rewards on a whim. In the early 1600s more than one penniless Scot whose only recommendation was a well-turned leg or the ability to survive one of the King's tedious monologues found himself the master of a fortune or a valuable office. Queen Anne's power to gratify her own fancy was much reduced, for she depended upon Parliament's willingness to finance her household. She had favorites—the fearsome Sarah, Duchess of Marlborough,

11. The gatehouse of St. James's Palace,
London, during the reign of Queen Anne

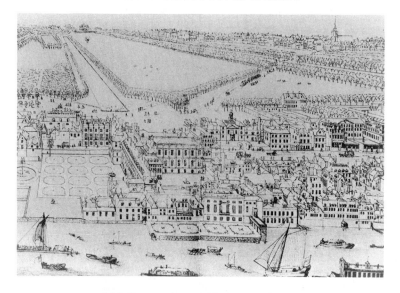

12. A bird's-eye view of Whitehall, about 1720

and her simpering successor, Abigail Masham, were the two best known. But charming the sovereign was now only one of the chores awaiting an aspiring politician, and it was possible to succeed—at least temporarily—even in the face of the Queen's dislike. Anne loathed the members of the Junto, yet sometimes found herself forced to employ them because of their parliamentary strength. Moreover, the Queen's regard might not necessarily save a minister in political trouble, as Robert Harley found in 1708, when the Junto combined to turn him out of office, and as Lord Godolphin found in 1710. James I had once claimed that kings were gods on earth, but his great-granddaughter Anne was now something of a minor deity: never wisely ignored, she still commanded considerable power, but she had learned, of necessity, to share the heavens with others.

Success and political power in British society now depended upon propitiating a range of powers: the Queen, parliamentary politicians, soldiers, and the moneyed men whose capital financed a state burdened by a costly Continental war. London, more specifically the territory bounded by Westminster in the west and Covent Garden in the east, was the temple of the new politics. Much of the work of the politically ambitious took place in Parliament. But the political art had more mysteries. The parks, taverns, and coffeehouses of the capital were just as important. Much of the business of politics and society took place there, as the few hundred of the politically important met, socialized, and planned the future for the Queen's six million subjects.

Both Mohun and Hamilton played an important role in the political order, and their London lives were typical of men of their rank and ambition. Hamilton, as befitted his rank, operated from his grand house in St. James's Square. Mohun, thanks to the Gerard fortune, used the imposing Macclesfield House as his headquarters. From these elegant premises, the two nobles worked to build their political careers. It was hard, if pleasant, work.

A typical day began as gentlemen shook off the effects of the previous night's excesses, rising sometime after nine. Most were not fortunate enough to awake in accommodations as lavish as Mohun's or Hamilton's. Even someone as important as General Maccartney in his best times made do with a couple of furnished rooms up a pair of stairs, rented at eight or ten shillings a week.[8] Many gentlemen called on their servants to provide them with a draft of one of the nostrums hawked in the apothecaries' shops, promising infallible cures for hangovers. Having choked down a miracle cure, usually with a mouthful of hot tea, a gentleman began the ritual of dressing: undershirt, breeches, shirt, waistcoat, neckcloth, and coat, all made of expensive material and provided, more often than not, on credit by a London tailor. The costume was topped off by a massive curled wig of human hair set firmly upon a shaven skull, and completed by the buckling on of a sword, the essential badge of a gentleman. Thus appareled, the ambitious London gentleman sallied forth into the streets of the West End ready for his day's work.

In a sedan chair hired for about a shilling per hour, his typical first stop would be the home of some great man: the Duke of Marlborough, if he were not across the Channel slaughtering Frenchmen, or Lord High Treasurer Godolphin, for example. From nine until eleven, ministers of state held their levees, receiving visitors and supplicants. Men and women in search of pensions, people with petitions or lawsuits, or those who merely wanted a chance to meet a man in the Queen's confidence packed ministerial drawing rooms. These suitors milled about as their hosts murmured promises or gracefully fended off uncongenial requests. Those in attendance could range from Sir Isaac Newton, the famous scientist and master of the mint, to people like Frances Hoffman, "a mad woman" who plagued Secretary Harley with ruminations on the wholesale wine trade and religious prophecy: "I have great hopes," she wrote in one of her missives, "that the Devil is come out of me having already dreamed so as will appear by the inclosed hymn which I have made thereupon as a specimen how Penchant I am to Divine things."[9]

Following his appearance at a levee, a gentleman then climbed back into his chair and made his way to his next stop: a chocolate house or coffeehouse. Coffee and chocolate had been part of the London social scene for over fifty years: hundreds of shops were scattered all over the metropolis. For a penny or two, these establishments provided a pot of coffee or chocolate and what amounted to a license to loaf for as long as the customer chose. Most coffeemen (and there were quite a few women in the trade, as well) kept their houses as simply as possible; cheap prints were tacked up on the walls for decoration—portraits of celebrated actresses and generals, advertisements for toothache cures or newly opened shops. Many coffeehouses provided free newspapers, and patrons sat for hours nursing their drinks, smoking tobacco in long clay pipes, and settling the great issues of the day. By late morning, most of the coffeehouses frequented by gentlemen of fashion were full. Ned Ward described the scene in Man's coffeehouse, which stood very near Parliament and catered to politicians and their hangers-on: "a pair of stairs led us into an old-fashioned room . . . where a gaudy crowd of odiferous Tom Essences were walking backwards and forwards with their hats in their hands, not daring to convert 'em to their intended use, lest it should put the foretops of their wigs into some disorder. We squeezed thro' the fluttering assembly of snuffing peripatetics, till we got to the end of the room, where at a small table we sat down . . . Bows and cringes of the newest mode were exchanged betwixt friend and friend." Ward was not impressed by what he saw, "being half-choak'd with the steem that arose from their soot-colour'd ninny-broth, their stinking breaths, and suffocating fumes of their nasty puffing engines, my friend and I pay'd for our Mahometan Gruel, and away we came."[10]

Despite Ward's complaints, coffeehouses were immensely popular among Londoners. News circulated in them, with their readily accessible newspapers and handwritten newsletters.[11] Some specialized; Lloyd's, for example, was the favorite resort of merchants, and by Queen Anne's day was becoming the center of the nascent marine insurance business. Others catered to political views: the Smyrna and the Cocoa Tree in Pall Mall were well-known Tory houses, while Mohun imbibed with his Whig cronies at the St. James coffeehouse, where in 1710 he wrote that he was "always . . . in an evening to be heard of."[12] Hamilton probably patronized the British Coffee House, which was the informal headquarters of London's growing contingent of Scots.

An hour or two would no doubt provide a gentleman with enough stimulation and news for the day, but knowledge of the latest parliamentary gossip, or the new arrivals at the dock, was only part of the information a successful Londoner needed. In fair weather, a gentleman took a turn in one of London's parks: St. James's or Hyde Park. Originally the private property of the Crown, by the early eighteenth century the parks were open to the public, and people of all sorts flocked to them. Unlike the

13. A London coffeehouse, about 1710

world of the coffeehouses, which was almost exclusively mascu-
line, the parks attracted both men and women. Business of a different order from that of the merchants at Lloyd's was transacted.
The business of sex went on straightforwardly. A young German
traveler was astonished at the number of high-class whores he saw
plying their trade in the walks of St. James's Park. They were so
finely dressed and elegant as they strolled behind their fashionable masks that poor Zacharias von Uffenbach had trouble distin-
guishing the professional courtesans from ordinary gentlewomen.

More complex than mere prostitution, however, was the daily
interplay between eligible men and women that went on in the
parks. Some trolled the walks on foot, ogling and being ogled, but
those who could afford it preferred to conduct their business from
a coach. The favorite place for this rolling social play was Hyde
Park's Ring—a large dirt-paved oval where hundreds of coaches
wheeled in a slow circle, their occupants displaying their finery.[13]
Nobles and heiresses made matches and tested the matrimonial
waters here, and many affairs had their beginnings in the covert

glances cast between coaches. "They have surrounded a circumference of 2 or 3 hundred paces diameter with a sorry kind of Ballustrade, or rather with poles set upon stakes, but 3 foot from the ground, and the coaches drive round and round this, when they have turn'd for some time round one way, they face about and turn t'other: so rowls the world." Von Uffenbach, visiting the park in the summer of 1710, was even less impressed: "Towards evening we drove to the Hay [Hyde] Park, which is by no means so large and pleasant as they would have us believe. On account of the number of coaches which drive around in a circle in a small enclosure, it is very unpleasant to ride through the terrible dust."[14] Nevertheless, as *The Spectator* said, "Neither frost, nor snow, nor an East wind hinders people from going" to the Ring.[15] This daily drama appeared to be a peaceful one: although reputations were routinely destroyed at the Ring, the casualties usually walked—or, rather, drove—away physically intact. But vicious rumors, social snubs, and confidence tricks ruined the prospects of many a promising young gentleman and, more often, gentlewoman.

Lord Mohun had sad experience with the ways of the park. One day, while still married to Lady Charlotte, he spotted her riding in the park with several gentlemen. Stopping the carriage, he demanded the names of his wife's companions—information that Charlotte was reluctant to provide. In Robert Harley's words, "My lord came up and would know who was there, she did not care to be found out [and] at last said that she would show her Bare Arse if that would satisfy him, he agreed and she put her arse out at the window to him and he went away."[16] The collapse of their marriage followed shortly, but for years afterward the story was still remembered.

Not every visitor to the park was in search of a wife or mistress, however. An ambitious gentleman might do more than flirt. He could get valuable information. The parks were among the few places that casually acquainted men and women could mix with relative freedom, and both did what they could to profit by the experience. The well-informed and the ignorant alike passed on the latest court gossip and tales of intrigue, and made contacts that might be valuable in the future. In the early eighteenth century, society strictly circumscribed a woman's life, but well-born women were always in a position to exercise influence over their men, and some accumulated considerable power. A turn in the park could yield unexpected benefits.

After an hour or two spent in the Ring, or sauntering through the walks at St. James's, the "world" sat down to dinner. An important aristocrat such as Hamilton kept a cook and probably took many of his meals at home. When it was convenient he ate out, as did gentlemen of more modest means. Meals taken in taverns or ordinaries kept up the daily round of socializing, as friends and acquaintances met to swap news and conversation. The meals were simple and hearty: the average tavern had large joints of meat (beef or mutton, usually) turning on a spit over an open fire. A customer pointed out what he wanted, which a servant immediately hacked off and served. Customers ate their meat with white bread and washed it down with either ale or wine. Vegetables, salads, and desserts were rarely available unless a customer made special arrangements. This constant diet of red meat and alcohol fattened many Englishmen. By his early thirties, Mohun had acquired a portly figure as well as a surplus chin. Those who, like Hamilton, escaped obesity often suffered agonies from nutrition-related illnesses such as the gout. The duke's was so acute that when it flared up he was barely able to hobble from one room to the next.

As with coffeehouses, there were taverns and cookshops for every taste and purse in London. Nearly everyone visited what were called "shilling ordinaries," where a satisfying meal could be had for only twelve pence. But the extravagant could dine at far more costly establishments, such as Pontacks, a house established as far back as the 1670s, where a meal might cost two pounds. Jonathan Swift, an occasional visitor there, complained bitterly of the expense, but despite the high prices, the place remained a favorite with Londoners down to the 1780s. There were other expensive houses, such as the Thatched House, one of Hamilton's favorites, a tavern not far from St. James's Square. Some places catered to Whigs, others to Tories, but many drew their customers from across the political spectrum. Both Hamilton and Mohun were familiar with one of the more famous, the Rose in Covent Garden. A long-established tavern, it was popular with the nobility, who often rented private rooms for extended meals, drinking bouts, and card parties. The Duchess of Hamilton's father, Lord Gerard, had dropped dead there in the course of a monumental drinking bout in the 1680s, but the duke, unfazed, continued to frequent the place.

A midafternoon meal taken in a place like the Rose could be relied upon to satisfy a gentleman's hunger for the rest of the day, and give him the opportunity to plan his next move. He could always join one of the interminable card games being played somewhere on the premises. Gambling was a favorite pastime, and more than a few luckless gentlemen rose from the table ruined men. The most serious gambling took place later in the day, after dark, but anyone with a few guineas in his purse could find a game at any hour of the day or night. If prudence dictated avoiding the tables, at least for the remainder of the afternoon, a gentleman might seek out other attractions. If he was a newcomer to the city, there were sights to see: the Tower, with its flyblown collection of lions and tigers. Or he could climb to the top of the immense dome of St. Paul's Cathedral, with its panoramic view of London and the surrounding countryside. Having scratched his name into the stonework of the cathedral as a souvenir (a universal practice), he might go on to one of the theaters to while away the early hours of the evening. Even the most jaded Londoners went to the theater: companies were kept busy throughout much of the year performing new plays written by a legion of playwrights. Runs were generally short, but audiences returned to watch the same plays again and again. They were sophisticated judges. Woe betide a performer who failed to meet a critical audience's high standards. It was not uncommon for drunken gentlemen to disturb unsatisfactory performances. Among even the most exalted playgoers rowdiness was commonplace. In the winter of 1712 the Duchess of Hamilton treated London gossips to a delicious story when she brawled publicly with a young man at a performance, "soe loud that everybody heard it, with language as is seldom used but at Billingsate, and he taking it in the best manner that could be, laughing extreamly at her." The duke, laboring to increase his standing among the inner circle of court society, could hardly have been pleased by his wife's behavior.[17]

Performances ended by 9 or 10 p.m., and afterward the audience poured out into the streets in search of more amusement. Women returned home, or attended the occasional balls or suppers given by their neighbors. Men more often returned to the taverns and gaming houses, carousing far into the night. Many gentlemen formed clubs. These organizations met regularly in taverns around the city, and members shared the expense of an elaborate meal and large quantities of alcohol. They were frequently politically oriented. Hamilton, for example, belonged to an exclusively Tory society called the Board of Brothers, while Mohun was a prominent member of the best-known club of all, the ardently Whig Kit-cat Club.

Many an observer might have speculated that the clubs' real function was to provide an excuse for heavy drinking and sophomoric behavior. When Lord Mohun was inducted into the Kit-cat in 1707, his first act was to break the special chair of one of his fellow members, the famous free-thinking printer Jacob Tonson. Appalled, the old printer grumbled that "a man who could behave so badly would cut a man's throat."[18] The Board of Brothers was not much more decorous, despite the fact that its members included the devout clergyman Jonathan Swift.[19] The Brothers had to decree limits on toasts in order to prevent excessive drinking, and the Kit-catters were famous for their vigorous toasts in honor of Whig beauties.[20]

Though often raucous, club meetings still had considerable political and social importance. The Junto frequently plotted strategy at Kit-cat meetings, and Tories made schemes over loyal toasts to the Queen and established Church. Gaining admission to the elite clubs was an important step for any aspiring politician. Hamilton and Mohun belonged to the most important clubs of the day. But entering the first rank of politics required investment. Clubs were expensive, as members took turns organizing feasts and paying for wine and food. Less wealthy gentlemen often had trouble keeping up. Without his Macclesfield inheritance, it is hardly likely that Mohun would have been invited to join the Kit-cat, and Hamilton's parlous financial state made every penny spent on his Tory Brethren a sacrifice.

One could end an evening in other ways, as Mohun did on a night in 1711. Peter Drake, an Irish adventurer recently back from Marlborough's army, had returned to the arms of his lover, Mrs. Goodman. Drake and Goodman were in bed shortly after midnight when they heard the rattle of a coach stopping before their lodgings. The coachman then knocked hard at the door of the darkened house, bringing the landlady, Mrs. Roberts, down to investigate. She and the driver spoke for a minute or two, and she learned that a "person of distinction" had come to call on Mrs. Goodman. It was Lord Mohun, who evidently had become well acquainted with Goodman during Drake's eighteen-month absence. Goodman was very likely one of the many apparently genteel women in London who lived by their wits, maintained by gentlemen who provided support in exchange for company and, very often, sexual favors.

Mrs. Roberts stole into Goodman's bedroom, and tried unsuccessfully to wake her lodger without disturbing her bedmate. Drake had been awake all along. He swore that Goodman would stay in bed, and demanded that Roberts send the visitor away. The

landlady returned to the door and, after a brief negotiation with the
occupant of the coach, came upstairs bearing Mohun's watch and
seal. Drake, whose claim to gentility was shaky at best, thought
twice about insulting a peer of the realm, and tried to defuse the situation by using his not inconsiderable wit. He sent a message
downstairs, claiming his status as a veteran of Marlborough's army,
and asserting that no soldier worth his salt would give up his conquest (in this case, Mrs. Goodman) "upon a bare summons."
Mohun, who by this time had made his way into the hall, was mag-
nanimous. He was, after all, a devoted supporter of Marlborough
and had become a general in the army thanks to the duke's patronage. Drake, whose military career was a checkered one—he had
served on both sides in the war with France, and was more adept at
desertion and flight than combat—had hit upon just the formula to
disarm his rival.

Mohun invited Drake and his mistress into Mrs. Roberts's parlor for a late-night supper—which he had already ordered from a
nearby tavern, no doubt expecting to share it with Mrs. Goodman
alone. Drake knew that a refusal to come down would be an open
insult, and he knew the baron's reputation. Fifteen minutes later,
Drake and Goodman appeared downstairs, despite the lady's fear
of a quarrel. The two men, Mrs. Roberts, and Mrs. Goodman sat
around a table, Drake warily eyeing the sword that Mohun placed
on a chair next to him. Drake carefully sat between Mohun and
Goodman, but the peer still managed to say "many soft obliging
things" to the young woman as the night wore on. Though clearly
suspicious, Mohun behaved politely toward Drake, quizzing him
closely about the details of the latest campaign.

Gradually, however, after the food arrived and the wine began
to flow, Mohun became less hostile toward his rival. "My lord
lov'd bumpers, and ply'd me pretty hard with the same," and a
lengthy round of toasts followed, drunk in burgundy and cham-
pagne. The bottles arrived from an apparently inexhaustible supply provided through a dumbwaiter by one of Charles's servants

in the basement. Not until 8 a.m. did Mohun, "pretty well over-come with liquor," order his coach. Drake walked him to the street, where Mohun turned and embraced him before climbing unsteadily into the coach and rolling away.[21]

Lord Mohun's behavior was hardly unusual for his time. His friend Maccartney probably accompanied him on many nocturnal expeditions. Mohun's excesses apparently did no harm to his rising political fortunes. Although contemporary moralists complained, a culture of dissipation thrived among many of the most important people in the kingdom. Men like Mohun cemented their political and social standing through excess. Hard living cut many lives short, as drinking and the violence it often generated took a high toll among fashionable men in the early eighteenth century, but many believed that fast living was crucial to their success.

Lord Mohun's life showed the advantages of profligacy. By flaunting his wealth and connections, he smoothed his way into political prominence. Though no favorite of the Queen's, Mohun had by 1710 won from the Electress Sophia of Hanover, Queen Anne's heir, appointment to the board of regency. The regents, most of whom were prominent Whigs, would ensure a peaceful transition to the new dynasty after Anne's death. Meanwhile Charles enjoyed his high standing among the Junto and other Whigs.

A lifelong resident in the tawdry world of London society, Mohun was an expert by the 1710s. For some he exemplified everything wrong with the metropolis, but many found his example an alluring one. He had admirers, even imitators. Mary Delarivière Manley told the story of his courtship of the woman who became his second wife with a tone of admiration that belies the illicit nature of the couple's relationship. As a vicious Tory propagandist, she had no reason to treat Charles tenderly, but in *The New Atalantis*, her barely disguised recounting of court gossip, she describes Mohun as "a handsome Atalantic lord," reformed after a dissipated youth. She seems to relish his antics.

Mohun's first marriage might have converted him to less formal arrangements, such as the one he had with Mrs. Goodman. He also had an affair with Elizabeth Griffith, daughter of one of the Queen's doctors, Sir Thomas Lawrence. Her husband, Colonel Edward Griffith, was a minor official at court, connected to the Duchess of Marlborough, to whom he owed his position. "Duck" Griffith, as his wife was called, was well known at court for her wit and her Whig partisanship. She and Mohun first met in the studio of a London dance master. By 1709 everyone but Colonel Griffith seemed to know of their affair. Mohun and Elizabeth met regularly at card parties in Whig homes, where she passed him notes, taking them from "between those no-small-beautiful breasts of hers." These billets set up clandestine meetings where the affair could be pursued beyond the prying eyes of gossips like Mrs. Manley.[22]

After Elizabeth Griffith's husband died early in 1711, Mohun married her—very likely not for her wit but for her connections to the Marlborough clan. Some professed surprise. "I wonder he should give himself the trouble to marry her, for everybody says he has for some years taken the same libertys he can do now."[23] A minister named Mr. Bradfield performed the marriage less than a month after Griffith's death. Bradfield's qualifications remain murky; he had no church living and presumably earned his keep performing clerical odd jobs, such as this clandestine marriage. Not long afterward, reports said that he went bankrupt and fled London. Charles and Elizabeth exchanged vows in a friend's dining room at the Middle Temple before a small group of witnesses.[24]

The marriage was less satisfactory than the affair that preceded it. Elizabeth had a sharp tongue, and no doubt Mohun offered her more than enough opportunity to exercise it. Within a year of the wedding Mohun had moved out of Macclesfield House to lodgings of his own not far away in Great Marlborough Street.[25] Yet the marriage was politically useful to Mohun. Elizabeth used her long-standing relationship with the Duchess of Marlborough to further her husband's ambitions. Not long after the wedding,

Elizabeth sent gushing letters to Sarah, assuring the duchess of Mohun's devotion and adding some choice flattery of her own.

Mohun campaigned to strengthen his political standing between late 1710 and 1712, because, after years of steady ascent, he had entered a more dangerous period. The Duke of Hamilton had arrived upon the London political scene and broader complications threatened the baron's position. Partisan warfare between Whigs and Tories approached a crescendo. For the first time since Queen Anne's accession, the balance threatened to shift decisively toward the Tories.

The Queen's sympathies had always been moderately Tory, but for much of her reign power remained with the Whigs. Marlborough and Godolphin found themselves more and more dependent upon Whig assistance in carrying out government policy. The Queen disliked the Junto Whigs intensely, but in 1708 had been forced to cooperate with them in order to keep her favorites in office. Depending upon men like Lord Wharton and his disreputable allies such as Lord Mohun mortified Anne, and by 1710 she was increasingly anxious to free herself from their bullying.

Hope came in the form of Sir Robert Harley. His moderate Tory politics were too much for the Junto, which in 1708 had demanded and obtained his dismissal as Secretary of State. But Harley was a consummate backstairs politician. His enemies contemptuously described him as "Robin the Trickster," and even his friends confessed that he had an uncanny ability to take every side of an issue. He planned to construct a ministry composed of moderates from both parties, committed to a victorious—but swift—end to the war with France and the restoration of the Queen's political maneuverability. He would head this new government himself.

Breaking the grip of Godolphin and the Junto would not be easy, but Harley went about his task skillfully. He was lucky that Godolphin's loyalty to the Duchess of Marlborough had strained Anne's relationship with her Lord High Treasurer. By now Anne's relationship with Sarah, once her most intimate friend, had broken down. The duchess's ungovernable temper and her devotion to the Junto (one of whose members, the obnoxious Earl of Sunderland, was her son-in-law) led her to badger the Queen unmercifully. Sarah's impatience and rudeness to her mistress went far beyond the bounds of propriety. Gradually Anne turned to others for companionship.

Harley, aware of the tension between the Queen and her favorites, quietly cultivated a relationship with Abigail Masham. Masham, a gentlewoman who had secured her court office by Sarah's favor, was one of the Queen's dressers, a relatively humble post involving menial service. Abigail was everything Sarah was not: quiet, unassuming, a good listener, and a Tory. Through Mrs. Masham, Harley presented to Anne his plan for a new ministry. Abigail demurely supported his views, and they slowly made headway through 1709 and 1710.

Intrigue was important in Harley's plans; he could not work openly against Godolphin. He often assured the Lord High Treasurer of his support. Yet the Junto were suspicious. They allowed Harley no official contact with the Queen. They could not, however, control Anne's bedchamber. There Abigail worked to undermine the government. Finally, Anne's growing lack of confidence in her ministers tipped the balance. A misstep by the government sealed its fate.

On Saturday, November 5, 1709, Dr. Henry Sacheverell preached a sermon before the newly elected lord mayor of London. The mayor, an uncompromising Tory, had invited one of his own kind to preach. The service ostensibly commemorated a favorite Whig holiday: the anniversary of the Gunpowder Plot, a failed attempt by Catholics in 1605 to blow up King James I and his Parliament. Sacheverell's targets were Lord High Treasurer Godolphin and his Whig allies. Sacheverell was a notorious preacher, whose standard theme was "The Church in Danger." In his view, Whigs, allied with Protestant Dissenters, sought to destroy the Church of England and its greatest champion, the monarchy. He preached political sermons, and he took no prisoners. This Saturday he entitled his message "On False Brethren in Church and State." He did not need to name his targets: Godolphin and the Junto. It was a typically intemperate performance, insulting and strident. The lord mayor was pleased. He treated Sacheverell to a ride home in his official coach, dinner, and high praise.

Godolphin was furious. As the war had lengthened and political battles at home grown ever more bitter, the Treasurer found himself more and more often the victim of political libels. Political pamphlets, lampoons, and lies poured from the press, each more scandalous than the last. But a fanatical preacher standing in the pulpit of London's own cathedral denouncing the government as the lord mayor vigorously nodded agreement was too much to bear. Then Sacheverell published the sermon, and within weeks tens of thousands of copies had been sold, fueling public disgust with government policy. Something had to be done.

The Junto agreed. At a meeting of the Kit-cat Club, probably including Mohun, a plan of action emerged. Sacheverell would be impeached. The House of Commons would charge him with high crimes and misdemeanors: slandering the government. A trial in the Lords, with its comfortable Whig majority, would be a lesson for loud-mouthed Tory preachers. After a guilty verdict, Sacheverell would at least be deprived of the right to preach, if not jailed.

The decision to impeach the doctor was a mistake. Although parliamentary sentiment favored exemplary punishment, in the kingdom at large the case seemed overblown and vindictive. The Whigs had overstayed their welcome. The war, now in its eighth year, dragged on, while Whig intransigence at the negotiating table ensured that France would keep up the fight despite Marlborough's superior generalship. Taxes were high and the harvest in 1709 had been bad. A weak economy created a pro-Tory climate of opinion.

Sacheverell's trial unleashed political passions beyond the control of the Whigs and made Harley's plan to create a new ministry possible. The government took an unconscionable time to prosecute. Not until late February 1710 did the proceedings begin. By that time, interest in the doctor's cause had risen to near-hysterical levels. Whenever he made a public appearance, usually to answer some charge brought by the Commons, he was surrounded by cheering Londoners. Women swooned at his approach, and engraved portraits of the pudgy, double-chinned doctor sold in thousands. Sacheverell's clerical supporters whipped up hostility against the Whigs, and Tories used the trial as a lever against Godolphin's ministry.

When the proceedings opened in Westminster Hall, the building was jammed with spectators, most of whom were vocal supporters of the defendant. Popular excitement spilled out of Westminster. Any known opponent of the doctor's learned quickly to keep his opinions to himself. Thousands of people filled the streets around the Houses of Parliament, wildly cheering Sacheverell as he arrived and departed for his trial, as well as abusing Whigs as they made their furtive way into the hall. Mohun, an enthusiastic supporter of the prosecution, chaired a committee of the House of Lords charged to investigate the disorders that surrounded the trial. Mohun's reliability as a Junto man made him a worthy conductor of this enterprise, but in the end it was little more than Whig whistling in the dark: the popular mood grew still more ugly as the trial continued.[26]

On March 1, 1710, the streets of London erupted in the most serious riots anyone had seen for decades, as hysterical mobs targeted those they believed responsible for their hero's prosecution. London's Dissenters suffered most. To chants of "High Church and Sacheverell!" their meetinghouses were systematically destroyed. Organized crowds battered down doors of chapels, stripped them of their pews, psalm books, and pulpits, and built bonfires with them in the streets. Some buildings were burned to the ground, while others were leveled, their remains carried away by the rioters. Some rioters intended to repeat their performances on the homes of prominent Whigs such as Lord Wharton and Lord Chancellor Cowper, but before they could accomplish their plans, the authorities had finally begun to act.

The government's first response to the riots was to dither; Lord Sunderland, the Secretary of State, hesitated to use the Queen's guards in the streets, for fear of leaving her unprotected. But Anne apparently did not fear the mob, and she ordered the troops out herself. By dawn the next day, the rioters had gone home, leaving behind the smoking ruins of dissenting London, and the Whig cause in deep trouble.

The doctor's trial dragged on for days, though the outcome was a foregone conclusion. With the Whig majority in the Lords, Sacheverell would certainly be convicted. Nevertheless, in a sign of the government's increasing weakness, the Lord High Treasurer and his allies worried about the punishment that would be imposed on the arrogant divine. Sacheverell carried himself like a conquering hero, basking in the adulation of the mob, and the government wanted desperately to vindicate itself with a stiff sentence. Unfortunately, all too many members of the House of Lords began to develop scruples. The peers would determine Sacheverell's sentence, and the overwhelming popular sentiment had its effect even on unelected lords of Parliament. Tories would nearly all vote to acquit in any case, but even moderate Whigs were beginning to waver. The Junto scrambled to shore up its support. Those thought bribable were approached with promises of favors should they stand firm, and the vulnerable feared government reprisal. Hamilton, for example, confided to one of his cronies that his heart was with Sacheverell, but he worried that his lawsuit against Mohun—which was moving toward a crucial hearing before the Whig Lord Chancellor—might suffer.[27] Everyone expected the duke, a Tory and known Jacobite, to side with the doctor, but Hamilton's position was more complicated than it appeared.

In the end, James voted with the doctor. He knew that he could expect no favors from this government anyway. And Mohun was one of the leading figures in the debates, arguing passionately for a conviction and harsh punishment. Once Hamilton and Mohun faced off on the floor of the House, on one of the rare occasions when their long-standing enmity was publicly displayed. The duke argued Sacheverell's innocence, and Mohun his guilt. In this exchange Hamilton once again found himself bested by the upstart baron.[28]

The Lords voted on March 20. Westminster Hall was packed with the doctor's supporters. Some, like the Duchess of Cleveland, went to great lengths to stop the Whig juggernaut. She locked her husband, who favored a conviction, in his room so that he could not vote against her hero. Fortunately, the Duke of Richmond, an ally of the Junto, rescued his friend with the aid of a ladder propped against his window. The Whig majority mustered the necessary votes: 69 to 52. Sacheverell was convicted. But the government's humiliation from the whole fiasco became clear the next day. The doctor's punishment was only a three-year suspension from preaching. Junto attempts to impose anything more serious failed, as many of their former allies voted with the Tories.[29] Sacheverell was received with adulation in the streets, and after his suspension returned to his partisan preaching, this time from the comfort of a valuable London church living.

Robert Harley watched the proceedings against Sacheverell with rising hopes. The ministry's weakness in Parliament was complemented by the Queen's growing impatience with her ministers. She had stood by Godolphin, but her support waned as he grew more dependent upon the Junto. His energy and enthusiasm for government declined noticeably during the trial, for he became convinced that his position was being undermined. And every day, while she dressed her mistress, Mrs. Masham presented Anne with an alternative: a return to a middle way, a ministry led by moderates like Harley, whose sympathy with the

Church of England was balanced by their determination to seek a victorious end to the war. Harley would be the Queen's servant, and the presumptuous demands of the Junto would be a thing of the past.

Harley's plans ripened over the summer of 1710. He worked slowly to build a coalition that would overthrow Godolphin. Many politicians had to be tempted to abandon the ministry, a task that was never very easy. Even a weakened government had many ways to maintain its majority: patronage of all sorts, and, as Hamilton feared when he contemplated voting for Sacheverell, an ability to punish.

Some were easy to win over. Tories, sensing the Queen's shifting attitudes, stood solidly for Harley. Scottish peers and MPs were more difficult: there were sixteen in the Lords and forty-five in the Commons, and many depended upon government largesse. It took a leap of faith for some to abandon what appeared to be a secure position at the ministry's trough for the possibility of favor in a new regime. The Duke of Hamilton was a key player. His flirtation with the Junto in 1708 was long over: the presence of Lord Mohun on the other side made any compromise with them impossible. But he could still stand aloof to increase the price of his support, for Hamilton had considerable influence with his fellow Scots, and Harley needed their support.

As rumors of the imminent demise of the ministry spread in the summer of 1710, Hamilton's name cropped up more and more often as a potential beneficiary. He was mentioned as a possible Master of the Queen's Horse, he would receive a British dukedom, and town gossip expected that the duchess, too, would win court office. The duke could barely contain himself in these months, and he redoubled his pursuit of political aggrandizement. At no time since his palmy days at the court of James II was Hamilton ever so near success. The prospect of regaining the place that the Revolution had deprived him of—and vanquishing Mohun—almost made him giddy.

James badgered Harley for preferment for himself and his family. To his chagrin, progress was not as easy as he expected. The duke's overeager pursuit of favor alienated many, not least Queen Anne, who had never trusted him. The duke's youngest brother, Archibald, was appointed governor of Jamaica, but Hamilton's grander ambitions were put off with fair promises. Harley could be fairly certain of Hamilton's support in any event, and he had many other more delicate negotiations in train.

The revolution proceeded slowly, following the dismissal of Godolphin as Lord High Treasurer on August 8, 1710. Harley, now Chancellor of the Exchequer, proceeded cautiously, working to build an effective coalition. Anne decided to part with her faithful Treasurer reluctantly. She had no desire for the new ministry to be a mirror image of the old: hard-line Tories who would allow her no more freedom of action than the Junto. Harley, like his mistress, hoped to follow a middle way, and did his best to co-opt some of the more useful supporters of the old regime—including the arch-Whig Lord Mohun. "Robin the Trickster" was well aware of Mohun's talents, and in September and October he made a concerted effort to win him over. His intermediary was a curious one: Charlotte, Lady Orby, Mohun's former mother-in-law and erstwhile opponent in the courts. In any event, she did know Mohun and was a reliable Tory. Early in October, the recently resigned Lord Chancellor, Lord Cowper, received a call at his home from an agitated Mohun. Charles sought Cowper's advice. Lady Orby had brought a proposition to him from Harley: "any preferment he would chuse" if he defected from his friends. The Whigs, she argued, had done nothing for Mohun despite his devoted service in the Lords, while the new ministry was prepared to reward its friends. Mohun had made an effort to put Lady Orby off, insisting that he had never asked for anything from the Junto, and so could hardly be disappointed by them. But as he was well aware, she was not a woman to be put off, and she made repeated overtures on the ministry's behalf. The pressure grew intense, and Charles's continued demurrers provoked his suitors to take a less amiable tack. Charlotte hinted broadly that the government could punish as well as reward, and that it was watching his lawsuit with Hamilton closely. Harley believed that there might be a flaw in Mohun's title to the Gawsworth estate, and implied that the courts might not, as they had in the past, rule in his favor. Mohun knew that in only a few weeks one of Hamilton's suits against him would be heard in Chancery—before a new, Tory, Lord Keeper. His estate was at great risk, and with it his political and social standing.

To Mohun's credit, the threats and bribes offered by the new government did not tempt him. He wanted to reject Harley's offer in the rudest possible terms. Cowper, who himself had rejected Harley and resigned rather than betray his colleagues, offered more moderate counsel. He suggested that Charles stand firm in his refusal, but that he present a conciliatory outward appearance. Mohun should tell Lady Orby that he intended to lead a quiet private life and was not interested in office. Furthermore, he would support the new ministry "while they acted in the interest of his countrey." In this way, Cowper suggested, Harley might not be provoked into acting on his threats about Gawsworth.[30] It is not clear whether Mohun took Cowper's advice. He never joined Harley's administration; from the first he vigorously opposed every move the new government made. For this Robert Harley, soon to be Earl of Oxford and Lord Treasurer, would exact his revenge.

The rivalry between Hamilton and Mohun reached an important turning point in 1710. Since he had taken possession of Gawsworth after the third earl died in December 1702, Mohun, allied with the Whigs who dominated government, had won every trial of strength. In case after case, the judges had decided against his enemies, especially Hamilton. Mohun's grip on the Gerard estate had grown ever tighter. He built a stylish new home next to the old manor house at Gawsworth, and renovated Bocconoc, providing himself accommodation fit for a man of his growing stature.[31]

14. Gawsworth's New Hall, built by Lord Mohun after 1702

Gawsworth's considerable income had financed an increasingly successful political career. The financial embarrassments of his youth had receded, and though he still took part in frequent escapades, Mohun was by 1710 an important man.

But in the waning days of Godolphin's ministry Mohun's position began to look less secure. The first, and most telling, blow was provided by Lord Chancellor Cowper himself. Cowper's impartiality on the bench was a byword and accounted for the respect with which he was viewed by both political parties. On May 20, 1710, he heard a case between Mohun and Hamilton on one of the many points of conflict between the two peers. The suit had been grinding its way through Chancery at the usual glacial pace, and revolved around Mohun's position as the heir of the second Earl of Macclesfield, former executor to the Duchess Elizabeth's mother.

Lady Gerard had become her daughter's guardian after Lord Gerard met his untimely end under the tables of the Rose Tavern. His only child, Elizabeth, a minor, then inherited a fortune of her own, independent of her mother's. It was this very considerable fortune that had made the hot-tempered young woman such an attractive match for Hamilton, whose own finances were in their usual state of crisis. It was Lady Gerard's responsibility, as guardian, to administer her daughter's fortune in her behalf, and to account for her actions when the girl came of age. The main issue at stake in this current round of legal warfare was Hamilton's 1698 promise to Lady Gerard that he would not insist upon an accounting if she allowed his marriage to Elizabeth.

Although the duke had made a solemn promise to his mother-in-law, he did not keep it. As soon as the couple married, he began to press Lady Gerard for an account. She indignantly refused, citing his bond, and the issue festered until her death. Lady Gerard's brother the second Earl of Macclesfield inherited his sister's feud when he became her executor, and through him, Mohun became involved. As part of his multifaceted campaign to harass Mohun in the courts, Hamilton filed suit reiterating his demand for an accounting, claiming that Mohun owed his wife thousands of pounds.

Mohun's lawyers skillfully resisted the duke's claims, but they could not prevent a review of Hamilton's twelve-year-old promise to Lady Gerard. Lord Chancellor Cowper heard the arguments and rendered a decision that was a blow to Mohun's cause. James's promise to his future mother-in-law was not binding. Lady Gerard, Cowper reasoned, was in a position of power over both the duke and her daughter, and demanding such an important concession on the duke's part amounted to little more than blackmail. Such promises opened the way for a guardian to abuse her trust, for they essentially relieved her from the responsibility to act in her ward's best interest. If her son-in-law had no right to know how Lady Gerard (or any other guardian) spent her daughter's money, what was to stop her from misusing it? Lord Mohun, who became Lady Gerard's executor when he inherited the Macclesfield estate, was obliged to render an account.

Mohun's case provided an important precedent and is still cited in English courts.[32] The decision boosted Cowper's reputation as a fair judge, but it left Mohun with a potentially disastrous problem. Providing the information the decree required would be no easy job; Lady Gerard had collected and spent the money in question years earlier, and of course she was now long dead. The duke's claims were certain to be exorbitant. He insisted that Mohun owed him some £40,000. Fighting him off would not be easy. Mohun's best hope for winning a reversal of Cowper's decision was an appeal to the House of Lords, where political influence played a much more important role. But by early summer 1710 everyone knew of the ministry's tottering state, and Mohun's hold over his property looked less strong.

Hamilton, on the other hand, welcomed the new turn of events. He was still under financial pressure, as tradesmen clamored for unpaid bills and threatened to deny him credit. His mother's purse remained closed, and repeated attempts to borrow from his more solvent brothers failed. Nevertheless, the victory in Chancery and Robert Harley's vigorous wooing for his political support promised to rescue James from his troubles.

Harley found negotiating with Hamilton a trial. After such a long spell in the wilderness the duke pitched his demands very high. He wanted to be Master of the Horse. He wanted to be Lord Lieutenant of Lancashire. He wanted the Order of the Garter. He wanted, more than anything else, to be made a duke in the new, British, peerage, like his archrival Queensberry. A British duchy would greatly increase his prestige. Moreover, it carried with it the important practical advantage of a permanent seat in the House of Lords. He would never again have to scramble to secure a place as one of Scotland's representative peers.

Pressing these demands tactlessly, Hamilton did little to endear himself with the new ministry. He irritated some by boasting of his imminent advancement. Lord Berkeley snidely suggested that the rumor of Hamilton's appointment as Master of the Horse came from the duke himself.[33] Lord Balmerino, a Scottish peer in search of a judgeship for his son, complained about Hamilton's "endless importunities." In September 1710 Godolphin told Lord Seafield that satisfying the duke had proved impossible for Harley: "The ministry were very desirous to satisfy him so as that he might give his assistance to their measures. But his pretensions have been hitherto so unreasonable that they cannot adjust it with him."[34]

Despite these vexations, Harley needed Hamilton's help. The Earl of Mar, a Scot who was one of Harley's confidants, was also angry at the duke, but admitted that some accommodation must be made: "I see more and more the necessity of gaining [Hamilton] and the danger of not haveing him. [Hamilton's] the oddest man in the world, and the most uncertain . . . He has no less than five or six demands besides this [his British title]." Two days later, Mar was complaining, "it is a pitty that such a man must be imployed of necessity."[35]

Harley's attempts to co-opt supporters of the previous ministry had borne little fruit and the duke's value continued to rise. Harley was still trying to win Mohun over as late as December 1710, and a minor victory for Mohun before the new Tory Lord Keeper in Chancery in late November might indicate Harley's continuing desire to deal with Whig peers. It might also indicate exasperation with Hamilton, who had made clear his annoyance at Harley's reluctance to satisfy his every request. But the ministry could not hold out long, for parliamentary elections were coming up, and an accommodation with the duke was crucial.[36]

The government's first step came in October, when Queen Anne named the duke Lord Lieutenant of Lancashire, the Queen's official representative in the shire and commander of the county militia; the lieutenancy also gave James considerable influence over local elections. He hurried up to Preston, the county town, and labored successfully on behalf of Tory candidates, to the vexation of local Whigs. One claimed that James used his power to intimidate voters and had several falsely accused of desertion from the army. More important was his influence in the Scottish elections, where his standing was still very high. Harley's Scottish son-in-law described James as "the Scotch man thats by farr the most capable to do service in the elections," and the duke vigorously supported a number of government candidates north of the border.[37]

The elections were disastrous for the Whigs. Tory candidates swept the boards and were returned to Westminster with a huge majority. Harley would have been happier with a less decisive victory, for all too many of the new members were Tories whose idea of good government was a Whig dangling from every lamppost. For a ministry dedicated to the proposition that moderates of either party should serve the Queen, a House of Commons filled with rabidly partisan Tories was hardly more welcome than a House full of Junto supporters. Dozens of backbenchers joined the October Club, an organization committed to a thorough purge of Whiggery. Anyone who, like Hamilton, was prepared to hew to Harley's moderate line became even more valuable.

The duke was on the ascendant from the beginning of 1711; his political value made his support crucial, and he could no longer be fobbed off with promises. As early as December 1710 Harley secured his appointment as a privy councillor, giving him an official place among the Queen's advisers. His importance made him no more popular at court, however. Jonathan Swift, Harley's friend and most brilliant propagandist, found himself thrown into the duke's company all too often. He commented sourly on Hamilton's "tedious politics" and found his exuberance a trial, as on the occasion when the duke impishly carried the train of Swift's clerical gown on their way to dinner.[38] More important, the Queen still regarded him frostily. James made trouble for himself. In July 1711, as soon as the death of the Duke of Queensberry, Hamilton's old rival, was announced at court, Hamilton rushed forward in an effort to take Queensberry's place as Anne's Scottish adviser, "but did it with so little concern for him that she was offended by it."[39]

Gradually Harley, now the Earl of Oxford, began to make headway with Anne. By November 1711 she was at last prepared to give in to James's desire for a British dukedom. He had been pressing the issue for over a year, and Oxford knew it was a favor that must eventually be granted. One of Hamilton's fondest desires was at last a reality, and typically he used the occasion to fire another shot in Lord Mohun's direction. When he chose his new title, he declared that he would now be the Duke of Hamilton and Brandon. The reference to the Gerard inheritance, now in the hands of the usurper Mohun, was obvious, for everyone knew that the extinct Earls of Macclesfield had also been the Lords Brandon.

The duke's cause continued to prosper. Mohun had already suffered a major defeat in May 1710, and the decisive political shift at Westminster boded ill. That Hamilton, for all his unpopularity, seemed to be rising politically must also have been ominous for Mohun, who, since the May 1710 decision, had done his best to stave off the duke with delaying tactics. As long as Parliament was in session, Mohun claimed immunity from prosecution, which suspended all of Hamilton's actions against him. But the duke, flush with his recent successes, was relentless, and in late 1711 he challenged Mohun's right to immunity before the Lords.

The winter session of Parliament proved momentous for both peers. Mohun had not yet been pressed as hard as he was now: the possibility that he would lose his estate began to seem real. The government was hostile, and Hamilton, newly equipped with royal favor and a British dukedom, had taken the offensive. Mohun was fighting a rear-guard action. But fate intervened to offer him—his back almost to the wall—a respite.

The issue was Hamilton's new ducal patent.* Oxford's enemies saw it as a wedge they could use to split the government's very

* The Queen granted titles by issuing what were called letters patent, which rehearsed the new titles, and laid out any special conditions associated with them (for example, allowing a title to pass through the female line, as in the case of Duchess Anne).

slim majority in the Lords. Although the Tories had a decisive edge in the Lower House, in the Upper the parties were much more finely balanced. Oxford's majority largely depended upon the votes of the Scottish peers, many of whom were poor and dependent upon the government. Although Scotland and England were now officially one, bad feeling remained between the two nations. Even reliable English Tory peers often resented their northern brethren. So when Hamilton took his seat as a new British peer, the Whigs struck. They argued that no Scottish lord should be allowed a seat in the Lords based upon a British title. The attack was shrewd. It played upon the prejudice of English peers against Scots. Whigs argued that if Hamilton were allowed to sit as Duke of Brandon, it invited unscrupulous ministers to overwhelm the Lords with hordes of venal Scots. The argument was logically weak; it denied the Queen one of her fundamental prerogatives, that of ennobling whomever she thought fit. It also conveniently ignored the fact that the recently deceased Queensberry had sat and voted as Duke of Dover without protest. In this case, however, logic retired before prejudice. Anti-Scots feeling was powerful among the lords and Hamilton was unpopular. Oxford and other ministers fought desperately to prevent it, but enough Tories defected to ensure that the House denied Hamilton the right to sit as Duke of Brandon. He could continue as a representative peer, but that was all.

The Hamilton peerage case had great political importance, for it seriously damaged Anglo-Scottish relations. The Scots reacted violently: here was yet another example of England's trampling upon their rights. Many tepid Unionists turned against the idea of a united Great Britain altogether, and some were no doubt propelled into the Jacobite camp. "If he [the duke] lose it the Union must break . . . for one would think that this will force Scotland to espouse the Pretender's right."[40] The duke was frantic. His unrelenting complaints finally drove the Lord Treasurer to hide behind the flimsy excuse of ill health to deny Hamilton admittance to his

London home. For Oxford it was potentially a political disaster, because all of the Scottish peers, whose votes were crucial to the government's survival, withdrew from the House in a fury. Whence would the margin of victory come without the Scots?[41]

For Lord Mohun, the Whig victory was a godsend. In February 1712, while the Scots sulked in their tents, his case against Hamilton came before the House.[42] The duke had been pressing Mohun for the accounting ordered by Lord Chancellor Cowper over eighteen months before, but Mohun had avoided compliance through a combination of delay and the manipulation of his parliamentary privilege. Hamilton's usual disastrous financial situation added to his difficulties. When one of his brothers refused yet another request for a loan to pay his legal bills, the duke wrote in anguish, "you knew that I had soe considerable a law sieut which is in soe probably [a] way of suces to have it starve by want of monie now in terme tyme when it comes to be argued is the cruelest thing for me that the severest of my enimies could have brought me under."[43] Somehow, though, he scraped the money together, and eventually James's lawyers presented their client's petition. On January 29, 1712, they argued that Mohun was not entitled to claim parliamentary privilege. The duke claimed that Mohun had effectively waived his right to immunity when his attorneys examined witnesses in the lawsuit *after* the winter session of Parliament began. Hamilton argued that Mohun had thereby conceded that the case could proceed. On February 2, after the clerk droned through the duke's case, Mohun made his reply. Considering the expensive talents he employed to support his cause, his response seems feeble. He argued that the trouble began when Hamilton broke his promise to his mother-in-law, that the duke was himself claiming privilege in another one of the multiple suits at issue between them, and besides, as merely "an Executor of an Executor of an Administratrix" he was hardly familiar with the case at all. This disingenuous reply did nothing to answer Hamilton's charge of waived privilege, the central issue

over which the battle in the Lords was to be fought. After a pre-
liminary skirmish on February 7, both sides appeared the next
day, ready to make their case.

Beneath the faded but still-impressive tapestries depicting the
defeat of the Armada, the lords sat in their frosty chamber and listened to the arguments on both sides. Ordinarily, the legal work of
the House interested few members. Some of the more dedicated
peers complained that their fellows were "scandalously remiss"
when the lawyers began their work, chattering among themselves
and ignoring the legalisms trotted out for their benefit. Most peers
were bored by the lawsuits over estates and debts, and they stayed
away from such hearings. In 1703 William Nicolson, the Bishop of
Carlisle, sat through a case "about some houses in Dublin" with
barely a dozen of his colleagues.[44] In the usual course of events,
cases were often decided by a tiny minority of interested lords.
But the case of Mohun versus Hamilton was not ordinary.

Edward Hyde, Earl of Clarendon, was in the chair on February
8 and presided over the hearing of the committee of privileges.
Clarendon, who as governor of New York had cemented his fame
by commissioning a portrait of himself dressed in a woman's gown,
was nevertheless one of a small group of reliable members upon
whom such duties frequently devolved, and he was probably not a
bad choice. The lawyers who practiced before the House were
usually the most successful and talented practitioners at the bar,
and consequently often legal prima donnas; an eccentric character
like Clarendon could at the very least upstage them. Appearing for
the duke was Mr. Serjeant Pratt, while in Mohun's corner was Sir
Joseph Jekyll. Sir Joseph was one of the most successful barristers
of his generation, and was eagerly sought after both for his skills,
which were formidable, and for his political connections, which
were extensive. His fees reflected his standing, and Mohun would
have had to pay him a great deal for his services.

The House suspended its usual nonchalance in anticipation of
the public clash of its most bitter rivals. The Mohun-Hamilton

feud was a matter of common knowledge and had broken out on the floor of the House at various times since the duke had joined as a representative peer. Many members had been present when Mohun had humiliated Hamilton in debate over the Sacheverell affair, but this was the first time that their famous legal battles had come before the House. Consequently, the benches were unusually full for the hearing. Instead of the typical ten or twenty lords listening inattentively to the lawyers, almost sixty were present. One of them was Baron Mohun—but Hamilton, still smarting from the rejection of his patent, refused to appear.

The lords heard a rehearsal of some of the arguments in the duke's petition and Mohun's answer. Charles's lawyers had now come up with some more plausible reasons for maintaining their client's privilege. They implied that Mohun had been forced to examine witnesses—the act that Hamilton had claimed was a waiver of privilege—as a result of orders from the Court of Chancery. The clerk of the House, taking notes as Sir Joseph spoke, wrote: "Question whether our proceedings were voluntary or compulsory by the order in Chancery." Pratt seized upon this line of argument; it was irrelevant whether the examinations were voluntary or not. The issue was that by examining witnesses, which Mohun admitted that he had done, he had effectively waived his privilege. Further replies worried this issue. Eventually the lawyers concluded their presentations and left the chamber while the peers debated. Mohun's case, though argued by one of England's most talented lawyers, looked shaky. It was further weakened during the debate when the duke sent a message to the House announcing that he would waive his own privilege in his countersuit against Mohun. Hamilton was offering an apparently reasonable compromise, and Mohun was on the defensive. He took the floor to speak in his own behalf, insisting that he was entitled to privilege: "I hope I will not be forced to waive my privilege," he said. After still more debate, the question was put: whether "the Lord Mohun in this case as it now appears before the committee has privilege?"

The Earl of Bridgewater, a Whig, stepped forward to count the "contents"—that is, those voting for Mohun—and the Earl of Abingdon, a Tory, rose to count the "not contents"—the duke's supporters. Fifty-two lords, an extremely large number in such a case, voted. The result was a narrow victory for Mohun: twenty-nine contents and twenty-three not contents. But Hamilton's side had not lost yet. When Clarendon reported the committee's decision to the full House, another vote would accept or reject the report. In the full House the outcome might be different.[45]

Mohun took a dangerous gamble. If he lost the vote in the full House, Hamilton could open a new flank in his campaign, where Charles was particularly vulnerable. Accounting for the Duchess Elizabeth's estate after such a stretch of years would be immensely difficult, and there would be endless complications. In the changed political climate, he could hardly expect a more sympathetic hearing in the Lords in the foreseeable future. Tory dominance there seemed inevitable, and Hamilton's star continued to rise, despite the denial of his patent. Rumors at court said that he would be given an important office to compensate for his disappointment.[46] Now was the time for Mohun to secure a victory, even though it must have been obvious that the triumph might only be temporary.

The House divided and suspense rose. When the count was done, the numbers were even: twenty-eight for each side. Had Mohun not violated the custom of the House and voted in his own case, he would have lost outright. The duke was not present for the division, but other members noted Mohun's exercise of desperation ethics. With the vote tied, the House next turned to proxies. Even when not present a member could leave his proxy with one of his colleagues, and when they were tallied Mohun had scraped through: forty votes to thirty-six.[47]

It was a bitter blow for James. Had he and his Scottish colleagues not been boycotting the House over his British dukedom, he would have won his case handily. His argument was stronger on its merits; Mohun was for once on very parlous legal ground. But the Lords could not act dispassionately when party politics intruded into their proceedings.[48] When the matter at hand involved routine matters of law disputed between obscure litigants, cases could be treated fairly. In this instance, however, impartiality was impossible. Members were interested for political reasons and they took time to vote, if not to listen to the lawyers' arguments.

Mohun's success was temporary good fortune. The Earl of Mar wrote a friend a few days after the vote, "The Duke Hamilton was unluckie in it for by our absence he lost a point betwixt him and Lord Mohoun."[49] The Scottish boycott could not last forever. Hamilton's political strength at court was certain to increase, and Lord Treasurer Oxford would not rest until he had a reliable majority in the Upper House. Should his struggle with the duke be renewed in the Lords, Mohun could not expect a repetition of his good fortune. The outlook remained gloomy as the parliamentary session advanced, especially after Queen Anne created a dozen new peers, all Harley loyalists.

Charles had built a promising career after his misspent youth, thanks in no small measure to the Gerard fortune. The days when Queen Mary hoped he would hang for his misdeeds were over. He was now an important politician, well enough thought of in Hanover to be among the prospective regents after Anne's death. Gerard money had rebuilt his ancestral home in Cornwall, paid for the construction of the New Hall at Gawsworth, financed a fashionably debauched life in London, and even funded a new school for the children of Gawsworth, proof that, wicked though their lord might be, he was not without a conscience.[50] All of this was now in peril.

Political tensions, rising rapidly since Dr. Sacheverell's trial, threatened to degenerate into hysteria. Mohun himself had played a part in the creation of these tensions. He and his fellow Kit-cat Club members had planned a spectacular Pope-burning for Queen Elizabeth's accession night, November 17, 1711. At a rumored cost of one thousand pounds, the demonstrators provided a parade of effigies—the Pope, the Pretender, Satan, and a numerous crew of his confreres (cardinals, monks, and the like) to be pitched upon a roaring Protestant bonfire. Harley's government, wanting no Whig-inspired demonstrations in the streets of the capital, seized the club's toys and banned its celebration. George Maccartney, living on the charity of friends like Mohun since his dismissal, amused himself by organizing all-Whig performances at the opera, rudely excluding any Tory at the door. Lady Mohun, writing to her patron and erstwhile friend the Duchess of Marlborough, summed up the view common among many Whigs struggling to cope with their loss of power: "I can allow nothing to love you as I doe but he [Charles] disputes that point with me continually. I may own he hates your enimies as heartily and that is some merit for me for I doe protest I wish 'em all utterly destroyed in this world, for the next let the monsters take their chance."[51] As Marlborough's Whig crony William Cadogan wrote to his mentor in January, "Everything is in the utmost confusion, and every honest man looks on the common cause as irrevocably lost."[52] It was in these same troubled months that the Duchess Elizabeth had her public brawl at the theater. Everyone was on edge, the more so due to the mysterious activities of the "Mohawks."

"Here is nothing talked about but men that goes in partys about the streets and cuts peaple with swords or knives, and they call themselves by som hard name that I can nethere speak nor spell," Lady Strafford wrote to her husband. Thomas Burnet, a gentleman who knew riotous behavior, described them: "inspired by potent Bacchus," the Mohawks "run into the streets at midnight, beat watchmen, slit noses, and cut women's arms, stop chairs and coaches," and offer violence to ladies "even of quality." They were alleged to have crammed an old woman into a barrel and rolled her down Ludgate Hill in London; Lady Strafford claimed that they had assaulted a well-known playwright as he left the theater. For weeks London cowered behind locked doors in fear of these young men. Bishop Nicolson took shelter with his brother-in-law, Lady Strafford kept to her St. James's Square home, and even Swift refused to venture out after dark for fear of Mohawks. On March 18 the Queen issued a proclamation against them, in spite of the fact that no one, including the Queen, knew who or what they were.

In fact, "Mohawks" were to a large extent the product of the overstressed imaginations of Londoners, for whom political tensions were becoming unbearable. Under the circumstances there may well have been more violence in the streets than usual, and perhaps a few acts were inspired by the excited talk of Mohawks in taverns and theaters. But it seems doubtful that any organized movement existed. Certainly the authorities, who did their best to round up some of these mysterious creatures, arrested very few. Eventually Swift, no doubt tired of being kept from his late nights at the tables of great men like Lord Oxford, decided that there was no such thing as a Mohawk—in London, at any rate: it is "all a lie, and I begin to think there is no truth, or very little in the whole story." The phenomenon reflected the jittery state of mind of many in the upper ranks of society in 1712, as they grew increasingly fearful of political upheaval.[53]

The ministry's conduct of the war with France worsened matters. In pursuit of a quick peace, the government issued instructions ordering Marlborough's Tory replacement, James, second Duke of Ormonde, to cease campaigning in Europe. Whig fears of an Oxfordian plot to deliver England into the hands of the Pretender increased. Oxford desired peace, but the continued presence of the Pretender on French soil left the Lord Treasurer open to charges that he planned a Stuart restoration. His dislike of Britain's unreliable Dutch allies and his desire to leave them to their own devices enraged Whigs who had pledged that the Dutch Republic could rely on British assistance against French tyranny. His task was further complicated by the enmity of the mercurial Lord Bolingbroke, who had by 1712 established himself as Oxford's principal rival in the government. As Secretary of State,

Bolingbroke should have had a key role in negotiating a peace, but Oxford's distrust of him led to the Secretary's being kept in the dark. The atmosphere of intrigue and mystery surrounding the peace negotiations, carried on against a background of shrill Whig denunciations of the whole process, and a rising hysteria about the future, made Oxford's life a misery, one which he increasingly alleviated by turning to the bottle.

The fears of committed Whigs and other supporters of the Hanoverian succession grew during the summer of 1712. On May 28, Mohun, joined by twenty-six mostly Whig peers, entered his protest in the journals of the Lords when their motion to address the Queen for a resumption of the war failed. Oxford, however, was resolute. He intended to make peace with France, come what may, and though he was no less determined to secure an honorable peace than the staunchest Whigs, many feared something far more sinister. For Lord Mohun, whose legal battles with Hamilton resumed after the parliamentary session ended, life became more difficult. Although he continued to hold his own in the struggle, his prospects were gloomy. Not only was the Revolutionary settlement in which he believed under siege, but his own fortune trembled on the brink of ruin. His rival was in the ascendant and his own cause in decline.

The Queen gradually warmed to Hamilton. When Lord Rivers, the old reprobate and former lover of the Countess of Macclesfield, died, Oxford urged Anne to grant Hamilton one of his offices. "Duke Hamilton must certainly have one," she wrote rather peevishly to her Lord Treasurer, but "if it be General of the Ordnance I fear he may claim being of the Cabinet, and if he should I doubt one cant well refuse him because formerly those in that post have been of it." Obviously Queen Anne thought that Hamilton's "tedious politics," as Swift called them, held little attraction. Even so, soon he was the new Master of the Ordnance. If the Queen was reluctant to appoint the duke, he apparently failed to notice it in his interview with her. Peter Wentworth reported to his brother: "I saw him come from the Queen, and seem'd to have a great deal of sattisfaction in his face, whisper'd [to] lord T[reasurer] who squeas'd him by the hand."[54]

Hamilton had at last reached the inner circle of the Queen's advisers. The news was disastrous for Mohun. In late summer, Whigs were further shocked by Hamilton's appointment as ambassador extraordinary to France. His mission was to clear up some of the final details of the peace, but most people thought Oxford's choice dangerous. That the duke had been in touch with the Jacobite court at Saint-Germain for years was an open secret. Although he had given the Pretender little comfort since his brush with the Tower in 1708, few people—even among Oxford's friends—doubted that the duke had more than a passing acquaintance with Jacobite conspiracy. The appointment "was thought strange by wise men and those that were indifferent to either party . . . I have met several who have been amazed at it, and some have drawn conclusions from It . . . that the Pretender was at the bottom of it . . . A certain duke told me he was hard pressed to defend the M[inistry] in this point there is not a man more obnoxious in the whole kingdome, for the suspition of a favourite of the Pretender."[55]

Hamilton was, of course, overjoyed at his newfound prominence. His reaction to his good fortune was hardly discreet. He boasted to Lady Strafford that the Queen had granted him the largest gift of plate ever awarded to an ambassador—seven thousand ounces. The genteel surroundings of St. James's Square were enlivened when his appointment to the Ordnance Office came through; Lady Strafford reported that she had been "mightly entertain'd with drumbs and trumpets at Duke Hambleton's and that his servants say'd there lord was made master of the Ordnance." A month later the windows of the Hamilton mansion blazed with lights as he gave a party in Oxford's honor.[56] Feasting the Lord Treasurer was only a prelude to more honors. In September came the announcement that the duke had been

awarded the Order of the Garter, England's highest order of
knighthood. And Hamilton would be allowed the unprecedented
privilege of retaining his place in the Order of the Thistle, Scotland's equivalent to the Garter.[57]

The duke's progress continued through the autumn of 1712.
Though the Queen impatiently asked when he intended to leave
for France, James reveled in his new honors and delayed his
departure. At last he had returned to the charmed circle he had
once inhabited. Indeed, his position under Queen Anne sur-
passed the favor he enjoyed under James II. Duchess Anne would
have to be impressed by her son's successes now, even if they
brought some expense. The embassy would be very costly—he
might have put off his departure to give himself time to marshal
the necessary resources. But perhaps there would be a new infusion of funds—his legal battle with Mohun was finally turning in
his favor. The embassy could wait a little longer. In the meantime, the new Knight of the Garter received the homage of his
friends and dependents. Late in October he dined with the Lord
Mayor of London, met frequently with the ministers, and
planned his strategy for the establishment of his claim to the
French duchy of Chatelherault.[58]

While Hamilton grew in stature, his case against Lord Mohun
was in the hands of a Chancery master named John Orlebar,
who was to report the details of Mohun's account of the Duchess
Elizabeth's estate to the Lord Keeper. Orlebar, like his fellow
Chancery practitioners, earned a substantial living in the service
of the litigious. He had parlayed his success into a fashionable
house in Red Lion Square, within easy walking distance of his
chambers in a court just off Chancery Lane, the heart of London's
legal world. Here Orlebar, and many others, spun the intricate
webs of suit and countersuit that entangled so many of England's
propertied classes. As a Chancery master, he was an officer of the
court, but this was no bar to personal advancement. A master's
place was lucrative, for over the years masters had become expert

15. Hamilton after he became a Knight of the Garter
and Master of the Ordnance, 1712

in squeezing the last farthing out of their clients.[59] Yet Orlebar had no need for sharp practices in the Mohun-Hamilton case. The participants were so determined to triumph that the suit promised perpetual sustenance for the house in Red Lion Square. Orlebar must have been delighted when he, and not one of his fellow masters, was chosen. If anyone had reason for complaint it would have been the master's long-suffering clerk, whose job it would be to ride herd on two of the most dedicated litigants in the kingdom.

Orlebar's association with the case had begun in the autumn of 1711, when, after a round of Mohun's evasions, he received each party's claim. The duke's lawyers submitted a claim designed both to overwhelm Mohun by its staggering size and to seize the moral high ground. Hamilton was merely acting to right wrongs done to his duchess, an innocent child who had been badly abused as a minor by Lady Gerard, her mother. Lady Gerard had shirked her duty to protect her daughter's inheritance, and had instead betrayed Elizabeth, forcing her to live a Cinderella-like existence. Her mother denied her daughter servants, books, jewelry, and even a proper education. Lady Gerard's stinginess ensured that neither the dancing master nor the music teacher she employed for Elizabeth stayed long enough to be of any service. When she rode in the countryside, her mother refused to provide her with a side-saddle, forcing the young woman to ride astride, a method both uncomfortable and unladylike. To add to her humiliations, Elizabeth's courtship was also marred by her mother's parsimony. "When the duke came a wooing," as the lawyers said, his intended was so badly clothed that she was forced to wear her servant's "cote and ruffles." All of these facts demonstrated the duke's honorable motives in suing Mohun, Lady Gerard's executor-by-inheritance. But the real issue was the money he claimed from Mohun: here the lawyers translated sentiment into numbers: pounds, shillings, and pence. Hamilton insisted that he was due £43,979 12s. 7d. This massive sum included profits from the Gerard estates during Elizabeth's minority, before her marriage, as well as her parents' personal property. Nothing was overlooked in the list of debts: all Lord Gerard's horses were listed and valued, from Squirrell, allegedly worth £50, down to Slouch, valued at £4, and Skewball, £3. Never mind that the horses, not to mention Lord Gerard, had been dead for decades. The property legally belonged to the duchess, and it was Mohun's responsibility to turn it over, thanks to the Chancery decree of May 1710.

Mohun had a different view. His own liability for Lady Gerard's actions seemed tenuous at best, whatever his friend Cowper said. She had been dead for over ten years, and her husband, whose property he was now required to account for, had breathed his last drunken breath in the Rose nearly thirty years before. And yet, whatever Mohun's personal opinion, the order in Chancery could not be wished away. He would have to respond. After such a stretch of years, an adequate reply would be very difficult. Documents had been lost or destroyed, witnesses had died or been enfeebled by age. Moreover, Hamilton's star at court was on the rise, while Mohun's own party was in eclipse. The years of easy legal and political victories were over.

Mohun's strategy remained delay and obfuscation. His answer to the duke's claim before Orlebar was a long, wordy denial of every point. In eighty-eight pages he contradicted all that Hamilton had asserted. Although he was free with rhetoric, he was chary with fact. He claimed that Hamilton far overestimated the size of Lord Gerard's estate: all his money went to pay debts. There were no valuable paintings, no profitable leases, nothing that should have gone to Elizabeth but did not. The clerk no doubt groaned under the burden of recopying these documents, but Mohun could at least congratulate himself that the time it took to prepare his case had brought him safely home to the shelter of the new parliamentary session that began in late 1711.[60]

Mohun's luck in staving off Hamilton's attack in this session, thanks to the controversy over the ducal patent, could not continue, and no sooner had Parliament adjourned in 1712 than Chancery's machinery started again. Beyond the legal realm,

Hamilton's place in the government's favor grew more firm. At the same time, Orlebar, who had now had months to ruminate over the submissions of both sides, ordered the principals to appear at his chambers at four o'clock on June 23, 1712. At that meeting the principals would begin the work of thrashing out their different claims. Hamilton, who had been waiting impatiently for an opportunity to set his lawyers on Mohun when his privilege lapsed, wasted no time. When the adjournment was imminent, his lawyer petitioned the Lords in an effort to force Mohun to cooperate with the master. Mohun now changed tack; on June 24 he asked for time to examine witnesses to prove the assertions in the answer he had submitted the previous year.[61] There would now be more delay, a respite, Mohun hoped. With political tensions on the rise, and his own case inching toward what was most likely a disastrous conclusion, Mohun's actions began to take on a desperate tone.

The passage of the summer of 1712 had done nothing to calm Mohun's fears of catastrophe, and he found himself more and more often reflecting upon the ruin that impended for both the nation and his own fortunes. Everywhere around him his political friends and allies were under assault; despairing Whigs predicted the end of English liberty and the return of a persecuting Stuart tyranny. Mohun was more than willing to believe such fears, and he was encouraged in them by his bosom friend George Maccartney.

FIVE

The Duel

I N the last weeks of 1712 the Duke of Marlborough spent most of his mornings at home. His London residence stood at the end of Pall Mall, almost next door to St. James's Palace. Surrounded by stunted young trees and gardens planted only months before at vast public expense, Marlborough House's prime location bore mute testimony to the unrivaled position the duke had once held in the Queen's councils. But his position had changed dramatically over the previous two years. His former patron and neighbor, Queen Anne, had long since shifted her lodgings from St. James's to Kensington Palace, and her affections from the duke to others. Now, when he was not in the country, Marlborough lived for the most part alone, complaining of the damp and the ingratitude of his countrymen. The duchess preferred to avoid the London house, a stylish pile designed by Sir Christopher Wren as a gift from the nation to its most famous general. It was largely her fault that Marlborough had lost his eminence. Sarah, once Anne's intimate friend, had permanently alienated her sovereign by merciless pro-Whig hectoring, and had in the process undermined her husband's political position. Dismissed from his command in 1711, the great duke had plenty of time to ponder the fickle nature of courts and the possible consequences of political failure.[1]

Robert Harley's rise to power was a disaster for Marlborough. The new government's commitment to peace challenged the duke's lifelong conviction that Louis XIV's France must be irrevocably defeated before Europe's security could be assured. No less

16. John Churchill, first Duke of Marlborough

important was the threat to his livelihood that peace represented. Marlborough "possessed the Graces in the highest degree," as Lord Chesterfield later said, but beneath the elegant polish lurked a ruthless and grasping nature. The penniless son of a country gentleman, the duke had raised himself to international fame through a single-minded pursuit of his own interests. He—like Hamilton—was once a protégé of James II, and his desertion of his master in 1688 was one of the most bitter blows the King received in that fatal year. Since James's exile, Marlborough's success as a general—and his wife's intimacy with Queen Anne—had carried him to heights no one could have expected. Even as he attempted to ensure his future through a long-standing correspondence with Saint-Germain, Marlborough augmented his fame and power through his undoubted talents on the battlefield. The Battle of Blenheim, fought in 1704, secured his reputation as a military genius, as well as a series of more tangible rewards. The Queen's ally the Holy Roman Emperor Joseph I made him a prince of the Empire, and the government granted its hero a lavish pension, Marlborough House, and, closest to the duke's heart, Blenheim Palace in Oxfordshire. Blenheim was to be the duke's monument: a massive structure built at the cost of tens of thousands of pounds, to the designs of the great architect Sir John Vanbrugh.

Marlborough reveled in his hard-won fortune, and even his greatest admirers were forced to admit that their idol sometimes seemed gripped by a passion for money: "his private character was blemished by sordid avarice, the most unamiable of all vices."[2] By 1712, already past sixty, he was more than ever determined to hold fast to what fate and his own enterprise had brought him.[3] The duke's talents were well suited to the defense of his interests. Although Chesterfield described him as "eminently illiterate; [he] wrote bad English, and spelled it still worse," he excelled as a judge and manipulator of men.[4] Over the years he had cultivated a circle of soldiers and politicians whose abilities were sometimes matched only by their vices. Both Mohun and his companion George Maccartney had risen thanks to Marlborough's patronage;

17. Marlborough House, London

the general was fond of the Irishman and attempted to revive Mac-cartney's career after he was accused of rape in 1709.[5] With the help of such men, Marlborough had faced the worst Louis XIV had to offer and been consistently victorious. Now, however, the duke was fighting a very different sort of campaign against an enemy at least as skilled as the Sun King's marshals: Robert Harley, Earl of Oxford.

Political parties had rarely disturbed Marlborough's thoughts; while much of his life he was identified as a moderate Tory, he had never scrupled at acting with Whigs. Yet Harley's pursuit of peace with France, opposed by Whigs of nearly every stripe, pushed Marlborough into opposition. His views increased in vehemence as the conviction grew that the Tory regime contemplated a settlement with the exiled Stuarts. The duke's dalliance with the Pretender had probably never been serious. By 1712 Marlborough counted himself a strong supporter of the Hanoverian succession. Queen Anne, now Sarah's implacable enemy, supported Harley's policy with increasing determination. Both Marlborough and his wife had now lost their lucrative posts under the Crown, but the Stuart restoration they feared would have brought even more drastic consequences: Blenheim might become a tomb instead of the palace of a thriving aristocratic line. Marlborough could hardly have expected much sympathy from Saint-Germain. Everything the duke had built since his arrival at court over forty years before seemed threatened.

The ministry's ire against the duke grew. A man of his prominence and fame was dangerous, and Oxford knew that the general must be brought to heel. Marlborough marshaled opposition in the House of Lords against the ministry's peace policy, denouncing it as cowardly and dishonorable. His speeches circulated throughout the realm, and even though the Tory majority in Parliament rendered his activities there futile, his voice was heard and made the government's task more difficult. Reducing Marlborough's influence became an important goal of Oxford's policy. The duke was the subject of a barrage of critical comment from hired propagandists and friends of the administration, all the more effective because it often contained a grain of truth. Most devastating of all to the duke's reputation was the poisonously brilliant prose of Oxford's intimate friend Jonathan Swift. Swift's satirical "Bill of British Ingratitude" prodded Marlborough at his most sensitive point: his purse. Great Roman conquerors of old, Swift argued, counted themselves blessed when a grateful Republic honored them with a triumphal parade and a laurel wreath ("item, two pence"). Marlborough, famous general though he was, complained about the ingratitude of his people despite the £50,000 palace rising on the Oxfordshire landscape, the house in Pall Mall, the profits of his generalship, and a perpetual annual pension granted from Post Office revenues, for a total of £540,000.[6] Such criticism, so devastating to the honor of a great man in a culture where honor was a vital component of greatness, pursued the duke even to the floor of the House of Lords.

Earl Poulett, a Tory who frequently demonstrated his devotion to Oxford's policy by his rather confused speeches to the Lords, scathingly attributed Marlborough's opposition to his greed. In May 1712, as the House wrangled over the current campaign, Poulett claimed that the general courted battle in order to assure himself profits from the sale of the commissions of officers who had been "knocked on the head" by the enemy. This was too much. Before the day was out, the duke's friend Mohun appeared at Poulett's house with an invitation to the earl to "take the air in the country." Mohun would serve as second in a fight that would pit the sixty-two-year-old duke against a much younger man. Fortunately—probably for Poulett, for Marlborough's age was balanced by his extensive dueling experience—Lady Poulett overheard Mohun's challenge. She rushed a frantic letter to the Privy Council, begging its intervention. The duel was never fought.[7]

Marlborough faced a greater threat than the ill-considered words of a not very talented Tory peer: an official parliamentary investigation of his financial practices as Captain General. As commander in chief of the Queen's forces in Flanders, Marlborough had administered millions. His accounts, like those of most officers of his day, were more works of art than of science. The possibility of confusion and outright peculation was manifest in such a loosely regulated system, where standards of fiscal propriety were murky. If Marlborough profited by the manipulation of government funds, as he very likely did, so did many of his fellows. Yet his actions left him vulnerable to a charge of theft, and in a House of Commons dominated by Tories who believed the duke an apostate, there could be little doubt that, in the event of an investigation, disgrace, imprisonment, and the loss of his family's fortune would be his fate. Threats from the ministry began early in 1712, and the danger grew greater as the year progressed and the government's peace plan moved forward.[8]

Marlborough's troubles were nearing their height when in late summer Queen Anne named Hamilton her ambassador extraordinary to France. The knowledge that the Duke of Hamilton would bear the government's messages to Louis XIV provoked horror among Whigs and puzzled many Tories. Whatever Anne's motives, most observers believed that a secret agenda lay behind the move. Such suspicions of Hamilton's inclinations were well founded. Word of the duke's appointment caused great satisfaction both at Saint-Germain and at Versailles. Mary of Modena, James II's widow, believed that Anne's choice of ambassador was a good sign, and the Duke of Saint-Simon, Louis XIV's gossip-general, described Hamilton as "very highly esteemed" at the Sun King's court. Jacobite expectations were high, and the duke appeared ready to encourage them. George Lockhart, perhaps the most devoted Jacobite in Britain, later recounted his conversations with the duke about his plans: "he had got all his instructions concerning the negotiation of peace, and he understood there were some things besides of the greatest importance to be committed to his management; and tho' the Lord Oxford had not yet spoke fully out, nevertheless by His Lordship's innuendo's and some private conversation with the Queen, he cou'd guess at the import and design of them." Hamilton urged Lockhart to return to Scotland with a message of hope for his fellow Jacobites, and he counseled patience: "he desir'd all the Kings [i.e., the Pretender's] friends wou'd take care to do nothing to expose themselves, and by living quietly expect such an issue as it shou'd please God to give to what was now in agitation, and of which, he hop'd very soon, to give a good account."[9]

Given Hamilton's past record of vacillation in the Stuart cause, the hopes and fears of Jacobites and Hanoverians over his plans might have been exaggerated. In the increasingly hysterical political atmosphere of the time, however, an extreme reaction on both sides is hardly surprising. A second Stuart restoration remained possible, and the consequences would be far-reaching. Anyone who played a successful role in returning the self-styled James III to the land of his birth could expect lavish reward. The recent favors granted by Oxford and Queen Anne would pale in comparison to what would follow if Hamilton could claim to be the Pretender's patron. A new restoration offered Hamilton the hope that years of humiliation and bitter disappointment, political and financial, would be succeeded by a golden age of power and profit. Moreover, any lingering guilt about his failures in James II's cause would be wiped away: Hamilton now had an opportunity to triumph over his past, his creditors, and his enemies.

On the other side, a Jacobite victory would be catastrophic for those who had staked all upon the fortunes of Whiggery and a Hanoverian succession. The most prominent of these were the Marlboroughs, but they were joined by a host of others, including Lord Mohun and General Maccartney. Bitter comments about Hamilton's abilities and intentions were made in correspondence, clubs, and coffeehouses from Edinburgh to London: "he [Hamilton] sees himself despised and no wonder . . . It is easie to do mischiefe but hard if not impossible for some people to do good or be of use, and he has done more hurt to his country and countrymen then ever it will be in his power to do them good, and all this for no good but quite otherwayes to himself."[10] The duke's exuberant boasting about his new-won favor did nothing to reconcile his enemies to the embassy: "he says hes to have the greatest allowance any won with that carracter ever had"; he rattled his neighbors' windows in sedate St. James's Square with blaring trumpets and banging drums at each new triumph, and annoyed Dean Swift with his monologues at Windsor Castle.[11]

Fear of Hamilton's intentions rose as he continued to put off his departure: he announced he was ready to embark at the start of September 1712, but the house in St. James's Square remained occupied. James continued to receive visits from prominent Tories and well-known Jacobites such as Lockhart. In reality, the delay may have had as much to do with the duke's finances as with anything else. Organizing an embassy was expensive. Initial expenses were usually met from the ambassador's own pocket and only partially reimbursed by the government later. James must have been waiting anxiously for the arrival of rent payments from Lancashire, and making arrangements to borrow still more money to finance his trip. One economy he imposed upon himself—probably without much regret—was to travel as a bachelor. The duchess acceded unhappily to her husband's plan, according to Peter Wentworth: "I hear the French Ambasidors lady that is coming is A great beauty. Duke Hamilton does not carry his beauty with him much to her mortification."[12] James had another reason to stay. His struggle with Mohun was turning his way at last, and experience with the law had taught him that his presence could be vital. Crucial hearings before the Chancery master were scheduled for the autumn. The Queen complained about the duke's delays in November. On the thirteenth she wrote Oxford, "Should not Duke Hamilton be hasten again [*sic*], when I last saw him he talked as if he wanted several things for his journey; if that be so care should be taken that he has no just pretence for staying."[13]

Suspicion of Hamilton's plans grew, as did Whig fears, for Oxford's campaign to disgrace his enemies rolled forward unchecked by protests from his victims. The barrage of criticism from the press convinced Marlborough and other Whigs that their enemies were determined to destroy them. Even before he returned to England after his dismissal in 1711 the duke had written Sarah, "the dayly Vexations I meet with, dose not only break my sperit, but also my Constitution."[14] More threatening than the calumnies of the press was the steady progress of complaints about the duke's alleged peculation: by the autumn of 1712 Marlborough faced demands for the repayment of nearly £300,000.[15] Once an international hero, the duke nervously watched his reputation dwindle and his fortune teeter on the verge of seizure by a vindictive government. By late October he saw only one escape: exile. Oxford made clear to Marlborough that the charges against him would lie in abeyance if he left the country. The duke and duchess made plans for leaving, collecting £50,000 to finance their stay on the Continent.[16] Marlborough spent the first two weeks of November in London supervising preparations for his departure and consulting with his friends.

Whatever hope the duke had for the future rested upon foiling the Earl of Oxford's plans. The Pretender's accession, negotiated by the Duke of Hamilton—or anyone—promised to make Marlborough's temporary exile a permanent one. In reality, Oxford had no interest in helping the Pretender to the British throne, but Whigs and Hanoverians assumed that he meant to do so. The choice of Hamilton, a notorious Jacobite, as ambassador merely confirmed Whig suspicions. In later years Hamilton's illegitimate grandson had no doubt about who was his grandfather's greatest enemy: the Duke of Marlborough. Relations between the dukes were always bad, claimed Charles Hamilton, because his grandfather had "labored incessantly in keeping the eyes of the Queen opened upon the sinistrous designs of Marlborough, in combating her propensity to trust him, and in evincing the fallacy of his declarations." The Duke of Marlborough had no reason to be a friend of the new ambassador to France.[17]

At about 9:30 a.m. on November 14, 1712, two well-dressed men were ushered through the front door of Marlborough House. A servant showed the two serious gentlemen through a house disordered by preparations for imminent departure. The footman took Charles, Lord Mohun, and General George Maccartney into the presence of the former Captain General and closed the door silently behind them.

What exactly was said at this interview? For the best of reasons no notes were taken and the principals kept silent about what passed. Everyone in the room had cause for desperation. Marlborough could reflect upon a brilliant military career and forty years of successful court politics now in ruins, his reputation shattered by slander and libel. He and his wife faced permanent exile, deprived of the fruits of a lifetime's service to the Crown. Blenheim Palace, Marlborough House, the Ranger's Lodge at Windsor, the Post Office pension—all that John Churchill had coveted since his days at Charles II's court was slipping from his grasp. Lord Mohun had lost his secure political position. The legal onslaught upon his estate was gaining headway. Hamilton's Tory dominion threatened Mohun with poverty and obscurity; the Gerard estate was all that stood between him and his creditors. The Mohun estate in Cornwall could be sold and still Charles would be a debtor; £50,000 or £60,000 would hardly cover his debts. Mohun knew that without his Macclesfield inheritance he would again live the life he had known in his youth: cramped lodgings shared with a bitterly unhappy woman, under constant siege from furious shopkeepers. George Maccartney did not even have an estate to sell. Brave but possessed by a sinister temper, he had put an end to his career as a soldier by his outrageous conduct. Blasting away at effigies of Lord Oxford had ended all hope of a new, lucrative position: the governorship of Jamaica. Though Marlborough had tried to obtain the post for his friend, it went instead to an aristocratic dependent: Archibald Hamilton, the youngest brother of Duke James. Marlborough could not overcome the Queen's prejudice against a man she considered to be an immoral profligate.

In every case James, Duke of Hamilton, played the role of nemesis. As ambassador to France, he foretold peace and the return of the Pretender. As Mohun's opponent in the struggle over the Gerard estate, he threatened bankruptcy and penury. And after killing Maccartney's hopes for Jamaica, Hamilton threatened to deprive the general of his patrons.

On this morning Mohun had a tale to tell. The day before, he had met Hamilton at the Chancery Lane offices of John Orlebar. A personal presence, as both men knew, could help maintain a case in the dilatory netherworld of Chancery, especially in the closing phases of their struggle. For Hamilton, secure in his newly won offices and confident of the favor of the government—possibly even counting upon a more brilliant future as mentor of a new King—these meetings were gratifying. Years of failure and delay seemed miraculously reversed. Mohun, usurper of his family's property, was about to receive justice. Mohun's own presence reflected his determination to protect his waning interest.

Orlebar's chambers were on the fringes of Lincoln's Inn. His position as a master of the Court of Chancery ensured that the office would be a well-appointed one, proof against a November cold snap.[18] The building surrounded a courtyard, further shielding his offices from the weather. That evening the retinues of Lords Hamilton and Mohun picked their way through the narrow, gloomy lane, lit by the flickering lamps over doorways. The meeting was scheduled for 7 p.m., and both parties, accompanied by lawyers and servants, crowded into the building. The lawyers and their clients came prepared to engage their adversaries as their footmen listened in the outer room with varying degrees of indifference. The office door stood open a crack, so eavesdropping was easy.

Hamilton, who had just dined with his London man of business, Gavin Mason, met his old rival with a low bow. Mohun returned the courtesy. The lords sat down, followed by the rest of those present. The subject of that night's meeting was the dispute over accounting for the profits of the estate of the deceased Lady Gerard. The Chancery decree handed down in Hamilton's favor in 1710 ordered Mohun to account for all the money she had collected from the estate and show what was done with it. Hamilton claimed that Mohun owed his wife thousands, a claim Mohun rejected. In fact, he maintained that the duke owed *him* money, thanks to an unpaid mortgage now over a decade old. Both claims rested upon business transacted years—even decades—before. Mohun insisted that money spent on the duchess's dancing master in the 1680s be deducted from the profits of the estate, and claimed the expenses incurred at her father's funeral, nearly thirty years earlier. Proof for these claims and counterclaims was not easy, especially for Mohun, who was presumed to possess the documents relating to the estate, whether they actually existed or not.

On November 13, the litigants focused upon the deposition of Richard Whitworth. Whitworth was one of Mohun's last connections with the remote days of Lady Gerard and her father, the first Earl of Macclesfield (both dead for well over a decade). He had been a trusted servant of the family, steward to Macclesfield and his daughter. He was one of the few living people who knew how the Gerard estate had been managed—what its income had been, and how that income had been spent. As a link to the past, Whitworth was extremely important for Mohun's case, but he was a weak link: he was very old, and the reliability of his memory was subject to question. In 1711, when he was asked about the location of important estate papers, Whitworth declared that "he was then soe very weak and so farr by sickness and old age lost the use of his memory that he could not tell what papers he had or att least where to find the same."[19] Whitworth's standing as an honest witness might have been questioned in any case, had the duke's lawyers known anything about his past. In the 1660s Whitworth had acted as one of Lord Macclesfield's principal henchmen in his campaign to defraud the Fittons of the Gawsworth property.[20] In 1711 the old man's lapses helped Mohun, who had become Whitworth's patron following the death of the second Earl of Macclesfield. His memory had evidently not been a problem in 1708, when he claimed to have discovered a previously unknown will penned by the first Lord Macclesfield—a fortuitous discovery that had enabled Mohun to fend off charges leveled against him by his old adversary Charlotte, Lady Orby.[21] In this case, Hamilton was determined to use Whitworth's claim of disability for his own purposes.

Whitworth had submitted testimony in Mohun's behalf, and Mohun's footman, Rhys Williams, overheard the duke reading the old servant's statement aloud, and then exclaiming that Whitworth was an unreliable witness: he had "quite forgot himself about a year ago and was not now to be believed." Whitworth's evidence, to use the phrase Williams claimed to have heard, "had neither truth nor justice in it." Since Whitworth had acknowledged his memory to be imperfect, it is hardly surprising that Hamilton denounced his testimony. But an important part of Mohun's case rested upon the steward's evidence, and Mohun had no intention of allowing such a crucial witness to be branded as senile. He replied hotly to the duke that Whitworth was "an honest man and had as much honor and justice in him as his Grace."[22] Whitworth's status as a man of honor was questionable, but the duke listened to Mohun's outburst without comment. His friend George Lockhart later claimed that James "frequently, upon former occasions, to my hearing, declar'd his positive resolution to bear evry thing but blows" from Mohun.[23]

The momentary flaring of tempers then disappeared to the eyes and ears of the waiting servants when someone inside shut the office door. The men within continued their negotiations until sometime after eight o'clock, when the meeting ended in a dispute over when the parties should get together once again. Hamilton, whose departure for Versailles had already been put off far longer than the Queen or Lord Oxford liked, wanted to meet on Saturday the fifteenth, but Mohun, aware of the benefits of procrastination, insisted that he would be unavailable. Lady Mohun was in the country, and he declared his determination to join her. Hamilton, however, would brook no delay. Another appointment was fixed for Saturday. The meeting ended with the duke leaving the office first, and joining his servants, who were waiting for him in the courtyard.

The duke stood urinating in the court as Mohun emerged from the building. The younger man passed his rival without a word and their retinues went their separate ways. Hamilton went back to St. James's Square, first stopping for a word with one of his lawyers. Mohun, agitated by the unfavorable course of events, sought out his friend Maccartney. At about nine o'clock he found the general at home in the lodgings he rented. Maccartney listened as Mohun poured out his frustrations with his lawsuits and the duke. "I am prodigiously wearied out with my lawyers," he said. The latest meeting, with its attack on his key witness, brought the ruin he dreaded closer. Mohun directed his ire at the duke, "His Grace has, before a Master in Chancery, treated my witnesses so very ill, that I cannot help thinking it as meant to myself; particularly he said of Mr. Whitworth, that he was a vile old rogue, not fit to be credited, nor fitting for any honest man to employ, saying this in such an air and manner, as if I had procured corrupt evidence!"[24]

Joined by Maccartney's fellow lodger, Colonel Joseph Churchill—a kinsman of Marlborough's—the two men continued their conversation at White's Chocolate House. They then went to the Queen's Arms, an expensive eating establishment in Pall Mall, near Marlborough House. Maccartney would readily take a free meal in such surroundings, and he enjoyed Mohun's hospitality as the younger man fumed. Lord Mohun was a boon companion, a fellow Whig, and a valuable source of credit. Equally, the Duke of Hamilton's politics were reason enough for Maccartney to dislike him. Furthermore, Hamilton's kinsman and part-time factotum Colonel John Hamilton had been a rival in the army: the two men had nearly come to blows after Maccartney, benefiting at least in part from his Whiggish political connections, was promoted over Hamilton's head. And then there was the matter of Jamaica. Now the duke seemed on the verge of making Mohun as penniless as Maccartney. George Maccartney had been in tight situations; he had survived the disaster at Almanza in Spain and defied French shot and shell in Flanders. But this was a different sort of problem.

Maccartney and Churchill returned to their lodgings, and Mohun retired alone, telling his footman, Williams, "to let nobody speak with him next morning but General Maccartney."[25] Maccartney ordered his own footman to rise early and call in St. James's Square. The general wanted to know when Hamilton received company.[26] Mohun and Maccartney had apparently decided that they would meet again in the morning.

On Friday the fourteenth, Mohun rose: probably by seven. He dressed, climbed into a hackney coach, and rumbled off to Maccartney's lodgings. When he entered his friend's chamber, between eight and nine, he found the general drinking tea. Maccartney professed surprise: "My lord, you are very early!"[27] Within a few minutes the general's servant appeared to say that the Duke of Hamilton received visitors at 9 a.m. Maccartney dressed, and the two gentlemen took Mohun's hackney coach. The stay at the general's was brief: about half an hour.

Mohun's footman began to suspect that something might be afoot between his master and Hamilton—the night before, he had been one of the servants outside Orlebar's office and he had heard the angry exchange between the peers. He had witnessed his master's unusual early-morning activity. Fearing a disaster, he spoke to Colonel Churchill, Maccartney's neighbor. He was afraid, he said, that there might be a quarrel brewing. Churchill did not take the information to the nearest magistrate, as the law required, but told Lord Mohun that he had a talkative footman. Mohun asked Williams "Why he concerned himself with his [Mohun's] affairs?" He denied that there was anything amiss and warned Williams to keep his mouth shut: "the report of such a thing could do him harm."[28] Chastened, Williams kept his own counsel for the rest of the day.

Leaving Maccartney's rooms after arranging to meet Churchill for lunch at one o'clock, the men directed their hackney to Marlborough House: here occurred the interview already described,

which lasted between thirty minutes and an hour. Maccartney may
have gone first to St. James's Square in an attempt to call on Hamilton, but the duke's porter, John Hipsley, was vague about the hour
of the general's first visit—there would be others that day—and in
any event, Hamilton was not home.[29] By about ten or ten-thirty
Mohun and the general had left Marlborough's mansion.

The coach pulled up, around eleven, outside a well-known
establishment in Long Acre: the Bagnio. The Bagnio had been a
fixture on the London scene since the 1680s. It provided hot and
cold baths and massages in luxurious surroundings: marble floors,
hot and cold running water, and even a scale "for those who want
to see how much weight they lose." The owners boasted of the
health benefits they provided, and went to considerable lengths
to attract a high-class clientele: admission was five shillings, a sum
no casual bather could afford. The stone walls were decorated
with specially commissioned art. The establishment was popular
with London's high livers: many an aging gentleman, suffering
the effects of late nights and heavy drinking, came through the
Bagnio's doors in search of a soothing bath and a massage. The
staff's ministrations, claimed the management, ensured that even
the most jaded roué went away from the premises in fine fettle:
"leaving the Bagnio, he betakes himself to his pleasure or business, finding himself as brisk, active, and vigorous, as if he had
just skip't into the world."[30] The Bagnio also provided refresh-
ment and privacy—the reason that George Maccartney chose it.
Meals could be ordered and there were private bedchambers on
the premises; a room could be rented with few questions asked.
The general himself, not his footman, carried a portmanteau into
the building and reserved a room for the coming night.

Next, Maccartney retraced his steps to St. James's Square.
Once again Hipsley, the porter, was forced to tell the caller—who
wrote his name in the visitors' book but referred to himself as "a
northern gentleman"—that his master was out. This time Hamilton was at Lord Bolingbroke's house. After Maccartney's first
visit, Hamilton had asked Hipsley to describe the caller and then

told his servant that should the gentleman return, he should be asked to wait—something Maccartney refused to do, saying that although he "had business of importance to communicate" he would call again.[31] It is unlikely that Hamilton knew what was happening: mysterious "northern gentlemen" were frequent enough visitors to his house; Jacobite conspirators relished cloak-and-dagger methods, and even those who thought them distasteful found them prudent in the face of government vigilance.

On that Friday James had what was for him important business to attend to: the issue of his badge of the Order of the Garter. The Queen had awarded Hamilton the order two months earlier—a move that gratified the duke immensely, illustrating once again his unequivocal return to favor. But James's thirst for distinction, driven by his deep-seated insecurities, could not rest satisfied. The Garter was all very well, but James was also a member of the Order of the Thistle. Here was the difficulty: upon his being named a knight of the Garter, British nobles expected Hamilton to resign from the Order of the Thistle. Other Scottish peers were as anxious as James for signs of the Queen's favor, and the Thistle, whose membership (like that of the Garter) was strictly limited, was one of the most coveted rewards Anne could bestow. She could not create a new knight unless an old one died or resigned: and Hamilton refused to resign. It had been his ambition to combine membership in both orders; he was the only British peer entitled to wear the two gaudy stars and ribbons of these select companies. This attitude merely enraged his fellows, now deprived of the chance to append the letters "K.T." to their names. Some at court made trouble: Hamilton would need a license to wear his stars when abroad, and official footdragging threatened to deny him what he had sought. He spent part of his day complaining to his fellow Garter knight the Earl of Strafford, himself a newly inducted member; as a diplomat who would wear his star abroad, Strafford may have sympathized. Hamilton's focus on this matter gave no hint of any looming trouble with General Maccartney or Lord Mohun.[32]

The duke's pursuit of validation continued through the day as Maccartney fretted over his repeated near misses in St. James's Square. Chairmen in London's West End must have found the general's face a familiar one by Friday afternoon. Sometime between visits to the big house on the square, Maccartney joined his friends for lunch at the Globe in the Strand. The barman remembered that Maccartney and Mohun arrived first, and that they were joined by Colonel Churchill, and another of Mohun's friends, Sir Robert Rich. It was particularly noteworthy that the group—one ordinarily not accustomed to self-restraint—drank no more than "a flask of claret."[33]

While Mohun and his companions finished their meal, Maccartney returned to St. James's Square. On this fourth attempt, at about four o'clock, he succeeded. Maccartney's weary chairmen deposited their charge before the duke's door, and at last Hipsley could report that his master was in. Hipsley told Maccartney that the duke had given strict orders that no other visitors should be admitted to the house.[34] The porter announced Maccartney's arrival, and showed him in to the duke. Maccartney stayed about fifteen minutes. Representing his friend, he apparently told Hamilton that Lord Mohun, distressed by their meeting the night before, desired an explanation from the duke of his implied condemnation of Mohun's honesty. A request for an explanation was the first step toward a duel. Hamilton knew the possible consequences. Dueling was illegal. For a privy councillor and an ambassador, a duel with Mohun would be absurd. The Queen's views about duels were well known: she hated them. She might withdraw her favor. His mother the dowager duchess would once again be free to read a homily upon her eldest son's feckless behavior. He was nineteen years older than Mohun, and plagued with gout. Mohun had grown fat but could wield a sword, probably with more agility than could the gouty duke. But if Hamilton had to fight, he would.

During Maccartney's final visit to St. James's Square, Hamilton agreed to meet Mohun. He walked the general to the front door, and watched the chairmen bear their passenger off in the direction of the Strand. At the Globe, Maccartney had a quiet word with Mohun. They climbed into a coach outside, which

18. Trade card of a master swordsman

took them to a tavern in Covent Garden that Hamilton knew well: the Rose. A haunt of the fashionable world for decades, the Rose had seen many intrigues and tragedies. In its back rooms politicians combined privacy with the convenience of rapidly filled bumpers.

Walking into the Rose shortly before five, the two men cornered a barman and asked him "whether stars and garters used this house."[35] Puzzled, he told them yes, nobles of very high rank did patronize the tavern. The general and his friend then said that the Duke of Hamilton would be in, and should be given a private room—but *not* the room they took for themselves. Making their way through the noisy building, now beginning to fill up with gentlemen whose long night's pleasure was just getting started, Mohun and Maccartney settled into one of the Rose's private rooms. The sun was already down, so the tavern was dimly lighted with candles and coal fires; there would have been little light. Still, the barman could see the light glint on the duke's Garter star when he walked into the taproom.

Accompanied by his kinsman Colonel John Hamilton, Hamilton asked for General Maccartney. The general appeared, and the two men retired to an inner room. Colonel Hamilton waited, and Mohun remained in his own room. Maccartney called for a bottle of claret, which he and Hamilton insisted upon serving themselves. The waiter was ushered out of the room and the door closed. Minutes later, Maccartney emerged and rejoined Mohun. This routine was repeated. Although the Rose's staff must have wondered about the curious shell game going on before them, no one knew precisely what was happening. Eventually, Colonel Hamilton rejoined the duke, Maccartney returned to Charles, and the Scots left.*

---

* Maccartney's actions on Friday, November 14, cast doubt upon his later claims to disinterested peacemaking: if he was not deliberately fanning Mohun's resentment of the duke, it is clear that he did nothing to reduce the building tension between the two men. He never made any effort to warn the government of an impending duel. His early morning call upon Marlborough might possibly have been an attempt to

As the two noblemen and their supporters left the Rose, the Earl of Oxford was pondering a letter he had received that day. As the head of a government in an age of the most bitter political divisions, the Lord Treasurer was no stranger to intrigue. He had just recovered from the stab of a penknife wielded by a crazed French spy, and another, more ingenious mind had recently sent him a box booby-trapped with a brace of loaded pistols. Had the device worked properly, the person who opened the box would have had a pair of bullets fired at him at point-blank range. The Treasurer's friend Swift had opened this dubious gift, but fortunately the pistols misfired. In 1712 Oxford's postbag swelled with frantic appeals against enemies, real or imagined, with darkly worded threats, and with rambling tales of intrigue.

One message in that day's post had been written by a shady gentleman named Francis Lee. It warned the earl of unspecified "enterprizes of wicked and bloodthirsty men." Lee's letter said that he had received a young gentleman in "very uncomfortable circumstances . . . What he acquainted me with upon his first arrival at London, but, being unwilling to be Accessory to the blood of any, hinted only to your Lordship, is now I understand, and that from a good hand, consulted by some of the great ones of the earth to put into present execution."[37] The warning was obscure; there were no specifics, no names, no details. Did Lee refer to an assassination

---

enlist the great man in a peacemaking mission, but circumstantial evidence, as well as Maccartney's own character, points in a different direction. If a peaceful settlement were Maccartney's goal, why reserve a room at the Bagnio *before* speaking to Hamilton? The general later claimed that his visits to the duke were reluctant, and that after missing him the first time he "thought no more of going to my lord duke's." But the evidence shows that George made no less than four trips to St. James's Square that day. The meeting at the Rose, stage-managed as it was by Maccartney, hardly seemed destined to produce an amicable settlement. It did not last very long—one source says only about a quarter of an hour, hardly long enough to do more than present the standard compliments. Moreover, it was Hamilton whose interests most strongly dictated avoiding a duel. It is impossible to know precisely what George Maccartney's role was in the events of that November day, but the evidence suggests that he was not the evangel of peace he later claimed to be.[36]

plot? Who would be the victim? Who were the mysterious "great ones"? Without any further information, Oxford could do nothing, and that seems to be precisely what he did that night. The Lord Treasurer spent the evening with his usual drinking companions.

From the Rose, Mohun and Maccartney went to the Queen's Arms in Pall Mall. There, with Mohun's footman, Williams, in attendance, they dined with Rich, Colonel Churchill, and a new face, the Duke of Richmond. Richmond, whose talents lay mostly in his capacity for liquor and loudly proclaimed Whig politics, was an old friend of Mohun's. They had shared many a late-night debauch, and Charles could rely on him. The Queen's Arms catered to gentlemen of fortune and rank, and such knots of whispering nobles were common enough, especially in times as fraught as those of November 1712. If the drawers noted anything out of the ordinary, they saw that Lord Mohun was quieter than usual, and that he drank less. Five men drank only four bottles of claret over a period of some six hours.[38] The men sat nursing their drinks until past midnight.

Near midnight Mohun sent his footman on an errand, intending to throw the inquisitive Welshman off the track. When Williams returned, his master was gone. No one could say where Mohun and his companions might be found. Williams left in search of Mohun, stopping in at three different places. Eventually he gave up the search, returned home, and turned in, troubled by the day's events.

Hamilton returned from the Rose at about eight o'clock, and spent his evening at home, preparing for the next day. Contriving to avoid the duchess, he gave orders for his coach to be ready early the next morning. Sitting down in his study, he took a sheet of paper and began a letter to his five-year-old son and heir, the Marquess of Clydesdale.

> My dear son, I have been doing all I could to redeem your mother's right to her estate, which I hope shall be yours. I commend you to be dutiful towards her, as I hope she will be just and kind to you. And I recommend it particularly to you, if you ever enjoy the estate

of Hamilton, and what may, I hope, justly belong to you, (considering how long I have lived with a small competence, which has made me run into debt). I hope God will put it into your heart to do justice to my honour, and pay my just debts: There will be enough to satisfie all, and give your brothers and sisters such provisions as the state of their condition and their quality in Scotland will admit of.

I pray God preserve you, and the family in your person, My humble duty to my mother, and my blessing to your sisters. If it please God I live, you shall find me share with you what I do possess, and ever prove your affectionate and kind father, whilst,

Hamilton

I again, upon my Blessing, charge you, that you let the world see you do your part in satisfying my just debts.[39]

As he contemplated death, his thoughts turned to the condition of his house. James, fourth Duke of Hamilton, was uncomfortably near bankruptcy. His death now could destroy his family, as creditors descended in a mad scramble to secure their money. A man of Hamilton's pride could hardly bear the thought of the damage that unpaid debts would do to his reputation. His life had been a struggle for honor and respect, and by 1712 the struggle seemed near success. To lose now, so unexpectedly, preyed upon the duke's mind as he added the postscript to his finished letter in the candlelight of his quiet study.

At 11:15 p.m. a footman dressed in the Duke of Hamilton's livery hammered on the door of a house in Suffolk Street, near the Hay Market, not far from St. James's Square. Its owner, Paul Boussier, was a French émigré surgeon of some renown. He had already retired, feeling unwell, when he received the footman's message. Hamilton wanted the Frenchman to attend him at his house immediately. The doctor asked if the duke had taken ill. The footman said no; his master wanted to consult with Boussier on an important matter. The doctor told the footman to return His Grace his compliments, but as there was no emergency, he would call at St. James's Square in the morning.[40] The footman returned with the doctor's message and at last Hamilton could go to bed.

At one o'clock in the morning a gentleman arrived at the Bagnio in Long Acre. He asked whether General Maccartney had left a portmanteau on the premises earlier in the day. John Chaboner, who saw to late arrivals, told his heavyset customer that the general had indeed left a bag and reserved a room. Lord Mohun followed Chaboner up the stairs as the man lighted the way with the glow of a candle. Chaboner showed his lodger into a bedchamber and helped him remove his shoes and stockings, as another servant watched. Coat and waistcoat followed, and a quick search in the portmanteau revealed a dressing gown, which Mohun pulled on. He "seemed to be thoughtful, but was very sober" as he paced the floor with his arms folded.[41] He seemed melancholy and sighed as he lay down.

At two o'clock another knock came on the front door of the Bagnio. Once again Chaboner responded, and this time faced General George Maccartney. Unlike the previous visitor, Maccartney seemed to have no cares. He kept up a running chatter with Chaboner as they climbed the stairs. He was shown into Mohun's room, which he said he would share with his friend. Maccartney seemed merry with drink. He was not drunk, however; he certainly had his wits about him. After taking offense, for no apparent reason, at one servant, he demanded another to undress him. This new arrival, probably roused from a sound sleep, grew still more befuddled when the general peremptorily asked "whether he loved the French." Assuring the old campaigner of his hatred for France and all things French, the servant managed to get him out of his clothes and into bed, having first received orders to wake them no later than six, "for they were to go in a stage coach."[42]

Sometime after 2 a.m. on Saturday, November 15, Charles, Lord Mohun, and General George Maccartney went to their rest—the former evidently far more troubled than the latter. When Chaboner came to rouse them, he found Mohun in his bed, snoring. At about the same time that Chaboner shook the sleeping form of Lord

Mohun, James, Duke of Hamilton, was giving instructions to one of his footmen, John Lesley. Lesley hurried off to the Golden Peruke in Charing Cross, where Colonel John Hamilton lodged. The footman awakened Hamilton with word from the duke: he was to dress himself as quickly as possible, for His Grace would momentarily pay a call upon urgent business. The colonel had combined his military career with personal service to the duke—he oversaw some estate business, and helped collect rents; being roused at odd hours in Hamilton's behalf was not that unusual. He had also been with the duke the day before and could guess the nature of the duke's business.

When Lesley returned to St. James's Square at 7 a.m., he found his master already dressed, wrapped in a heavy cloak, preparing to walk out the front door. Just before he left, the duke told Mr. Ferguson, his master of horse, that he was going out to "vindicate his honour." Ferguson was to keep silent, and in the meantime pay another call upon Dr. Boussier.[43] Andrew Clark, the coachman, sat shivering outside on the box of the coach, where he had been ordered to appear by six. He was then joined by Lesley, who took his place standing at the rear of the vehicle, and the duke climbed in. A moment later the three men clattered out of the square, iron-bound carriage wheels and the horses' heavy shoes ringing over the cobbles in the cold morning air. When they arrived at the Golden Peruke, the colonel once again had a visit from Lesley, who told him that the duke was waiting for him in the street below. Before John Hamilton had finished dressing, the duke came into the room to hurry his second along. Before the colonel was aware of what was happening, the impatient aristocrat hustled him into his shirt and chivvied him down the stairs and into his waiting coach. At about the same time Ferguson arrived at the surgeon's house, this time with a more ominous message than the previous night's: "the duke would have him take coach . . . to dress him should there be occasion."[44] The doctor, a man who valued his rest, was not yet out of bed, and sent his footman, along with a promise to attend personally as soon as he was dressed and ready.

The duke hurried because he was late. He was to meet Mohun by dawn, and sunrise was near. Mohun and Maccartney, more methodical in their plans, were ready first. Chaboner's call came in good time. Providing a pot of hot tea and changing a guinea for Mohun, he left to call a coach. John Pennington, cruising the area in his hackney, answered the call, and Chaboner watched the two men clamber aboard, "in very great haste," leaving behind their portmanteau. Mohun was silent as the two men drove away; Maccartney directed the driver to take them to Kensington, and off the coach went, headed west in advance of the sunrise.

Rhys Williams, still anxious about his master's intentions, was also up early Saturday morning, searching for Lord Mohun and hoping that there was nothing more afoot than one of his employer's usual nights of riotous living. He could not be sure where Mohun was, for there were many taverns and lodgings kept by women of easy virtue and accommodating schedules. Nevertheless, considering Mohun's curious behavior since Thursday night, Williams thought it worth the effort to track him down. A round of some of the usual places turned up nothing, but the footman's suspicions grew when he saw Hamilton's coach in Piccadilly, headed west. Williams's encounter with Hamilton's coach was sheer luck, for the duke would have passed by earlier had he not been delayed for a few minutes. After he left the Golden Peruke, ordering Clark to drive to Kensington, Colonel Hamilton, still buttoning his clothes and attempting to set his wig straight, made an awkward discovery: he had left his sword at home. A second was worthless without a weapon; his job was to ensure fair play, and his only sanction was his sword. More often than not, seconds engaged each other even as their principals fought. He must not arrive on the field unarmed.

An impatient pull on the duke's signal bell stopped Clark in St. James's Street, and Hamilton called for Lesley, the footman.

Producing a large set of keys from within his cloak, he instructed Lesley to hurry home in search of a sword for the colonel. The house was only a few yards away, but the duke's impatience could hardly have been assuaged as the footman ran for home, returning a few minutes later with a mourning sword from the duke's closet.* Colonel Hamilton was not in mourning, but the three-cornered, razor-sharp blade would serve as well as any other, despite its somber blacking. Lesley, breath puffing in the cold air after his run, once again climbed aboard the coach and Clark drove on, passing Rhys Williams moments later. Williams, curious and apprehensive, ran down Mayfair to the brick wall that marked the boundary of Hyde Park. With considerable effort, and at some risk to his handsome green livery, he pulled himself over the wall. If his master was about to fight a duel, the park was the obvious place for it. At the western edge of the metropolis, the park was London's largest—its wall some six miles in circumference. Once part of a royal hunting preserve, Hyde Park was still stocked with deer, but had been opened to the public and wholly given over to the pleasures of the better sort.

But the park was also a place where those with irreconcilable grievances might silence their antagonists, though at the risk of their lives. Hyde Park was a popular venue for duelists. As Williams knew, if reputations were ruined by day in the park, they were restored at night or in the light of dawn, when most of society's coaches still stood in their houses. There were other quiet places where men settled their quarrels around London: the fields behind Montagu House on the northern outskirts of town were another favorite. But the duke's coach was rolling west, not north.

By the time Williams, clothes scuffed and disordered, dropped over the wall to the cold grass, his master had already passed through the park gates. Maccartney's unexpected order to turn

---

* A mourning sword was designed to be worn by gentlemen in mourning. Mourning swords were just as deadly as any other blade, but they were less ostentatiously decorated and their blades and scabbards were blackened.

19. A view of the western edge of London, about 1730; in the
background, Buckingham House, right, and Westminster Abbey, left

into the park instead of continuing along the road to Kensington
alerted Pennington, the coachman, to the possibility of a duel.
His passengers attempted to allay his suspicions, and those of the
park's gatekeeper, by asking whether they might "get anything
good [to drink], it being a Cold morning" in the park.[45] The gatekeeper, not prepared to balk two men of quality, allowed the
hackney to pass, directing the driver to Price's Lodge, a tavern
that catered to the needs of those fatigued by their circuit around
the Ring.

As the coach approached the lodge, one of its occupants
ordered a halt and instructed Pennington to go in and warm himself with a draught of burnt wine. They were going to take a walk,
and they would return for him in a few minutes. As the gentlemen
walked off in the direction of the Ring, a young groom, William
Morris, watched from a distance as he exercised his master's
horses. The well-dressed men walked for some ten or fifteen

minutes before Morris caught sight of two more figures approaching on foot from a different direction. The duke had avoided the gatehouse by ordering his coachman to stop at the edge of the park, where the road was separated from the grounds by a ditch. The duke alighted from the coach and instructed his servants to proceed farther down the road and wait for him. Lesley helped his master across the ditch, and he was joined by Colonel Hamilton. Clark, uneasy about his employer's actions, pulled away very slowly, casting backward glances at the duke on the grass below, until Hamilton "turned and looked very sternly at him, bidding him go where he was ordered . . . and not stir thence for their lives till he came to them."[46]

Mohun and Maccartney had arrived in the park at seven-thirty or a little after, and when Pennington walked into the lodge asking for burnt wine for his passengers, John Reynolds, the innkeeper, was immediately suspicious, "for very few came hither so soon in

20. Price's Lodge in Hyde Park

the morning but to fight." Reynolds refused to draw the wine and told Pennington to get back outside to keep an eye on his passengers. Pennington, protesting that he thought them "very civil gentlemen," was concerned enough that he went back outside to ease his fears. He might momentarily have persuaded himself of Mohun's innocent intentions, as he and Maccartney remained alone together, apparently taking the brisk early-morning air as they had claimed. But within a few minutes he realized that Reynolds had been right: Morris, the groom, rode up to inform him that two gentlemen were standing at his coach. Pennington abandoned his surveillance and ran to the two new arrivals, men dressed in heavy cloaks and wearing swords. "Who have you brought?" the older of the two asked. Pennington said that his passenger was Lord Mohun and another gentleman he did not know. The duke, whom the coachman did not recognize, asked, "Which way have they gone?"[47] Pennington, now certain that a duel was in the offing, pointed toward the Ring, where Mohun and Maccartney waited. Hamilton and his second walked on in that direction, and Pennington tore off to the lodge in search of help. He rushed into the building shouting that the gentlemen were going to fight and that "there wou'd be murder!" Reynolds must grab a stave and get help; Pennington dashed back out toward the field, stopping behind a tree about fifty yards from the Ring.

Reynolds picked up a pair of stout truncheons and ran out to find an assistant. The first person he came across was John Nicholson, a laborer pushing a wheelbarrow through the park. Hurriedly explaining, Reynolds gave the bewildered workman a stick and they ran toward the gentlemen, who were standing over a hundred yards away, near the rail that enclosed the Ring. Mohun remained silent at first: when Hamilton spoke, asking, "My lord, have I come time enough?" it was Maccartney who replied, "Time enough." Mohun and his second were separated from Hamilton by a shallow ditch, and after this exchange they jumped across to where the duke stood.

Pulling off his cloak, Hamilton followed the general and Mohun. Hamilton told Maccartney, "Let the event of this be what it will, you are the occasion of it." Stung, the general replied, "I had a commission for it." Almost simultaneously Mohun spoke: "My lord duke, these two gentlemen shall have nothing to do," indicating that the seconds should not engage. Maccartney would have none of that: "We will take our shares," he said, and the duke answered, "Here's my friend, he will take his share in my dance."[48] At the same time Mohun threw off his coat, and all four men drew their swords.

The onlookers saw, not the sort of parry-and-feint delicacy that gentlemen learned from fencing masters, but ferocious, unhesitating cut and thrust. No sooner had Mohun and the Duke of Hamilton's swords made their first clash than Maccartney attacked Colonel Hamilton. A desperate parry beat the general's sword down. The blade cut through Colonel Hamilton's shoe and wounded him on the instep. Despite the painful gash, the colonel managed to get the advantage. He disarmed Maccartney before turning to see what had happened to the two peers. As close as the seconds were to the fight, others had a much better view. Nicholson, the laborer, was farthest from the action, having tripped some forty yards away on the uneven ground. Morris, the groom, was closest: not much more than thirty feet away, he could plainly hear the clash of steel and the cries of the combatants. The others, Reynolds in the lead, were charging forward in hopes of breaking up the fight.

The duke was upon Mohun almost before he could raise his sword. His blade slashed at Mohun. One stroke bit deeply into his left side. Another plunged into his right side near the short ribs, the blade ripping through his trunk and emerging from his back. Mohun, thrown backward by Hamilton's violent attack, desperately lashed out with his own sword, cutting James badly in the right calf. Attempting to ward off his enemy, Mohun delivered a glancing blow to the duke's right arm. But now Hamilton's assault

seemed irresistible. Mohun made a desperate effort. Falling
backward, he raised his sword high and, with all the force he
could muster, plunged it downward into Hamilton's onrushing
breast. The blow struck home: the blade bit into the duke's waistcoat and entered his breast about three inches above his right nipple. The force of the thrust carried the sword more than eight
inches into James's body. But the enraged Hamilton was still
determined to finish his foe. Mustering his strength, he pushed
toward the gasping Mohun. Charles had backed to the edge of the
shallow ditch that he and Maccartney had jumped only a few minutes before. Now he stumbled into it. As he fell, the duke's sword
struck downward into the left side of Mohun's groin. In a last
futile effort to stave off death, Charles grabbed the sharp blade of
Hamilton's sword, trying to blunt its impetus. Three fingers of
his right hand were reduced to bloody ribbons, nearly severed.
The last, most violent, stroke cut an artery, emerging just under

21. A contemporary depiction of the duel,
showing Maccartney murdering Hamilton

Mohun's left buttock. The groom, Morris, ten yards away, heard Mohun cry "I am killed!" as he received this last blow, and saw him tumble into the ditch. He lay motionless in a pool of blood.

The duke staggered away, bleeding profusely. One of Mohun's wild blows had severed the artery in his right arm, and he was losing blood fast. Exhausted and badly wounded, he could now contemplate the end of his most bitter rival: Mohun lay dying in a ditch. The seconds rushed forward to assist their friends. Maccartney lifted the fast-weakening Mohun, who lay on his back, speechless. The general turned Mohun over, hoping to limit his internal bleeding, but Charles died almost immediately. Colonel Hamilton caught up with the duke, and asked him anxiously how he was. Glassy-eyed, James made no reply but continued to walk haltingly forward, his bloody sword still gripped in his right hand. The colonel asked again, and this time the duke answered feebly, "I am wounded," before sinking down with his back against a nearby tree. At that moment a panting Mr. Ferguson, with the surgeon's mate in tow, rushed forward to attend to him. Colonel Hamilton stood aside as the surgeon knelt to begin his work, but when he raised the duke's arm there was no pulse. The Duke of Hamilton was dead.

By now Reynolds and his helpers had arrived on the scene, and forced the seconds to hand over their weapons. The onlookers saw both seconds in attendance upon their principals, but no one knew what precisely the two officers had done between their own fight and the deaths of their friends—a question that would later be of considerable importance. Colonel Hamilton exclaimed, "By God, my lord duke is killed!" Maccartney said, "By God, my Lord Mohun is killed!" The colonel added, "We've made a fine morning's work on it." Maccartney, knowing the danger he was in, turned to John Nicholson, grasped him earnestly by the hand, and said, "Honest friend, bear witness that we endeavoured to part them, and pray remember that I in the grey cloaths and the silver-lac'd hat, tell you so."[49] Maccartney knew that if he came to trial, his survival might depend upon the testimony of people like John Nicholson, driver of wheelbarrows.

Mohun's body was moved first. Maccartney called Pennington's coach, and, with Nicholson and Williams, the footman, loaded the corpse into the vehicle. Maccartney ordered the driver to take it home. Pennington asked who was going to pay the fare. Maccartney indicated Williams. The driver took one look at the Welshman, and refused. The general had arrived with his lordship, and someone owed him the fare for the journey to the park as well as for carting a corpse. That someone was the general. Maccartney fished half a crown from his purse, and Pennington departed.

Waiting at the entrance to the park for their master's return, Andrew Clark and John Lesley grew more anxious. Eventually Lesley, ignoring Hamilton's orders, climbed down from his perch on the back of the coach and walked into the park. He had not gone far when he came across George Maccartney, in his blood-stained gray suit, walking in the direction of Kensington. Picking up his pace, he soon afterward came upon a disconsolate Colonel Hamilton and asked anxiously, "What has become of my lord?" The colonel said that "This was the worst morning he ever saw, for he feared his lord was mortally wounded."[50] Colonel Hamilton needed to get away from the park. His foot was bleeding and he had no desire to be arrested. He and Lesley returned to the duke's coach, where Clark was waiting.

Clark had just seen Maccartney, "with his arms folded," wearing a melancholy expression, walk by him, through the park gate, out into the road to Kensington. With the light of the rising sun following him down the road, he disappeared. Lesley and Colonel Hamilton arrived. With a hurried explanation, the colonel climbed into the coach and told Clark to drive. They went west to the gravel pits in Kensington, then changed course and headed back toward the city. Clark "was under such a consternation for fear of his lord, that he scarce knew where he drove, till he came to Holborn bridge, and there he stopped the coach, and told the colonel he would drive no further."[51] Colonel Hamilton asked Clark to go into a tavern and order a fire in a private room, which the driver did. After helping the officer out of the carriage, Clark left him and returned to St. James's Square as quickly as he could.

SIX

The Aftermath

ON the night of Sunday, November 16, 1712, southeastern England shook under the force of a tremendous gale: "the high winds . . . blew down severall firr trees . . . and the trees are so heavy that we cannot Stirr Em, with all the strength we can make, so I know not what we shall doe to raise them to their places again."[1] A political storm also followed the duel between Mohun and Hamilton. The weekend had dashed more than trees to the ground: the lives and careers of the two peers had ended in a welter of blood in Hyde Park, and their seconds were now fugitives. Oxford's plans for Hamilton's embassy to France were disrupted. Jacobites like George Lockhart convinced themselves that Hamilton's death set back the cause of a Stuart restoration: "This I know, that His Lordship [Oxford] regretting to a friend of mine, the Duke's death, next day after it happened, told him, that it disordered all their schemes, seeing Great Britain did not affoord a person capable to discharge the trust which was committed to His Grace . . . ; and what other than the Kings restoration coud then be of so very great importance?"[2] Whatever the intent behind Hamilton's embassy, the violently partisan atmosphere of the day ensured that the duel would instantly become a matter of supreme national importance.

The news of the duel quickly spread across the capital. Hardly had the coaches arrived home bearing their grisly burdens than word of the extraordinary affair flew. "Thare was a bad Exsedent hapen'd this morning about 7 a Clock, the Duke of Hambleton and my Lord Mone fought a Dewell in Hey Parke, and Lord Mone Deyed upon the Spott, and the other was Carried home and it is saide Deyed in a littel time after."[3] Swift, at home preparing to begin another day denouncing Lord Oxford's enemies, received the electrifying news a little after eight. His servant rushed excitedly into Swift's chamber with the word: there had been a duel and the duke was wounded. Swift sent the man directly to St. James's Square to inquire after James. When he arrived at Hamilton's door he had to press through a hubbub to speak to Hipsley the porter. Swift's servant saw the truth in Hipsley's face: he "could hardly answer for tears."[4] Hearing his man's report, Swift prepared to venture forth into the cold to comfort his friend the duchess. Although in January he had disliked Elizabeth, he had revised his opinion by November and become a frequent visitor to St. James's Square.[5]

The duchess had first learned about the duel from a servant. She was awakened with the news that her husband's body had arrived. At the front door, Hipsley, in tears, fended off inquisitive sightseers. Upstairs, Elizabeth fell into a paroxysm of rage and grief. Her distress was heightened by the rapidly growing mob outside in the square. The crowd, excitedly exchanging rumors and half-truths, was soon joined by hawkers with the first printed account of the duel. A single sheet describing the morning's events, including phony dialogue ("I see you have been pricked, Sir!") and a false account of the duke's death at home was on the street hours after the duel.[6] The publisher was determined to get the jump on his competitors. Every broadsheet sold for a penny, and within a few hours he could make a tidy profit. Listening to the grubby printers' boys bawling their wares directly beneath her windows was too much for the duchess. With her servants' help she moved to a nearby lodging. It was in this refuge that Swift joined a weeping

Elizabeth. "I never saw so melancholy a Scene For indeed all Reasons for real grief belong to her, nor is it possible for any one to be a greater loser in all regards. She has moved my very soul."[7]

Leaving the square spared the duchess the visits of the surgeons who came to examine her husband's body. Dr. Ronjat, who once had attended James's old enemy King William, arrived to find James fully dressed, laid carefully on his bed. He cut off the duke's clothes and examined his wounds: the severed artery in the arm, the slash in his calf, and the deep wound in the breast. The arm, which Ronjat considered to be the fatal stroke, caused the old man to wonder why no one had thought to apply a tourniquet. It is questionable that a tourniquet would have saved James's life, considering the severity of the thrust to his breast, but Ronjat, in making this conjecture, would not be the last to offer an opinion. There would be other examinations, and plenty of controversy over which wounds were the most deadly—and who inflicted them.

At Lord Mohun's house, John Pennington's coach rolled to a stop before the door, and the servants carried the corpse inside. No crowd gathered about Mohun's doorway. Rumor later said that Elizabeth, Lady Mohun, was as enraged as the Duchess of Hamilton had been, but for different reasons. The servants struggled into the house with Charles's heavy body and laid it upon a bed covered with "a magnificent counterpane," and Lady Mohun was vexed to have such a valuable object ruined by her husband's bloody body.[8]

A surgeon, Mr. La Fage, another French refugee, arrived to examine Mohun's remains. There was little doubt about what had killed him: the downward thrust that had pierced the groin and cut "the great artery." But La Fage was sure that another wound, the one that transfixed him, entering through the right side and exiting above his left hip, would also have been fatal. All that remained to be done was prepare the body for burial.

Witnesses had to be rounded up before a clear picture of what happened in the park could emerge. Both seconds were still at large: they could now be charged with murder and were, moreover, likely to prove the most important witnesses of the affair. The government launched a massive search. Mohun's body had hardly grown cold when a figure in livery turned up at the Bagnio in Long Acre: George Maccartney's servant. He had come to fetch the general's portmanteau. He told the servants at the Bagnio news they had probably already heard: "Lord Mohun was killed and his master would be hanged if he were taken." The general had not paid his servant's wages and the man was taking no chances.[9] Maccartney's disappearance succeeded as if he had planned it before the duel was fought. Some claimed to have seen the general's friend the Duke of Richmond near Hyde Park on the fatal morning—presumably intending to spirit him away from the scene. Maccartney's first stop in his flight was the duke's home near the Thames in Chelsea. If Maccartney walked from Hyde Park to Chelsea, as he probably did, he endured a few anxious moments. He would have passed through the lanes leading down to the river at a time when many people were just beginning their day. The roads leading to the city were filling with London-bound travelers. Peddlers and vagabonds made their daily tramp along the roads, bending under their burdens and hoping for a successful day cadging pennies from the quality. Travelers might notice a well-dressed gentleman on foot, his waistcoat smeared with blood. Nevertheless, Maccartney reached the Duke of Richmond's. He now dropped from sight for days, despite the uproar caused by his escape.

Maccartney's secret arrival at Richmond's home came just as Mr. Woodward, a surgeon, received a call to dress a wounded man at a tavern called the Half Moon in Cheapside. Cheapside, a bustling commercial district with no pretensions to elegance, was a good place for a gentleman on the run from the law. There was little chance that a fugitive would be recognized on the street. Plenty of housekeepers accepted lodgers with no questions asked—if they paid their rent. London's surgeons were uncommonly busy on the third weekend of November, but Woodward had no idea who his new customer might be. At the Half Moon, he was shown into a private room. There he met a man with a wounded foot who refused to give his name or explain how he came by his injury. Obviously, the wound, in the instep of the right foot, had been caused by a sword. The leather shoe and stocking were neatly sliced through. But the victim said nothing about what had happened, and Woodward, in the Cheapside manner, did not press for answers. His fee assuaged his curiosity. Gentlemen got themselves into scrapes all the time; this was a minor injury, and if somewhere in town there was someone with a worse one, well, that was some other surgeon's business. Woodward bandaged the cut, collected his money, and left.[10]

Colonel Hamilton, like Maccartney, went into hiding as soon as he could. Only a few friends of the duke's knew where he might be found. The duke's London agent had a hand in protecting him from immediate capture. Though he received visitors, his hiding place remained unknown for almost a week. George Lockhart was one of those who spoke with him, and there were others, people closely connected with the duke's family, and quite possibly with the government as well.[11]

Unlike Maccartney, whose fate if captured was clear, Hamilton was on friendly terms with the ministry. He might negotiate a surrender. As a Tory officer in good standing, Hamilton was fairly placed. Yet he stood in peril: the coroner of Middlesex, Mr. Lo, had already begun an inquest into the duel. Of course, a finding of willful murder would be the result. However exalted the victims, the coroner must observe the forms of the law. It was Lo's duty to assemble a jury of citizens and investigate the deaths. The inquest's origins went far back to the Middle Ages, but it remained a valuable means of establishing the facts surrounding violent death. The coroner was empowered to take depositions on oath from witnesses, and Lo's work provided the first real information the authorities gathered about the duel. While the inquest could not make criminal indictments, a grand jury would follow its lead. When the jury brought in a finding of murder by the seconds (as the law obliged in any fatal duel), the legal clock would begin ticking. After a grand jury indictment would come outlawry if the seconds remained at large. Outlawry, if not reversed, meant exile or death. Mr. Lo had begun his work on the day of the duel, and by the morning of Tuesday the eighteenth he had taken a variety of depositions from witnesses.[12] The jury would render a verdict soon. If Hamilton were to make a deal, he must act quickly.

The ministry wanted to get to the bottom of the duel as much as the coroner. As Oxford had already said, the duke's death had derailed the government's plans. The duel might have arisen from a plot orchestrated by Whigs determined to prevent an Anglo-French rapprochement—or some other rapprochement, perhaps with the man at Saint-Germain calling himself James III. Francis Lee's letter, warning of a plot afoot among "the great ones of the earth" must have leaped to mind the moment the Lord Treasurer heard the news from Hyde Park. The government assembled a cabinet committee to examine as many witnesses as could be found.

On Tuesday the eighteenth, in the presence of the Attorney and Solicitor Generals, a group of the most important politicians in Britain met at the Cockpit. The Cockpit, a house belonging to the Crown on the site of a former cockpit between Whitehall and St. James's Park, resembled its namesake only in that more than a few vicious political battles had taken place within its walls. This was the place, for example, where the Union treaty between Scotland and England had been negotiated. In 1712 it was a comfortable establishment reserved for the use of the Queen's ministers, who assembled there for meetings and political strategy sessions.

Both Lord Oxford and Secretary Bolingbroke were present, as was the other Secretary of State, Lord Dartmouth;* the Earl of Strafford; the Lords Steward, Chamberlain, and Keeper; and the President of the Council. The room was tense; Hamilton's death

---

* In this period there were two Secretaries of State, one for the Northern Department and one for the Southern Department, each formally responsible for affairs relating to their half of Europe as well as domestic matters. As with most early modern administrative practices, the reality was more complicated; their duties often overlapped, and ambitious Secretaries competed for influence, frequently poaching upon their colleagues' turf.

had been a serious blow. While many of the men around the table had disliked the duke, he had been an important man. A variety of factors conditioned the cabinet's response to his passing. His own political significance and the part he had played in the ministry's plans for the peace were obvious. But there were other, more subtle issues in play. The leading players in the government, Oxford and Bolingbroke, once the Castor and Pollux of Toryism, were now deadly rivals. Bolingbroke had been excluded from many of the negotiations for peace despite his official position as Secretary of State. He was determined to seize every advantage in his fight with the Lord Treasurer. The death of the Duke of Hamilton might give him a stick with which to beat Oxford. Oxford distrusted the younger man's mercurial temper and would have much preferred a world without such an irritating presence. Other members of the cabinet vacillated between the two, each pursuing his own interests.

Oxford and Bolingbroke sat with their cabinet colleagues before a roaring fire and began to question witnesses. The first man to appear was the coroner, Lo, who brought his depositions. He read through the evidence he had already gathered. The council's messengers produced a crowd of witnesses, ranging from the duke's lawyer, who testified about the meeting at Mr. Orlebar's the previous Thursday, to John Nicholson, wheelbarrow man. Most of the witnesses examined were humble people: tavern keepers, barmen, and others with whom Mohun and Hamilton dealt in their final days. The witnesses' accounts agreed on most points: the two peers had fought viciously and briefly, while the seconds had been much less active—some were unsure whether they had fought at all. Those who actually saw the lords fight offered similar stories, and all but Pennington, the coachman, seemed certain about what they had seen. Nevertheless, there were no material differences between his story and the others.

After several hours of testimony, the lords adjourned, having heard from all the eyewitnesses except the seconds. The origins of the duel remained a mystery. Why exactly had the peers quarreled?

Was the incident in Chancery Lane all there was to the story, or was there more to it? From the testimony of those present at Orlebar's it seemed as though Mohun had affronted Hamilton by questioning the duke's "truth and justice." And yet it was Mohun, through his second, Maccartney, who evidently had issued the challenge. Ordinarily, Hamilton, the injured party, would have challenged his accuser. Was the duke maneuvered into accepting the challenge as part of a conspiracy to derail the peace treaty? Mohun and Maccartney had reputations as swaggering bullies, deeply partisan Whigs, and clients of the Duke of Marlborough, the greatest enemy of the peace in the kingdom. Was it a coincidence that Marlborough and his duchess were leaving Britain very soon?

Without the testimony of the seconds, getting to the bottom of the duel would be impossible. Though both men had vanished, by Thursday the twentieth Oxford apparently was negotiating Colonel Hamilton's surrender. The colonel might hope for lenient treatment if he surrendered before he was captured. The government might even turn him to some account. His version of events—that of the only eyewitness of any standing—would carry the most weight with a public clamoring for information. Before Friday the colonel and Oxford reached an understanding. That morning the Lord Treasurer received a signed statement from Hamilton and a promise that he would surrender later in the day. The colonel confirmed all the government's darkest suspicions: this was no ordinary affair of honor. Hamilton

> declares that when the Duke of Hamilton, Lord Mohun, and Macartney came to the place agreed on for them to fight, the Duke and Lord Mohun had no sooner drawn their swords than Macartney drew his, as Colonel Hamilton did the same, and that Macartney immediately pushed at the Colonel, and he striking down Macartney's sword, by which he received a wound in his right leg, closed with Macartney and took his sword from him, by which time Lord Mohun was down on the ground and His Grace upon him. The Colonel, the better to help the Duke up, flung both swords upon

the ground, and he helping his Grace to recover with his Grace's back to his face; his head being to the right of the duke's head, Macartney came with a sword in his hand, and gave a thrust into the duke's left breast, which he believes was his mortal wound, the Duke at the same time saying, I am wounded, and whilst the said Colonel Hamilton was helping him Macartney escaped.[13]

This was no duel; this was murder. Maccartney had violated the rules of gentlemanly behavior: killing in the name of honor was acceptable, but seconds did not run through helpless victims as they lay wounded on the field. Oxford quickly rounded up the available members of the investigating committee, and another meeting took place at the Cockpit.

The Lord Keeper acted as chairman while Oxford and Bolingbroke discreetly kept themselves out of the forefront. The Lord Keeper instructed Colonel Hamilton to tell what had happened the previous Saturday between Mohun and his patron, "and that he might say nothing that could hurt himself desired him to confine himself to the transactions of Saturday." The colonel was thereby warned that his statement could be used against him in a later trial. Hamilton told how the duke rousted him from bed early Saturday, and hustled him, without a sword, into a coach. Before he knew what was happening, he and the duke were in Hyde Park facing Mohun and Maccartney. Hamilton repeated, in more detail, what he had claimed in his earlier statement: Maccartney had given the duke the coup de grâce while Hamilton, disarmed, was attempting to aid his friend.

The colonel's story differed from those provided by the other witnesses: none of their testimony described Maccartney's treachery. Even Morris, the groom who was only a few yards from the peers as they fought, gave Hamilton no support. The colonel may have been telling the truth, for once both lords were down, the attention of the witnesses had probably focused upon them rather than the seconds. But Hamilton had made no effort to prevent Maccartney's unhurried departure, neither pursuing him nor calling to anyone to pursue him. When George Lockhart asked him why he had done nothing, he responded, "he cou'd not apprehend him [Maccartney] himself, for the Duke was so lame and faint with the loss of blood, he wou'd have tumbled down if he had not supported him. And when people came up, he was so confusd and in such a consternation and withal so apprehensive of what woud befall himself, after the death of two such great men, that he did not know what he was doing, and after two of the duke's servants came up to take care of his Grace's body, thought nothing but getting off with himself."[14] No doubt Colonel Hamilton was frightened, but people less biased than Lockhart found his explanation a curious one. Even the Queen, no friend of General Maccartney's, was puzzled by Hamilton's behavior.[15] Some, however, preferred his account, for by accusing the general of murdering the duke, Hamilton gave the Tory government aid and comfort. There may have been a conspiracy. But whether or not the Whigs contrived to kill the duke, Hamilton's charge gave the Tories a far stronger case to make against them.

Did Colonel Hamilton's story emerge from his negotiations with Oxford? Robert Harley, Earl of Oxford, a sinuous politician himself, was capable of countering the Whigs with schemes of his own. Hamilton's charge was widely believed, and it gave the ministry further leverage in the war against its enemies. The charge also had the effect of redoubling the hunt for Maccartney. While Hamilton was sent to Newgate until his trial, the Queen issued a proclamation for the general's arrest. The government offered £500 for his capture, and the Duchess of Hamilton added £200. The reward was huge, enough for a family to live comfortably on for a decade or more.[16] Tips poured in with assurances that the general's capture could easily be arranged in return for a small advance on the reward. A gentlewoman solemnly assured a correspondent that Maccartney escaped "through a common sewer," and a Tory paper gave a description for bounty hunters: "He is a well-set, middle-sized man, of a dark, ruddy complexion, dark eyes, dark eye-brows, has a wide mouth and good teeth, generally wearing a black peruke, but of late hath appear'd in woman's cloaths, and other disguises."[17] Even the Queen repeated rumors: "She told me that Mackartney was seen crossing [the river Thames] to Putney two days ago," wrote her doctor.[18]

The search for the fugitive ranged across the kingdom, but many expected that he would make for Ireland. "We here [hear] Macartney is gone over to Ireland," wrote Swift in December.[19] In mid-December Lord Buckley sent a long, detailed account of his pursuit of a mysterious stranger in Anglesey, Wales, a man he was certain was the general; "he behaved himself very odly shifting his lodgings every night; he had two periwigs, a fair and a black one, wich latter he wore, when the packet went off for Dublin he would not venture aboard it with the rest of ye passengers, but hired a boat for himself." A local report clinched the matter. The stranger sat in the chimney corner of the inn one cold night when a pair of guests struck up a conversation mentioning "the murder of the Duke of Hamilton, whereupon he struck his breast in a great passion and fetched a most dismal groan."[20] This melodramatic behavior was sufficient to convince Buckley that he was near to capturing his man. But George Maccartney did not indulge in sentimental breast-beating. More like the general was the character reported under arrest in the Isle of Man in February: when the authorities arrived to take him into custody, they found on him four loaded pistols and bank notes worth £800.[21]

One quick-thinking gentleman turned the manhunt to his own advantage. Set upon by a gang of highwaymen in the country, he let slip that he was the famous General Maccartney. Realizing that such a prize was valuable, the robbers hauled their victim before the first justice of the peace they could find. A £700 reward was considerably more than they would make robbing the occasional coach or passing gentleman. The supposed fugitive then revealed himself to be someone else as soon as they were before the justice. The thieves soon resided in the county jail awaiting trial for highway robbery.[22] In fact, most of the attention directed toward Ireland and wandering strangers was misplaced, for, thanks to his friend the Duke of Richmond, Maccartney escaped to the Low Countries.[23]

Despite continued accounts of his capture and near capture, the next solid information about Maccartney's whereabouts came early in the New Year: he had arrived safely in the Low Countries and was living in Holland. On January 4 Swift wrote his friend Esther Johnson ("Stella"), "Lady Mountjoy told me that Maccartney was got safe out of our clutches, for she had spoke with one who had a letter from him from Holland; others say the same thing. Tis hard such a dog should escape."[24] By the spring of 1713 Maccartney's presence in the Netherlands was public knowledge; he published his own account of the duel in late March or early April. Swift noted its appearance on April 7: "Here is a letter printed in Macartney's name vindicating himself from the murder of Duke Hamilton. I must give some hints to have it answered; tis full of lyes and will give an opportunity of exposing that party."[25]

Maccartney's entry into the propaganda war that broke out after the duel was rather late, for it had raged furiously since the very first hours after the fight, and its ferocity mimicked that of the struggle between the two lords themselves. Ever since the government had loosed its control over the press following the expiration of the Licensing Act in 1695, cheap broadsides, newspapers, and pamphlets had become one of the principal venues in which the daily war between Whig and Tory was fought. Censoring everything published had become impossible even before the act expired: there were too many presses and too many opportunities to smuggle literature in from abroad. Rather than continue the futile struggle, politicians adopted a new strategy: they commissioned propaganda of their own. Whig ministries subsidized Whig newspapers and Whig writers; Tories did the same. Jonathan Swift's attacks upon Marlborough proved just how effective the new methods could be, and success encouraged imitators. By the

1710s the political press was huge and growing rapidly. Coffee-houses and taverns served as clearinghouses for this information; most of them provided copies of the latest papers for their clientele. Customers spent hours passing the tattered papers from hand to hand, commenting on their contents and compounding their lies with their own brew of rumor and half-truth. Some political literature was more or less accurate, but it was more often neither fair nor truthful, and commonly downright scurrilous: Mary Delarivière Manley, for example, produced thinly disguised allegories in which Whig stalwarts were accused of every imaginable vice, although her specialty was salacious commentary upon her victim's sex lives. Every major incident in public life and many minor ones provoked an outpouring of printed commentary given a particular spin by one side or the other—or larded with "facts" made up for the worthy purpose of doing down the opposition and appealing to the prejudices of the readership.

The news of the most sensational duel to have taken place in Britain in decades set presses everywhere to work. Printers saw an opportunity to make both political points and large profits, and a stream of accounts poured from the press on an almost daily basis. The story presented in the first printed accounts were relatively unbiased: the first description, despite its errors and inventions, was nonpartisan, as were several other accounts. The lord mayor ordered the publication of a transcript of Colonel Hamilton's trial that was substantially correct in its details.[26] But after Hamilton accused Maccartney of the duke's murder, the partisan press went to work. One of the most virulent Tory papers of the day, the *Post Boy*, gave credence to almost every anti-Whig rumor bandied about in the confused days following the duel. The Duchess of Hamilton was herself closely associated with the editor of the paper, and the journal reflected the violence of her views. *The Examiner* was no less certain of Maccartney's villainy. "I cannot but observe," wrote the editor, "that the Whig-party are now resuming their Old Way of Management, wherein We never can pretend to be their Match. They have try'd all other Methods in vain, and return with fresh Vigour to their last Expedient of Murder." Noting that Marlborough had set a precedent for "political duels"—and had used Mohun to carry a challenge to Lord Poulett—the journalist worked himself up to his peroration, focusing upon "the Bloody Tragedy of *Saturday* last, where the two most ABANDONED WRETCHES that ever infested this Island, I mean the Lord *Mohun* and *Maccartney conspired* and perfected the *Murder* of one the greatest among Her Majesty's Subjects."[27] Other papers, such as the *Evening Post*, were less strident but still sympathetic to the Tory line, and gave the story tremendous play; developments in the case completely dominated the front page of the *Post* for several issues. This was extremely unusual; ordinarily the most prominent place went to foreign news—domestic affairs rarely made the first of the paper's three pages at all.

The Whigs responded. Swift had a worthy opponent in Daniel Defoe, who probably wrote *A Strict Enquiry into the Circumstances of a Late Duel*. This pamphlet, which argued that the Tories had manufactured a "sham plot" for political gain, presented itself as a reasoned examination of the case, designed to clear away the fog of bias in the Tory accounts. "The duel which was lately unhappily fought between a certain Duke, and a lord, has not been more strange in its circumstances, than are the unaccountable Notions which the abused common people have had put into their heads about it."[28] But Defoe lied when he said that Hamilton had issued the challenge. If an unnamed "certain servant" were allowed to testify, he claimed, readers would see that Hamilton had been the aggressor. Defoe followed this with an attack on Hamilton's character: the duke was "a tryed man, [who] had on many such occasions given eminent proof of a fire in his temper not easy to be dealt with."[29]

For all of the reams of paper devoted to the battle, there is little evidence that the accounts of either side did much to sway public opinion: most Tories took Colonel Hamilton's story as gospel, while Whigs denounced it as a "sham plot." The propaganda battle did, however, illustrate the depth of political divisions in Britain. The reclusive Jacobite antiquary Thomas Hearne, for example, eagerly adopted Swift's version of the duel from the comfort of his Oxford study: Maccartney—"a bloudy, ill man"— was the villain. "The whiggs appear glad at the duke's death, and declare that they are sorry for the death of Mohun, whom they cry up for a saint, tho' he was the greatest debauchee and bully of the age."[30] Thomas Burnet, on the other hand, a son of the Whig Bishop of Salisbury, got his account of the duel from the Duke of Richmond at Tom's Coffee House. His opinion of the colonel's accusation against Maccartney was quite different: "This oath is wondrous strange and I think a true picture of a ———— man I would not keep company with."[31] Perhaps Lord Chesterfield's opinion, rendered nearly fifty years later, was the more likely: as for the charge that Maccartney "murdered Duke Hamilton; nothing is falser, for though Maccartney was capable of the vilest actions, he was guiltless of that."[32]

Both seconds, Colonel Hamilton and Maccartney, were subject to such vilification on either side that they tried to defend themselves. The colonel made his case public first, at his trial. The Middlesex Grand Jury charged the colonel with murder, and the trial was scheduled for Thursday, December 11, at the Old Bailey. The trial was the first test of strength between the surviving families, and both widows were determined to succeed. Lady Mohun wanted a harsh punishment, while the duchess was committed to an acquittal. If Lady Mohun was willing to spend her money to see Hamilton hanged, the Duchess of Hamilton worked to protect him. She took the lead in lining up character witnesses for the colonel and, true to form, pursued her goal with a passionate intensity that carried her beyond prudence. Her husband's brother the Earl of Orkney reported that Elizabeth had alienated the Duke of Roxburghe, an important Scottish aristocrat. She had badgered him to testify on Hamilton's behalf, despite his protests that he did not know the colonel at all. Rebuffed, the duchess told Orkney that she intended to have Roxburghe pilloried in the *Post Boy*.[33] Orkney talked her out of her intention, but keeping Elizabeth under control was difficult.

After a twenty-four-hour delay, the trial opened on Friday the twelfth, in a packed courtroom. Public interest had been heightened by the vituperous exchange of charges between Whigs and Tories in the press, and now at last people would have a chance to hear testimony given under oath. Colonel John Hamilton stood before the bar of the court and heard the indictments as they were read to him and an attentive jury: he stood accused of "comforting, aiding, abetting, and assisting" in two murders: those of Charles, Lord Mohun, and James, Duke of Hamilton. As a second in a fatal duel, Hamilton was equally responsible for the deaths of both men: thus the double indictment.

The first witness was Rhys Williams. He recounted the story of Lord Mohun's meeting at Mr. Orlebar's chambers and all that followed. Then came a parade of witnesses, most of whom had already testified at the coroner's inquest or before the privy councillors, or both. There were, on the whole, no surprises in the testimony, but the most uncomfortable moment for the Whigs came when Williams testified to Mohun and Maccartney's stop at Marlborough House on Friday, November 14. Nothing further was said about this visit to the former Captain General, but many in the courtroom would have drawn their own conclusions. No doubt to the great disappointment of the spectators, the colonel himself gave very little satisfaction when he took the stand in his own defense. Rather than repeat his testimony about General Maccartney's role in the duel—information that was irrelevant to the case—Hamilton confined himself to his own part in the affair. He maintained that when the duke came for him on November 15 he had no idea that a duel was in the offing: "he knew not anything of the matter 'till he came into the field." Did he tell the truth? Hamilton had accompanied the duke on his visit to the

Rose Tavern the evening before the duel, when the meeting was arranged. It is hard to imagine that he knew nothing of the impending fight. But there was no positive evidence to the contrary. The barman who had served Mohun and Hamilton testified only that the duke had not been alone. He could not identify the colonel.

After Hamilton testified, a long line of Scots noblemen took the stand to vouch for the defendant's character. They "all gave him the character of a very Honest, Gallant, Inoffensive Man." Evidently the duchess had done her work. Bringing up the rear in this parade of virtue was the prosecutor himself, who summed up the case for the jury. The jurors spent very little time arriving at their verdict: guilty of the lesser charge of manslaughter. Because there was no convincing proof that Hamilton had known of the duel in advance, he could not be guilty of premeditation, which saved him from the harsher penalties of murder. As was the form of the day, the jury's foreman announced the verdict and, before sentence was passed, the colonel pleaded for benefit of clergy.[34] The judge granted Hamilton's plea, and he walked from the court a free man.[35]

The colonel's real trial was in the press and among the public. Testimonials from Scots peers carried very little weight with London society. The key charge against Hamilton in the court of public opinion was that he lied about Maccartney's role in the duel. He had behaved dishonorably. A gentleman's honor was more valuable than life itself, as the deaths of the Duke of Hamilton and Lord Mohun so clearly demonstrated. Partisan though they were, Whig accusations about Hamilton's dishonorable behavior stung. By the end of December doubts about the colonel's story had begun to spread, prompting him to publish a letter in the *Post Boy* reaffirming his charges against Maccartney. This made the Queen "wonder that it had not been done before, he having sworn it, soon after the duke was killed."[36] But the opposition would not let Hamilton rest; a Tory correspondent wrote that

Lord "Southerland" (probably the Junto Whig Lord Sunderland) "hath confronted that Account you had in the *Post Boy* given by Col. Hamilton."[37]

The colonel, at least, had the benefit of a sympathetic government and the advantage of a London base from which to defend himself. George Maccartney had neither. His successful escape to Holland rendered him safe from capture and trial. He could laugh at the futile address of the Scots nobility to the Queen calling upon her to pursue his extradition—it could have no effect. There was nothing the government could do. But if the general's body was safe in exile, his character was exposed from every side. George Maccartney had an evil reputation to begin with, and his involvement in the duel increased it. Nevertheless, as a gentleman and an officer, he must vindicate his honor. Very few people, even the most partisan Whigs, could plausibly assert that he had led a blameless life. There was a parson's widow who could testify eloquently to the contrary. His wife and family, despoiled of their fortune, could add volume to the chorus. Comrades-in-arms had watched Maccartney peculate his way across Europe at the expense of his regiment. Not surprisingly, the efforts of Whig propagandists to burnish the general's image failed. Defoe feebly referred to his subject as "a man of honor" on several occasions, without being able to specify how the appellation fit. Only the Whig John Oldmixon threw caution (and veracity) to the winds, describing Maccartney as "so ingenious, so delightful, and so inoffensive a man."[38] Queen Anne was extremely vexed with her former Whig Lord Chancellor, Lord Cowper: "she said that she saw he [Cowper] was in the Party, by his vindication of Mackartney" when he presumed to question Hamilton's account of the duel. His legalistic quibbles, she contended, could not efface the general's reputation.[39]

Beyond the central charge made by Colonel Hamilton, a host of other rumors, soon converted into solid fact by constant circulation, sprang into being as the partisan battle raged. "Tis said that

Mackerty had five hundred pounds given him the morning he fought the duel, the Lord have mercy upon us." "I hear from all hands of the rage of the party about Mackartney's villainy. It is said public collections are made for his support. This looks as though there was a combination of assassins." Maccartney was even accused of having once offered to assassinate his patron the Duke of Marlborough.[40]

These charges threatened to destroy Maccartney's honor, and they inspired his partisans to produce pamphlets in his defense. Finally, in February 1713, his own defense appeared: *A Letter From Mr. Maccartney to a Friend of His in London.* This account, which says nothing whatever about the fight in Hyde Park, gives Maccartney's version of events leading up to the duel. In it the general takes on the role of peacemaker, putting a generous construction upon Lord Mohun's meeting with the duke at Orlebar's: "My lord, says I, everybody knows those harsh and warm expressions are not unusual among lawyers and sometimes their clients, for I can't but think that if the duke meant to affront your lordship, he should have spoken more directly." The next morning, Friday, November 14, he urged his friend not to be hasty in challenging Hamilton: "Says I, my lord, you are . . . come, I hope, to forbid your message, for to tell you truly . . . in my opinion this message is not absolutely necessary."[41] Although George's memory of his conversations with Lord Mohun was precise, he omitted important details from his account: his visit with Lord Mohun to Marlborough House; his trip to the Bagnio; his dining partners at the Queen's Arms, and the number of times he called at the duke's house in St. James's Square. Maccartney's account hardly answered the charges leveled against him, but the issue was less the production of a believable defense than an assertion of the general's honor. Society's demands were simple: for men like Maccartney, as well as Colonel Hamilton and, for that matter, their principals in the duel, appearances were still crucial; one's behavior was a different matter. George Maccartney was treated as a "man of honor" because he maintained the façade society required.

In this case, the general benefited from a standard of behavior that was under siege. Everyone knew that he was in fact a dangerous thug—and his political opponents used his obvious character flaws as evidence of the hollowness of his claim to honor. In effect, the vicious partisanship of the day made the sort of cheerful hypocrisy about public behavior, honor, and morality so common in the days of Mohun and Maccartney's parents increasingly difficult to sustain. For the third Lord Mohun, or contemporaries such as the libertine Earl of Rochester, honor was a private attribute, subject to the judgment of private persons: gentlemen at court, for example, assessing the behavior of their fellows, decided what was acceptable and what not—or, more accurately, which *forms* were acceptable and which not. Such assessments were intimate, the product of direct interaction among the "better sort." Hypocrisy was a crucial part of this social system, for it acted as the veil behind which competition and the less attractive aspects of human nature operated. But this cozy world was changing. Now, thanks to the rise of a partisan press and constant political warfare in a divided society, hypocrisy was becoming less a social lubricant than a charge to hurl at one's enemies. The George Maccartneys of the world found themselves held up for public inspection and, indeed, condemnation, by the likes of Jonathan Swift—a bog-trotting Irish parson. Colonel John Hamilton, connected to Scotland's most noble house, found himself abused and derided by a nobody called Defoe—a bankrupt merchant and tile manufacturer who scribbled lies to avoid starvation. That Maccartney and Hamilton were no match for Swift and Defoe is hardly surprising: the new game was played by rules that favored the scribblers. But it is also evident from both seconds' attempts to present their own versions of the duel to the public that they were adapting to the changes taking place around them, as their deceased friends Lord Mohun and the Duke of Hamilton had not done. At last, it had become apparent that the pen really *was* mightier than the sword.

Both peers left their widows to learn the lessons they themselves had missed. Yet the Elizabeths were apt, and determined, pupils. Despite unhappy marriages, after the duel they strove to defend their husbands' social and financial legacies. Both were still in their thirties, and neither could be dismissed as weakwilled or easily moved. The duchess had given ample evidence of her strong opinions all her life and had been unrelenting in her campaign to prove Colonel Hamilton's innocence.[42] Lady Orkney, whom Elizabeth despised, was scandalized by her sister-in-law's temper in the weeks following the duel. The duchess "is all storme and so warm in her expressions unfit for melancholy or true grief, that I am in a wonder every time I see her and pity the poor young ladyes her daughters if they are to be bred up by her, who can give them an example but il-judged storm and passion and resentment . . . in short I see it is beyond all I ever heard of."[43] Even Swift, who had much less cause to resent the duchess, made the same complaint. For her part, Duchess Elizabeth had been at odds with her husband's family for years: "for your family I'm sure those of it that don't care for me have not ye gift of justice in 'em," she wrote in 1705. In 1710 she told James, "I must beg you'l not hearken too much to your owne family who have I must say ever been too fond of themselves and too little of you."[44]

Duchess Elizabeth's unpopularity with her Scottish relatives reflected her own difficult personality, but it was also based upon her consistent refusal to defer to the dictates of her mother-in-law, and especially to the views of her husband's brothers. Now that the duke had gone, and while her son was still a minor, the duchess intended to live as she chose. Her life would be centered in London, where she could indulge in lacerating court gossip and enjoy the attentions of brilliant social climbers like Jonathan Swift and Alexander Pope. There would be no more trips to the pompous misery of Hamilton Palace, no more listening to lectures from the hectoring old duchess. Duchess Anne would not have been amused by the note written by Elizabeth's secretary to Pope in June 1717: "Sir, My Lady Dutchess being drunk at this present & not able to write her self has commanded me to acquaint you that there is to be musick on the water on Thursday next; therefore desires you to be that evening at her house."[45] The new Dowager Duchess of Hamilton, as Elizabeth had become, had two principal goals in life: to stay as far away from Scotland as possible, and to pursue her husband's legal battles against the estate of Lord Mohun.

Waging war against the Mohun estate pitted the duchess against a formidable opponent: Elizabeth Griffith, née Lawrence, Baroness Mohun since the spring of 1711. Lady Elizabeth had been raised at court; her father, Sir Thomas Lawrence, had served every monarch from Charles II as a personal physician, and had avoided offending the partisan politicians determined to fill every post at court with one of their creatures. "I have been plagued this morning with sollicitors," wrote Swift in March 1712, "and with no body more than . . . Dr. Friend; who must need have to gett old Dr. Lawrence the Physician Genrll turned out and himself in. He has argued with me so long upon the reasonableness of it, that I am fully convinced it is very unreasonable."[46] Given his daughter's rabid Whig sympathies and connections with the Marlborough and Mohun clans, the doctor's survival must be taken as evidence of an effective bedside manner.

Lady Mohun herself was a tough woman. She was no beauty (Mrs. Manley described her as "forbidding, not to say frightful"), but she was endowed with charm.[47] Her marriage to Lord Mohun lifted her far above her modest origins. Her husband's income was ample, and suddenly shopkeepers, noting a whiff of solvency in the air, were respectful and attentive. Her rise had been almost miraculous, but the miracle was a self-generated one.

How much did Lady Mohun know about her husband's affairs? It is unlikely that Charles confided in her—though it is possible that she had her own informants. Charles's death gave her control over the estate—she had seen to that, presiding over the creation of a new will immediately after their marriage. There could be no doubt that she would have to fight to preserve her gains against a powerful array of opponents. Charles's death had catapulted her, without warning, into the forefront of his struggle. She was determined to defend her station in life, and the income that went with it, regardless of the challenges ahead.

On November 25, 1712, Lady Mohun bundled her husband into his grave under the floor of St. Martin-in-the-Fields—the same church in which his father, also killed in a duel, lay.* She then prepared to ward off the inevitable assault upon her property. Particularly vexing was the case of Lord Mohun's daughter. Unfortunately also named Elizabeth—clearly one of the most popular female names of the period—young Mistress Mohun was born to Charlotte, the first Lady Mohun. Though only about eighteen at her father's death, young Elizabeth found, like most women in the family, that bearing the Mohun name was a heavy burden.[49] Her parents' marriage had disintegrated while she was still an infant, and Charles had abandoned her to the care of her Orby grandparents. Lord Mohun paid little attention to his daughter over the years. Convinced that she was fathered by one of Charlotte's lovers, he referred to her as his "pretended daughter." According to the second Lady Mohun, after young Elizabeth's birth Lord Mohun "cou'd never be perswaded to lye in the same house with her [Lady Charlotte]." Moreover, continued the adamant peeress, the young woman did not even resemble her alleged father. "I never saw the young lady, so that I can say nothing of her likeness, but those who have, that have neither prejudice to her nor partiallity to me, have sworn there was never two faces more unlike."[50]

Shortly after his second marriage, Charles made a new will at his wife's urging. An attorney named William Peisly drafted a new document on Lord Mohun's instructions, one that left nearly his

---

* Mohun was buried near his father; his final resting place remains unknown because the church was completely remodeled from 1722 to 1726.[48]

entire estate to his new wife. His feelings about the younger Elizabeth had not changed. When Peisly brought a fair copy of the document to Charles for his inspection, Charles was annoyed to discover that Elizabeth was not described as "my pretended daughter." This was a deliberate move on Peisly's part, because, he told Mohun, she was, as he had heard, born "in lawfull wedlocke," and therefore it would be a reflection upon his honor, to which "he [Mohun] replied with some warmth he knew what he did" and ordered the phrase restored.[51] Elizabeth received a legacy of £1,000 from her father and nothing more.[52]

With the support of her grandparents—who had already been beaten once in legal combat with Lord Mohun—Elizabeth decided to challenge the will. One thousand pounds was a handsome legacy for a bastard child, but if, as she maintained, she was really Mohun's daughter, it was scandalously inadequate. Such a

22. The old church of St. Martin-in-the-Fields,
where Mohun was buried

sum guaranteed that Elizabeth would be unable to marry well; as the daughter of a peer, custom demanded that she receive much more. Lord Mohun's will condemned her either to spinsterhood, eking out a living on the £40 or £50 a year her legacy might earn in interest, or to marriage to an impoverished gentleman or someone below her rank (a tradesman or petty merchant). The prospect was unpleasant. Her father's estate—discounting the load of debt it carried—was worth well over £100,000, and Lady Mohun intended to hang on to as much of it as possible for herself and her own daughters.[53]

For the second generation, Elizabeth could argue, the Macclesfield estate had been hijacked by usurpers.

Elizabeth and the Orbys launched their case upon the sluggish waters of the Court of Chancery in January 1713. The plaintiff first refused to accept the very existence of a will, but then argued that if a will did exist, she "hath great reason to suspect and believe that he [Lord Mohun] was by some sinister contrivances drawne to execute the same when he was intoxicated with wine or other strong liquors." Lady Mohun's answer relied upon the testimony of William Peisly, who had drawn the document. Charles was not drunk when he made the will, but Peisly did admit that the circumstances were somewhat unusual. First there had been the debate between Mohun and Peisly about Elizabeth's legitimacy. Then Mohun had insisted that no clerk be allowed to make the final copy, "for he would have it kept very secrett."

Mohun's insistence on secrecy hints at the force of Peisly's comments about asserting his daughter's illegitimacy: Charles evidently wanted her status known after his death rather than before it. In this way Mohun could escape the obloquy of cuckoldry, at least in life. Charles really did believe that Elizabeth was not his daughter; his first wife's conduct gave him every reason for suspicion. Even if he had been drunk when he made the document, the sense of the will represented his wishes. Nevertheless,

Lady Mohun did play a role in making this particular will, and she stood to profit from the disinheritance of Mohun's daughter. On the morning when Peisly returned to Lord Mohun's house with the final copy of the will for signature, he found the couple in Lady Elizabeth's dressing room, shortly after they had risen, at about eleven. Mohun signed, and the witnesses were his step-daughter, Elizabeth (yet another) Griffith, Peisly, and Elizabeth Bamford, a friend of Lady Mohun's. After everyone signed the paper, the lawyer asked who should receive it. "Who hath most right to it?" Mohun snapped. "Pray give it to my wife." Peisly left, two guineas clinking in his purse, and heard no more about the matter until young Elizabeth Mohun surfaced with her claims of fraud.[54]

Mistress Mohun's charges were flimsy. Lord Mohun's will appeared to be genuine, and during his life he had demonstrated his lack of interest in his daughter's fate. But Lady Mohun was in a vulnerable position. Her enemies included powerful individuals who were prepared to use Elizabeth Mohun for their own purposes. Lady Mohun would have to deploy every one of her wiles to avoid disaster. She had sympathy from no one in government but could rely on the support of some of the ministry's enemies. The Duke of Richmond lent her money, and she relied most heavily upon the Duchess of Marlborough, whose generosity was motivated less by affection for the widow and her cloying letters than by a desire to annoy the Earl of Oxford. "Heaven can be my witness," wrote Elizabeth to the duchess in January 1713, asking for a £400 loan, "I have no prospect or thought of any joy now on earth but the continuation of your friendship."[55] In June she asked for another £1,000, and at about the same time she pleaded with Duchess Sarah to intervene on her behalf with her creditors. Soon afterward Elizabeth asked for no less than £10,000. Sarah grew weary of these wheedling letters very quickly and replied that no one, not even she, had such a sum lying about. Sarah was scandalized by Elizabeth's treatment of her stepdaughter. The duchess took Lady

Mohun to task for refusing to settle any money upon the younger Elizabeth. The baroness defended herself against this charge in her most pitiful style: "for the young lady, I am not surprized she meets with compassion and charity, for her case is indeed very melancholy, and may deserve the pitty of those she has not distressed, and had I not experienced the fatal consequence of her persecution, I believe I shou'd not have been the last to relieve her . . . I have hardly ever known a mean in joy or grief, all was exquisit, with this difference: the happiness was short, the pain will last forever."[56] However plaintive Lady Mohun could be, once the duchess set her mind against her, there was no recovery. Within a year Elizabeth was reduced to using her daughter as a mediator, for Sarah refused to answer Lady Mohun's letters.[57]

Lady Mohun's charms were lavished in the most unlikely places. A distant cousin, Mr. Coke, Vice Chamberlain of the Household, received one of her letters asking for his influence with an unnamed privy councillor: "I beg therefore dear cousin that you will try to feel his mind, for I am under the greatest impatience to know the cause: and if you meet with a fair occasion, it would be the greatest obligation to do me justice, as I think you would to all the world, and, I flatter myself, more particularly to your most faithful humble servant."[58] Still more audacious was her pursuit of Lord Oxford himself, a man who had once been anathema to her. Begging for his support, she gushed: "I am so satisfied of your lordship's humanity and justice that I cannot doubt of your ready compliance to my request."[59]

Lady Mohun needed Oxford's favor because by November 1713 the fight to keep a grip on her estate had reached a critical phase. Her enemies had combined forces and launched their assault very quickly. A London attorney received a visit from Sir Thomas Orby, Lord Mohun's former father-in-law, on the very day of the duel. Acting on Orby's instructions, and with the support of the younger Elizabeth, the lawyer went north, and on November 25 he seized Gawsworth. By the twenty-ninth he had also taken possession of Mohun's Lancashire property. Two weeks later the Duchess of Hamilton joined with the Orbys, promising to support their case.[60] Thanks to the generosity of the Duchess of Marlborough, Lady Mohun fought back, and after months of wrangling in the county courts of Cheshire and Lancashire, she secured court orders ejecting the Orbys. But decrees rendered in county courts were merely the opening salvo in a legal war. Throughout 1713 the two sides battled on a variety of fronts: Chancery, the Court of Exchequer, and the House of Lords. More important for Lady Mohun was the case opened by the Duchess of Hamilton and her allies at court. The law, unreliable as it was, had the virtue of complexity: defeat in one battle rarely killed a cause, however weak. There were always new avenues to pursue and delays and exceptions to take advantage of. The history of the Mohun/Hamilton lawsuit could serve as a textbook for litigants. But when participants brought a case before Queen and Council, the process became subject to the vagaries of politics and personality. It was in Lady Mohun's interest to avoid having her affairs brought before this particular Council, commanded as it was by Tories.

The Council's bias against Lady Mohun made it the obvious venue for a major attack from her enemies. Within a few weeks of the duel, they had petitioned the Queen, the first step to secure a hearing. Submitted jointly by the heirs-at-law of the Macclesfield estate—the duchess, Charlotte, Lady Orby, and her nephew John Elrington (son of the first earl's third daughter)—the petition returned to an argument that the duke had once thought promising.[61]

The petition was based upon a technicality, and one that had already failed when argued in court. But the important point was to get the case before the Council, where, thanks to their political influence, they might beat Lady Mohun. While the Attorney General investigated their claims, the litigants on both sides plied Oxford with letters and visits. The Gerard heirs troubled the Lord Treasurer most, particularly the indefatigable Charlotte,

Lady Orby. "I humbly entreat your Lordship will doe us ye Honour of your presence to morrow at ye Committee of ye Lords of ye Privy Counsill . . . for without it wee shall be undone, which I am absolutely sure it is in your Lordship's power to prevent." Her husband joined the effort: "I have had great encouragement given me that you would be our friend in this affair."[62] The Orbys also pressed their granddaughter into service. "I understand the [Attorney General's] report is now before your Lordship," Elizabeth Mohun wrote, "who I beg will remember she that is the most unfortunatest of all."[63]

The heirs suffered an unexpected reverse in their campaign: relying upon Oxford as their champion proved to be a mistake. The Lord Treasurer's government was already tottering. Although the Treaty of Utrecht, signed in 1713, was in retrospect a diplomatic triumph, ending the long war with France on relatively favorable terms, the contemporary view was different. Whigs denounced it as a betrayal of Britain's allies on the Continent, especially the Dutch, and many Tories found the abandonment of one of the war's principal aims—preventing a Bourbon prince from inheriting the Spanish crown—humiliating. The Tory majority in Parliament was dangerously fractious; Jacobites remained committed to James Edward Stuart, while a growing number of "Hanoverian Tories" grew alarmed by what they saw as a drift toward the Pretender. Adding to Oxford's woes was the now open hatred of Bolingbroke, who was determined to undermine the ministry. In the midst of these troubles the Treasurer's concern about a dispute between the peeresses was limited. Oxford seemed increasingly uninterested in any sort of business; he was now rarely sober and more lethargic than ever. Swift, whose hopes for the ministry had been so high in the beginning, despaired. He prepared to return to Dublin, where he might avoid the consequences of the government's collapse.

Whatever the heirs thought when they petitioned Queen Anne, by early 1714 their hopes for a quick defeat of Lady Mohun faded. She had regained her property through the courts, and in May the heirs lost yet another round in the House of Lords. Another petition from the Duchess of Hamilton against Lady Mohun failed. The Whig Bishop Nicolson described the duchess's case as "a Roguish cause," and not even a Tory majority was sufficient to rescue it.[64] Earlier in the same month the Council had rejected the heirs' argument, thanks to the strong opposition of the Duke of Argyll. Argyll—whose wife, a "fatt hogg in armour," the Duchess Elizabeth despised—had never been a friend of the Hamilton family. He used his influence to press Lady Mohun's cause. Her case was strengthened by the argument that her husband had made many leases and contracted debts over the years, and any decision to grant the estate to the claimants threatened the rights of innocent parties.[65] In the end, this argument and Argyll's personal enmity for the duchess prevailed: the Council rejected the Gerard heirs' petition.

The blow was especially bitter for the Orbys, who had spent a great deal of money in their pursuit of the estate. Tories, they expected better treatment at the hands of the ministry. Charlotte wrote a bitter letter to Oxford:

> I did entirely depend upon your Lordship's word, which has been the occasion that Mr. Orby and I persued the matter and have undon ourselves and not only that but have engagd all our friends in being bound for us . . . My Lord my condition is deplorable having noe other prospect but to see Mr. Orby perish in a gayle and I and my family starve, whilst my enimie run away with my father's estate, which in law they have no title to, but given her by the interst of ye Duke of Argile . . . My lord this is very cruell for me to see the servis of [my] husband and my family soe little regarded and all ye reward I am like to expect is to want bread.[66]

The failure of Orbys' case was at least partly the result of the political crisis. Queen Anne's health was failing. Concern about what would follow her death rose to a fever pitch. The Hanoverian succession appeared to be in grave danger, the ministry was in serious disarray, and everywhere politicians were hedging their bets. Without important men to press it, the case of Mohun versus Hamilton had become a nuisance. Neither of the widows, despite their strength of character, was politically important, and their affairs simply could not command the attention that their husbands' had. Lady Mohun, already in possession of the estate, was fortunate that the status quo favored her; circumstances militated against dramatic action. Soon Oxford would be unable to help even if he wanted to. When the Queen's final illness struck, he was dismissed and replaced by a ministry dominated by Hanoverian Tories. The Queen, so often suspected by Whigs of Jacobitism, proved her detractors wrong. She died on August 1, 1714, still firmly committed to the succession of the House of Hanover.

Lady Mohun was not the only person for whom the death of Queen Anne and the arrival of George I were fortunate. The Duke and Duchess of Marlborough returned from exile. In their wake came the duke's friend George Maccartney. He must have led a hand-to-mouth existence during his two years abroad, though he had ingratiated himself with the Elector of Hanover. George's transformation from Elector to King had hardly taken place when Maccartney's petition to return to England arrived. The general wanted his outlawry reversed so that he could stand trial for his part in the duel. Now that Oxford was headed for the Tower, Maccartney was sure that he could get a fair trial.

On December 6, 1714, the Council considered Maccartney's request. Marlborough argued strongly for his friend, although several Scots, including, surprisingly, Argyll, opposed him. The councillors agreed to allow the Duchess of Hamilton an opportunity to speak against the general. But the King's sympathy for Maccartney was enough to tip the balance, and his outlawry was reversed.[67] He was now free to return from Ostend to face the outstanding indictment against him.

The Court of King's Bench did not hear the case until June 1716. The results could not have been surprising. Colonel Hamilton, called as a witness, could not swear that Maccartney had murdered the duke. Maccartney had powerful friends, and Hamilton, who had already been dismissed from the army, had a small pension to protect. The general was convicted as an accessory, pleaded benefit of clergy, and was "burned" with a cold branding iron, as the young Charles Mohun had been many years before. George Lockhart later claimed that the case had been rigged: King George (or, the Elector of Hanover, as the Jacobite Lockhart always called him) had insisted that neither the Attorney nor Solicitor General should appear against his favorite. Furthermore, Lockhart said, the government had engineered a sympathetic jury and packed the gallery with prominent Whigs: a favorable result was a foregone conclusion.[68] What Lockhart did not mention, however, was that Colonel Hamilton had enjoyed the same treatment when he stood his trial.

With George Maccartney's trial, over three years after his friend Mohun died in Hyde Park, the duel seemed finally to have been relegated to the past. Both lords were in their graves, but the political and personal issues over which they fought had outlived them, and the great storm that heralded the news of their deaths had still not blown itself out.

Daniel Defoe tried to sum up what he believed was the futility of the Mohun-Hamilton struggle:

> But let the miserable rest in their Graves, why should the Age be Duelling every day, about who was kill'd fairly, and who not, and who fought bravest and who not? They either of them wanted Grace more than Courage, and the fear of God, as much as the fear of one another; both Desperate in this Quarrel; both Furious, both Mad, both Dead; they are past Pity now, and the Action no Christian Rules can justifie, let the Memory of it be buryed with them.[69]

But Daniel Defoe was wrong. James, fourth Duke of Hamilton, and Charles, fourth Baron Mohun, lived far longer in the memory of those who followed them than many of their contemporaries could have imagined. They themselves might not have been pleased by the uses to which their lives were put, but both men could at least rest satisfied that their lifelong struggle for recognition had succeeded at some level. Echoes of their story appeared in many places; in 1774 Malachy Postlethwait used them in his *Universal Dictionary of Trade and Commerce* as a lesson in the dangers of excessive litigation: "For men to make a dispute at law a formal quarrel, engage their passions in the difference, and turn their trade-breaches into breaches of charity and breaches of temper, is to put off the Christian and the man of sense together."[70] When in the 1850s William Makepeace Thackeray searched for a tale of the early eighteenth century around which to build a novel, he chose the story of Mohun and Hamilton, which provided the foundation of the plot of *Henry Esmond*.[71] As late as the 1760s publishers were selling ballads describing the duel, and Lord Mohun remained a stock figure in some cheap jest books.

The resonance of the duel changed over time, as the story was put to use for whatever contemporary purpose seemed appropriate. In the months immediately following the fight, most ballads and popular accounts were highly partisan. *The Lord M———n's Ghost* has that sorrowful specter offer wise (that is, Tory) counsel to his friend Richmond in the dead of a gloomy night,

> When pale faced Cynthia, sparing of her light,
> In smoaky clouds conceal'd her radiant head
> And oer the earth a sable veil had spread.

Charles, covered with gore and regretting his manipulation by the sinister George Maccartney, urged Richmond to fall in with the ministry and seek forgiveness from a generous Queen:

> Then let *Rebellious Whigs* no longer strive
> By Plots to keep their sinking cause alive.
> Due homage to their Sovereign let them pay
> And prostrate at her feet for mercy pray.

Not to be outdone, a Whig scribbler replied with "The Embassy":

> A Great Man once, that was to go
> Embassador to *France*, was sent below;
> And by mischance was forced to tell
> Instead of *France* his Embassy in *Hell*.

Pluto, as Satan is euphemistically named in the poem, received the Duke and said:

> But now Great *Mohun's* become my friend,
> By putting to your life an end.
> Be not dismay'd, nor dread this Hot-land,
> You'll find it not so bad as *Scotland*.[72]

Swift and Pope both produced some verse touching on the duel; Swift, the most partisan of literary geniuses, predictably lambasted the Whigs. In a 1713 poetical attack on his former friend Richard Steele, George Maccartney and Lord Mohun—described as the general's "pious patron"—performed as exemplars of Whig treachery and debauchery. By 1734, however, politics of any sort, much less party politics, was less intrusive. Pope satirized Lady Mohun for brandishing her backside to her lord in Hyde Park:

> A lady's face is all you see undress'd;
> For none but Lady M—— shows the Rest,[73]

but distinctions between Whig and Tory had disappeared—much as they had done in Britain under Sir Robert Walpole's long political dominance. By the 1730s the passions that roiled politics in Lord Mohun's day had cooled: Jacobites still conspired on behalf of their forlorn king in exile, but with every passing year James Edward Stuart became more and more irrelevant, a hostage to the cynical policies of Continental powers, and at odds with his volatile son and heir, Prince Charles Edward. There were still Tories, but, denied the fruits of office and excluded from the national political stage, most of them sat in their country houses cherishing grievances against the "moneyed interest" and the bloated foreign kings it served. The hysterical tenor that so characterized politics and society in the reign of Queen Anne was incomprehensible by the time of George II.

While Mohun and Hamilton continued to reside in the popular memory, their significance was changing to suit the times. By the second half of the eighteenth century, with both peers long in their graves and the political passions they animated no less defunct, ballad writers preferred to tell the tale of their relationship as a personal tragedy, the consequence of two tragic heroes set upon a collision course. In *Duke Hamilton and Lord Moon*, a ballad published in about 1760, the Duke is described as "as fine a lord / As ever Scotland could afford," while his rival is always referred to as "Brave Lord Mohon."[74] The author gives no reason for the duel—either political or personal—but merely focuses upon the bravery of the principals and the treachery of Maccartney, who, following the old Tory line, stabs Hamilton after he is wounded. Although the ballad does credit Colonel Hamilton's long-discounted testimony, it is interesting that it never assigns a reason for Maccartney's action. He has simply become the Snidely Whiplash of the story, necessary to complete the tragedy:

> This cowardly wretch is run away
> And ne'er was heard of unto this day.

A generation after their passing, Mohun and Hamilton were well on their way to becoming moral exemplars into whom Thackeray breathed life almost a century later—while still using them as object lessons in the school of Victorian morality. Although this was hardly what they set out to achieve in their tragic lives, Mohun and Hamilton had become the stuff of myth, fodder for the very finger-wagging moralists they had once held in such contempt.

The legacy of the duel went beyond poetry and ballads, however, for Lords Mohun and Hamilton left friends and family to shoulder the burdens they had laid aside. Their seconds, Colonel John Hamilton and General George Maccartney, both flung their careers and reputations onto the altar of friendship, with very different results. Hamilton's Faustian bargain with the government before his trial—if there was one—was of only limited benefit. Oxford (or his minions) may well have promised to protect John if he gave them evidence to use against Maccartney, but within two years Oxford was more interested in protecting himself from the fury of triumphant Whiggery. Accused of treason and thrown in the Tower, the former Lord Treasurer defended himself stoutly, rousing from the alcoholic torpor that beset his last years in office. He had neither time nor energy to rescue every person who had served him, and the colonel went to the wall. John lost his commission after George I's accession; deprived of his rank and much of his income, he faded into obscurity. Given his politics, Hamilton might have been dismissed in any event, but by swearing to what many people—and all Whigs—came to believe was untrue, he had destroyed his reputation. "Colonel Hamilton lived obscurely the remainder of his days, becoming so odious to all men of honour, that he was obliged to sell his company in the Guards, and died October 17, 1716, of a sudden vomiting of blood, which could not be stopped."[75] The price Hamilton paid for performing his duty to his patron was a high one indeed—an anonymous ballad writer had it about right when he put these words into Hamilton's mouth when the Duke asked him to serve as second:

> The colonel cried I am your slave,
> To follow you unto my grave.[76]

George Maccartney, too, followed his patron to the grave—but at a very great distance. The risk he ran as Mohun's second—and perhaps as the instigator of the duel—was high, but ultimately paid off handsomely. After over two years of impoverished Continental exile, when the general came home after George I's accession, he expected rewards appropriate to his fortitude. These were not long in coming. Even before his trial he was a favorite of the King, and within a month a Scot noted that Maccartney "is every day at Court and in Great favour. There is great talk he will get the Scotch foot guards." He did not, in fact, get this plum command, but the King made up for the loss first by offering him the governorship of Jamaica—the place he once wanted so badly, only to be supplanted by the Duke of Hamilton's brother Archibald. This post, so attractive to a penniless officer fighting off a rape charge from his landlady a few years before, was now not sufficient, and Maccartney declined the honor. The potential for profit was good enough, but the governorship might require a personal presence in the West Indies—something he preferred to avoid.[77] But better things would soon come along, thanks to George I's affection for this urbane desperado—the King and his friend the general dined together almost nightly. Maccartney was appointed colonel of a Scots fusilier regiment, and in 1718 given the governorship of Berwick. Berwick was an enviable post, on the English-Scottish border, requiring little direct attention but providing plenty of money for its commander. Maccartney went from honor to honor in the King's service: lieutenant general, colonel of a regiment of horse (far more prestigious, and profitable, than mere fusiliers), a place as one of the comptrollers of the army (laughably inappropriate for a man of his venality), governor of Portsmouth (much more important than Berwick), and, finally, commander of all of the King's forces in Ireland.[78]

Maccartney's dubious character did nothing to hinder his distinguished career as long as his patron sat on the throne, and he served his country by looting every command he held. The accession of George II in 1727, however, threatened to bring a halt to his plundering, and by then his misdeeds were catching up to him. A new Secretary at War audited his accounts, and a whole series of frauds emerged: he had peddled captain's commissions, gaining in one case almost £1,000 from an aspiring officer. He had pocketed government money that was supposed to be used for weapons and equipment. He had stolen funds appropriated for new tents for his men. He had neglected no possible malfeasance, provided a few pounds could be squeezed from the government—usually at the expense of his troops. They shivered in decrepit tents and shouldered inadequate weapons while he misappropriated his regiment's petty cash. The government's audit proved Maccartney's cupidity beyond doubt—not that anyone who knew him was surprised—but he retained his commands and, moreover, continued his lifelong practice of robbing the Treasury. When in 1730 Lieutenant General George Maccartney, beloved of George I, the Duke of Marlborough, and every Whig polemicist, finally died, the government discovered that he had stolen yet another £500 from his regiment.[79] He died peacefully at his home in Surrey, a pile bought with the ill-gotten gains of a career of striking immorality, proof that for some people crime can in fact be made to pay.

For much of the last years of his career, Maccartney stuck close to London, spending his time and money in the same taverns and coffeehouses he had haunted with his friend Lord Mohun. Did he ever encounter the Dowager Duchess of Hamilton? Elizabeth, too, spent much of her time in the capital, and occasionally appeared at court. In 1716 she gave up the house she and James had shared in St. James's Square and moved to another in Bond Street. She had already sold many of her husband's personal effects at auction, and now began a life unencumbered by a husband and meddlesome in-laws. She remained the incorrigible free spirit she had always been. Unlike many of her peers, Elizabeth relished the company of what were called "men of parts"; she continued her relationship with the literary men who had courted her, particularly Alexander Pope, now that Swift had returned to Ireland.[80] Her Lancashire property kept her comfortably, and the income from James's Scottish lands received a boost when in 1717 the long-lived Duchess Anne finally joined her ancestors.

Elizabeth's social circle was very different from George Maccartney's, but London, despite its size, was a small world for people of their rank. It is very likely, then, that their paths did cross from time to time; if so, Elizabeth's reaction would probably have been well worth watching. For the duchess did not mellow with age; if anything, she became even more cantankerous as time passed, feuding endlessly with her in-laws and anyone else who crossed her. Her children were no less subject to their mother's lash than James had been; in 1723 she sued her son and heir, James, for presuming to cut down timber on what she claimed was her property, and in 1736, when she was in her fifties, she distressed Queen Caroline by denouncing two of her own recently married daughters at court. "One cannot help wishing you joy, Madam," said the Queen, "every time one sees you, of the good matches your daughters have made." "Considering how they behaved," Elizabeth replied, "I wonder indeed they had any matches at all; but for any other two women of quality, one should think it no great catch for one to be married to a fool and t'other to a beggar." "Oh, fie, fie!" said Caroline, "my good Duchess! One cannot help laughing, you are so lively; but your expressions are very strong."[81] One imagines that Lady Charlotte and Lady Susan, the daughters in question, would have found much less to laugh about.

Elizabeth's children managed to avoid entangling themselves in their mother's continuing feuds with everyone about her, and must have experienced a certain relief when she died at the age of sixty-three in 1744. She had lived her life as she chose. Though very often she scandalized the family and her contemporaries, and her temper made her a legion of enemies, she was an independent woman of strong character who made a place for herself in a world where women of her kind were rarely appreciated. She left behind her an estate far stronger than that which her husband inherited, a flourishing family, and no regrets.*

Although they hated each other with a passion no less strong than their husbands had once reserved for one another, Elizabeth, Duchess of Hamilton, and Elizabeth, Lady Mohun, had much in common. Both women of determination and drive, they had raised themselves beyond society's expectations, and in the process incurred society's disapproval. Lady Mohun had further to travel as the daughter of a physician with a limited estate and no very exalted connections. The duchess succeeded thanks in part to her considerable beauty, her not inconsiderable fortune, and her strong-willed wit, but Lady Mohun's tactics were different. No beauty, and certainly not rich, Elizabeth Lawrence progressed though the strategic application of agreeability: she charmed the old-fashioned way. Where the duchess used her sharp wit as a blunt instrument, charming and wounding in equal measure, Lady Mohun preferred to exercise her own undoubted talents more subtly. Her first two husbands had time to regret their choice, but when working to secure their affections, Lady Mohun had been far more attractive than her rival, and far more effective. Not until she secured her position by inheriting Lord Mohun's fortune did she assert her personality with more freedom.

After Charles's death she maintained her ties to what the more staid Lady Cowper described as the "libertine Whigs," and in 1717 Pope noted that she "still makes the chief figure" in London society, through her pursuit of yet another potential husband, Charles Mordaunt, brother of the Earl of Peterborough, and a man considerably younger than herself.[82] The marriage duly occurred, and Elizabeth set herself up as the grande dame she had always wished to be. Both of her daughters had married well, thanks to the Gerard estate. After tedious negotiations with the

* Her third son, Lord Anne (born in 1709 and named for both his grandmother and the Queen), was the progenitor of the current, fifteenth, Duke of Hamilton.

fabulously rich Thomas Pitt, famous for his ruthless extraction of a fortune from India, Elizabeth sold Boconnoc, "universally allowed to be the finest seat in Cornwall" and her former husband's patrimony, for £54,000.[83] Pitt, a classic example of the "moneyed interest" denounced so bitterly by Tories, had wrestled a diamond worth an incredible £125,000 from his Indian hosts and was in pursuit of a landed estate to obscure his origins.[84] Boconnoc was the perfect site, although dealing with Lady Mohun was no joy, and she drove a hard bargain. The purchase price was enough to pay Charles's debts, pay off the impudent girl who called herself her stepdaughter, and probably leave a little in her purse besides.[85]

Thanks to the sale of Charles's patrimony—land that had been in the Mohun family for centuries—Elizabeth could finish her days in comfort, dividing her time between London and Gawsworth, although as she grew older she preferred Cheshire, where she could terrorize her tenants and Tory neighbors with her rabidly Whig sentiments. She sponsored an annual orgy of pro-Hanoverian bell-ringing on the King's birthday: "Our bells have rung ever since four a.m.," wrote the Countess of Suffolk, on a visit to Gawsworth in 1722, "which is more proof of Lady Mohun's power than the people's inclinations." Elizabeth masterminded the discomfiture of Tories from the pseudo-military fastness of her parlor, "adorned with all sorts of firearms, poisoned darts, several pair of old shoes and boots won from the Tartar by men of might belonging to this castle," and what must have been her favorite relic, "the stirrups of King Charles I taken from him at Edgehill."[86] When not pestering government ministers with her views on the loyalty of nearby Macclesfield, "which is at present very much wanting," Elizabeth worked to ensure the future of her two daughters.[87] In the years before her death in 1725, she demonstrated once again her talents for social success.

Lady Mohun was neither virtuous nor beautiful, but she nevertheless successfully overcame her relatively modest origins. By contrast, the stepdaughter whom she had so cruelly neglected fared less well. After fighting for years for even a modest part of her father's estate, in 1717 Elizabeth Mohun finally wrung a settlement out of Lady Mohun, whose plans to sell Boconnoc might have been complicated by further litigation.[88] The sum was not particularly large, but it was at least enough to make a marriage. Elizabeth could hardly expect to marry as well as her stepsisters. Lady Mohun provided each of her two daughters a handsome dowry of £20,000; Elizabeth would have to take her £5,500 and do the best she could.[89] In the event, Elizabeth probably did as well as could be expected: in June 1717 she married Arthur St. Leger. St. Leger, while no magnate, was at least the heir to a title—albeit an Irish title. His father was Viscount Doneraile, and though Irish peerages received scant respect in England—too many Irish lords were uncouth and impoverished—Elizabeth was not in a very strong negotiating position. In the event, any humiliation inherent in marrying a mere Irishman could not have lasted very long, for Elizabeth fell victim to the primitive obstetrics of the day, dying two months after she gave birth to a son, Arthur Mohun St. Leger. Arthur, who may—or may not—have been Lord Mohun's grandson, died in 1750, the last of a line that could trace its origins back to the Norman invasion.[90] Elizabeth's life had certainly been an unhappy one; shunned by her father, abused by her stepmother, deprived of her birthright, and batted about by angry relatives as a legal shuttlecock, she enjoyed little peace in her short life. Judging by the name she gave her son, she died unreconciled to the judgment of fate: her son, she made clear, was indeed the grandson of Charles, Lord Mohun, whatever his second wife might maintain. It was a futile but poignant gesture.

More durable than nearly all the people involved in the struggle between the Mohuns and the Hamiltons were the interminable legal actions both sides took for years, even decades, after the duel. The first skirmishes after the duel ended with Lady Mohun firmly in possession of the Gerard property. But the

Duchess of Hamilton was by no means prepared to concede defeat, and she continued the struggle. Her lawyers launched attack after attack upon Lady Mohun's position. Old arguments—about the validity of Lord Mohun's will, about Lord Macclesfield's attainder, about debts owed Lady Gerard's estates—were systematically revived and argued anew. The battle raged in nearly every possible venue: the common law courts, Chancery, Exchequer, and the House of Lords. On every occasion Lady Mohun stymied the duchess's lawyers, and she remained in possession of the property. But by 1720 or so the duchess's object seems to have been to harass her enemies rather than to triumph in the courts: this legal battle had gone on so long that it had become habit, an enmity so ingrained as to seem wholly natural.[91] The Hamiltons would fight the Mohuns (or their heirs) as the snake fought the mongoose: forever and without respite.[92]

The furious assault upon Lady Mohun's right to the estate failed in the end: the duchess never did dislodge her opponent, although she must have forced Lady Mohun to spend a great deal of money defending herself. But the passion in the struggle resided with the duchess, and not her family. When she died in 1744, her cause died with her. The remaining legal actions all petered out: her son, the fifth duke, was soon busy extricating himself from his entanglement in the ill-fated Jacobite rebellion of 1745; the family lawyers had far more important things to do. And so a legal battle that had consumed over forty years—eighty, counting the previous struggle between the Fittons and Gerards—countless thousands in legal bills, and, more important, the lives of an entire generation, was at last over.

Conclusion

W HY did they do it? James, Duke of Hamilton, Queen Anne's ambassador to the French King, friend of the exiled Pretender, a man in his fifties and crippled by gout, fought Charles, Baron Mohun, a general, member of the Hanoverian Council of Regency, and friend of Anne's legal successor, the Elector George. Dueling was illegal. Dueling was extremely dangerous. Moreover, for both men—Hamilton in particular—a duel was foolish. And yet after a decade of political and legal wrangling two of the most prominent peers of the realm met at dawn in Hyde Park armed with swords. They exacted from one another the highest price honor could demand—but why?

The duel that shattered the calm of that cold Saturday morning in Hyde Park was more than a personal tragedy. The men who fought on the field that day died in the grip of a hatred which brought them violently together and which was founded upon a personal quarrel. But forces that they neither recognized nor fully understood hurried them toward their doom. Since their youth, the world Mohun and Hamilton believed they were born to dominate had changed rapidly, heedless of their noble birth and high rank.

The eighteenth century has been characterized as "aristo-cratic," and there is no doubt that as a group the peerage emerged from the turmoil of the later Stuart period strengthened and more dominant than it had been since at least the days of the noble kingmakers of the fifteenth century. The sixteenth-century Tudor dynasty had tamed the nobility, ruthlessly suppressing restive aristocrats once used to far more power. The early Stuart monarchs inherited a peerage so thoroughly subdued that its very identity was inseparable from the idea of royal service—when Civil War erupted in 1642 most peers did not hesitate when choosing sides: Charles I won the loyalty of an overwhelming majority. Yet by the end of the seventeenth century aristocrats were reexamining their relation to the Crown. Their loyalty had led them to disaster in the 1640s and 1650s, and by 1688, under the zealous Catholic James II, disaster loomed again. The revo-lution that toppled King James was made by peers, and the settlement that followed reinstalled them in their old role of kingmakers. William III and his successors dealt with a House of Lords emboldened by a newfound confidence.

But the creation of this aristocratic dominance was no easy task. The Lords did not operate unilaterally, for they were joined by their junior partners in the Commons, and faced the rise of new and powerful interests: men whose wealth and power sprang from commerce rather than the land. Nobles had to master social, polit-ical, and economic change, and changing circumstances required adaptation and innovation. The "aristocratic century" was in-fused with many of the values and attitudes of people whose claim to gentility would have been laughable only a century before. The ability of the British peerage to co-opt the likes of Thomas Pitt, Indian merchant and progenitor of the Earls of Chatham, played a vital role in the creation of a new social order. Like most of the rest of their peers, Charles Mohun and James Douglas-Hamilton were both the beneficiaries of this change, but they were also its victims. Their story tells us a great deal about

the nobility's transition from seventeenth-century crisis to eighteenth-century dominance.

The shifting focus of power in Britain, from the court to the
Parliament at Westminster, gave Mohun the opportunity to rise to
prominence despite the enmity of Queen Anne. Hamilton, initially a creature of the court, endured years of political misfortune
before he, too, finally adapted to the changes wrought by the Revolution of 1688. Unlike his younger English rival, Hamilton was
steeped in an older, court-centered tradition. He had far more difficulty abandoning the tenets of his predecessors; indeed, if his
last mission as ambassador to France was a Jacobite plot, he might
still have been devoted to the old ways. Nevertheless, his role in
the Union and more obviously his alliance with Oxford's Tories
illustrate his gradual assimilation of the lessons of 1688. The
monarchy would henceforth have to live with Parliament, and
politics would become a complex exercise in the manipulation of
votes and ideology. Hamilton, with his influence in Scotland,
became a force to be reckoned with, and it is hard to imagine that
the Tory Board of Brothers would have endured his personal insecurities were it not for his political value.

For Mohun, those lessons were self-evident. After all, his
father, the third baron, had played a part in the birth of what
became party politics in the 1670s. The family's civil-war court-
centered royalism brought them to the edge of financial ruin; the
vistas opened up by Parliament-based party politics promised a
brighter future. Mohun escaped the gallows after the murder of
William Hill in 1697 because of William III's need to ensure reliable votes in the House of Lords. Loyally supporting the Junto
gave Mohun a prominence in society he would otherwise have
been denied. The Gerard inheritance that sustained him came
not because of his blood ties to the second Earl of Macclesfield
but rather because of the political bond between the two men. An
invitation to join the Kit-cat Club came thanks to Mohun's Whiggish reliability.

The conflict between the two men also reflected the new relationship between the kingdoms of the British Isles: Hamilton's Scottishness played an important part in his search for respect and acceptance in the newly formed Great Britain. His aggressive pursuit of what he believed was his right to a share of the purely English Gerard estate was of course about money, but it was also about his standing in Britain. The Act of Union gave him all the rights and privileges of an Englishman, but for those rights to be vindicated he required an English being. That meant the possession of English land; the deference of English tenants; the patronage of English clerics and politicians. And for Mohun, as for many other Englishmen, the Union represented a threat to their interests. The arrival of a legion of ambitious Scots like Hamilton, now entitled to legal and social equality, led inevitably to tension and, at times, violence.

The duel was society's way of limiting, and regularizing, the violence of an order trained from an early age in the use of arms. Mohun and Hamilton grew up in a culture in which violence was endemic: casually inflicted upon servants, spouses, children, and animals, it was often the first resort of a frustrated or angry man. Both men had fought duels, and Mohun had been involved in outright murder. Britons were ambivalent about the murderous propensities of their better sort: ministers railed against dueling and casual fighting; the Crown enforced laws against them. But when Lord Mohun killed Captain Hill, William III granted him a pardon. When George Maccartney was tried for his role in the deaths of Mohun and Hamilton, he walked away a free man. The army militarized a large portion of the British aristocracy; Mohun and Hamilton had military experience, as did many of their peers. The sermons of moralists had little effect until well into the eighteenth century, when political passions had cooled and peace returned. Even then, a soldier's belief in the virtue of the duel would linger for a generation, making resort to the sword natural for many.

Insecurity was a dominant theme in both men's lives—as it was in the society in which they lived. Even as they made their way successfully though the complexities of British politics, their place was under constant threat. Hamilton could testify to the treachery of fortune; his stretches in the Tower gave him plenty of time to reflect upon the nature of party politics. After the 1710 election Mohun, too, knew about the dangers inherent in the new political regime. Tory dominance of government threatened to deprive him of his estate; a biased House of Lords would reduce him to penury. More threatening still by 1712 was the prospect of a vengeful James III, returned from France and restored to his father's throne.

Political insecurity fed economic insecurity among the peerage. Since the reign of Charles II, Britain's economy had grown rapidly, led by colonial trade and increased agricultural production. There was a great deal more wealth in the kingdom in 1710 than there had been in 1660, but it rested in many more hands. Merchants and City money men amassed unprecedented fortunes. The bounty of the Indies and the profits of financing war against France funded a newly powerful order of men, rivaling the peerage and gentry. Many nobles adopted the methods of the moneyed interest, buying bonds and investing in stocks, harnessing these new forms of wealth for their own profit. Many, however, were like Mohun and Hamilton, struggling to keep up. Sometimes the allure of large profits caught the unwary off guard: the duke, always perilously near bankruptcy, lost all his investment in the Darien Company. Both men accumulated crippling debts. They were in the power of the moneyed interest—from the financiers who held the mortgages on their property to the small tradesmen who provided clothes and furniture on credit. The cycle of debt grew more and more dizzying, as each man borrowed to shore up his political and social position and became still more dependent upon political success to avoid bankruptcy.

Much of their money disappeared into the voracious maw of the courts. The Mohun-Hamilton feud provides an object lesson in the pitfalls of the law in the early modern period. The legal system was biased toward the status quo, which enabled Mohun, in possession of the Gerard estate, to fend off Hamilton's assault for over a decade. But the law was also subject to political influence, which made Mohun's possession increasingly tenuous as Hamilton's Tory allies entrenched themselves in power after 1710. The courts were incapable of expedition; indeed, nearly everyone involved relied upon the complexity and dilatory procedures of the courts. Lawyers waxed rich, clerks piled up fees, and litigants such as Hamilton and Mohun manipulated the system to their own advantage, encouraging unnecessary delays. As Abraham Granger discovered in the 1660s, the truth was a "weak and naked thing" when pitted against the high-priced legal talent available in London's Inns of Court. Had the two peers not fought each other so tenaciously in the courts for such a long time, the bitterness that led to their deaths might never have existed.

The money and time spent on legal warfare was necessary, however, for Charles and James were engaged in a struggle over far more than simply an inheritance. They fought to defend their positions in a rapidly changing world; they fought for the one thing that could provide stability for themselves and their families for generations to come: landed property. The rich acres of the Gerard estate would make all the difference for both; they would underpin a political career, they would provide status and respect. They were vital, and so each man desperately needed victory.

In their pursuit of that victory, Mohun and Hamilton were forced to live beyond their means. Both lords maintained expensive establishments in London and the country. Mohun built the New Hall at Gawsworth; Hamilton rented in St. James's Square. Both spent freely entertaining their friends and clients. Mohun footed the bill for more than one riotous evening at the Kit-cat, and Hamilton handed out gifts to valuable acquaintances like Swift. Money spent on lavish clothing, portraits painted by high-priced artists like Sir Godfrey Kneller, and jewelry drove the debts of each man higher and higher. Yet such expenses were necessary; much of the duke's personal anguish as an adult resulted from lack of the money he needed to play the role to which his rank entitled him. Sour complaints about his meanness and grasping only pushed him forward in the pursuit of a full purse. As a boy, Charles knew the humiliation of scarce resources, when his mother wrangled with the family trustees over the meager estate left by his father. Money bought political security, but it also bought personal affirmation.

Both men had deep-seated personal insecurities that they sought to assuage through the possession and use of their fortunes. Mohun built a school for the children of Gawsworth. Hamilton supported persecuted Jacobites. Mohun, literally fatherless, and Hamilton, spiritually so, chased praise and prominence all their lives. Mohun, raised in a house where disorder and incivility were routine, searched for affirmation as his father had done: through opposition politics and riotous living. Hamilton developed a taste for disorder on his own. Hamilton Palace was no place for riot. Yet after he came to Charles II's court, James, too, found that politics and dissipation served a need.

The rake's life satisfied the two peers, as it did many of their contemporaries. The complaints of moralists and clergymen only encouraged further outrages. The notorious actions of Rochester, Wharton, Mohun, and others, such as the infamous Mohawks, were a means of self-assertion. Made insecure by the shifting political and economic sands of the day, they responded defiantly, making a dramatic claim upon the attentions of society. Often coarsened by military service and spurred on by alcohol, through their violent antics they proclaimed independence from a society where moderation and civility were slowly becoming the standard of gentlemanly behavior. Mohun exemplified the model of the rake; the pleasures of drinking and whoring were compounded by the attention they garnered him, and he proved that debauchery could be combined with hard work on the floor of the Lords. A miserable childhood and two unhappy marriages taught him that personal satisfaction lay in the world beyond the home, and he spent his adult life chasing satisfaction through the taverns and bedrooms of London.

Hamilton, tamed by his marriage to Elizabeth Gerard, was even more driven. James II's exile had deprived him of the affection and patronage of a royal father, and his true parents did nothing to make good the loss. The third duke, his father, urged his imprisonment in the Tower; his mother denied him the money he needed to take his rightful place in British society. Financial pressure and political disappointment made James crave success more than ever. The noble heritage to which he was heir was pitiless in its demands: the head of the House of Hamilton had an obligation to his kingdom and his successors, and to fail, as his mother was sure her son would do, was intolerable.

In the end, Charles, fourth Baron Mohun, and James, fourth Duke of Hamilton, so representative of their time and their order, were drawn together in conflict and clashed fatally, driven by demons of their own making as well as social forces beyond their control; their insecurities merged and became personified in each other. Years of struggle in the courts engendered bitterness that political enmity could only intensify. As each man sought to guarantee his own survival it seemed ever clearer that the other stood in the way. Possession of the Gerard estate, that evil inheritance, would be the difference between honor and ignominy. Their tragic deaths ensured that neither peer would triumph.

NOTES

ABBREVIATIONS

BL British Museum/British Library, London
DNB *Dictionary of National Biography*. 22 vols. Oxford, 1885–1901
GEC G. E. Cockayne, *The Complete Peerage*. 14 vols. London, 1910–59
HMC Historical Manuscripts Commission
NLS National Library of Scotland, Edinburgh
PRO Public Record Office, London
SRO Scottish Record Office, Edinburgh

INTRODUCTION

1. Jonathan Swift, *Prose Works* (Oxford, 1940), vol. 3, p. 5.
2. Gilbert Burnet, *History of My Own Times* (Oxford, 1823), vol. 4, p. 176.
3. Quoted in G. E. Mingay, *English Landed Society in the Eighteenth Century* (London, 1963), pp. 145–46.
4. Thanks to Charles Royster for this excellent story.
5. For the Anglesey divorce, see HMC, *House of Lords Mss.* N.S. (London, 1900–53), vol. 4, pp. 148–50, 188–204. Anglesey's threat against his wife is on p. 195.
6. For Grafton, see Henri Misson, *Memoirs and Observations of His Travels Over England* (London, 1719), pp. 305–6; for Leeds, see Margaret Verney, ed., *Verney Letters of the Eighteenth Century* (London, 1930), vol. 1, p. 373. I owe Charles Royster thanks for the latter reference.
7. See Ben C. Truman, *The Field of Honor* (New York, 1884); for a more recent survey of the duel in Europe as a whole, V. G. Kiernan, *The Duel in European History* (Oxford, 1988).
8. There has been some confusion about the year of Mohun's birth—there has even been confusion about whether he was the fourth or fifth Baron—but Robert Forsythe has convincingly demonstrated that Mohun was born on April 11, 1677. See Robert Forsythe, *A Noble Rake: The Life of Charles, Fourth Lord Mohun* (Cambridge, Mass., 1928), p. 6, n. 1.

1: A SEASON OF YOUTH

1. HMC, *8th Report* (London, 1881), App., p. 166.
2. Ibid., pp. 114, 154.
3. Lorenzo Magalotti, *Lorenzo Magalotti at the Court of Charles II*, W. E. Knowles Middleton, ed. (Waterloo, Ont., 1980), p. 50.

4. HMC, *Eighth Report*, App., p. 161.

5. Both remarks are quoted in GEC, under "Anglesey."

6. HMC, *Thirteenth Report* (London, 1893), App. 6, p. 274 (Anglesey Diary). For the marriage market in general, see H. J. Habakkuk, *Marriage, Debt, and the Estates System: English Landownership, 1650–1950* (Oxford, 1994).

7. HMC, *Thirteenth Report*, App. 6, p. 277.

8. HMC, *Ninth Report* (London, 1884), App., Pt. 2, p. 110; HMC, *Seventh Report* (London, 1879), p. 493 (Verney Mss.).

9. See Robert Forsythe, *A Noble Rake: The Life of Charles, Fourth Lord Mohun* (Cambridge, Mass., 1928), pp. 8–9; HMC, *Rutland Manuscripts* (London, 1888–1905), vol. 2, p. 32; BL, Add. Ms. 38,141, f. 47; Francis Bickley, *The Cavendish Family* (London, 1911), p. 153.

10. For Mohun's illness and death, see BL, Add. Ms. 38,141, f. 47; HMC, *Rutland Manuscripts*, vol. 2, pp. 32, 35, 37; HMC, *LeFleming Manuscripts* (London, 1890), pp. 130, 141. For the doctor's complaint, see GEC, under "Mohun."

11. Henry Ringwood of Bristow Sale Catalog 233 (1977), item 96. I owe Charles Royster thanks for this reference.

12. Quoted in Rosalind Marshall, *The Days of Duchess Anne: Life in the Household of the Duchess of Hamilton 1656–1717* (New York, 1973), p. 134; this account of James's education is based upon Marshall's in ibid., pp. 131–43.

13. Ibid.; see especially the third duke's comment quoted on p. 143.

14. Ibid., pp. 174–77; see also chap. 8, "The Marriage of the Heir," passim.

15. Arthur Dasent, *The History of St. James's Square* (London, 1895), p. 166; *DNB*, under "James Douglas."

16. See Marshall, *Days of Duchess Anne*, p. 186.

17. Huntington Library, Loudon Papers, LO 8973, "A Speech made by ye E. of Arran . . . ," January 8, 1689. I owe Charles Royster thanks for discovering and transcribing this document for me.

18. For the attempted assassination, see HMC, *Kenyon Manuscripts* (London, 1894), p. 218.

19. For his debts, see Marshall, *Days of Duchess Anne*, p. 177. Much of this biographical information comes from the *DNB*.

20. For details of the Love incident, see HMC, *Ninth Report* (London, 1884), App., Pt. 2, p. 110, and HMC, *Rutland Manuscripts*, vol. 2, p. 49.

21. For Orby's background, see Forsythe, *Noble Rake*, p. 12, n. 2. See below, chap. 2, for the unfolding of the Mohun/Orby connection.

22. HMC, *House of Lords Manuscripts, 1677–88* (London, 1887), pp. 118–19. For more information on the Cornish estates, see PRO, C22/271/34, 397/40, 806/35. Orby claimed that the estate was worth about £4,000 a year; C9/449/87.

23. See James E. Thorold Rogers, ed. *A Complete Collection of the Protests of the Lords* (Oxford, 1875), vol. 1, p. 108; Narcissus Luttrell, *A Brief Historical*

Relation of State Affairs (London, 1857), vol. 2, pp. 628, 636; Forsythe, *Noble Rake*, pp. 22–23.

24. Quoted in Edward Callow, *Old London Taverns* (London, 1899), p. 281.

25. Dramatis Personae in Thomas D'Urfey, *Love for Money: Or, the Boarding School* (London, 1691).

26. The official account, *The Tryal of Charles Lord Mohun Before the House of Peers in Parliament* (London, 1693), gives this date as *Tuesday*, December 5, evidently a mistake for Monday.

27. The bulk of the Mountford story comes from the printed *Tryal of Charles Lord Mohun*. These quotes are from pp. 8–9. There is another set of handwritten notes on the trial in the Huntington Library, San Marino, California. I owe Charles Royster sincere thanks for transcribing these for me. Other information about the case is in Luttrell, *Brief Historical Relation*, vol. 2, pp. 637–38; vol. 3, pp. 9, 11, 13–14, 24, 26–27, 28–30, 46, 48; newsletter accounts in BL, Add. Ms. 70,081; HMC, *House of Lords Manuscripts, 1688–93* (London, 1894), vol. 4, pp. 294–99, and the *Journals of the House of Lords* (London, 1767–   ).

28. *Tryal*, p. 34.

29. Mary II, *Memoirs of Mary, Queen of England*, Richard Doebner, ed. (London, 1886), pp. 58–59.

30. *Tryal*, pp. 52, 56.

31. Ibid., p. 62.

32. Forsythe, *Noble Rake*, recounts all these incidents, pp. 52–64; see also Luttrell, *Brief Historical Relation*, vol. 3, p. 381; vol. 4, pp. 207, 278, 280, 296, 303, 318, 321–22, 351, 368; *Calendar of Treasury Books* (London, 1904–57), vol. 13, p. 71.

33. For Forsythe's account of the Coote murder, see *Noble Rake*, chap. 5, passim. Other sources are Luttrell, *Brief Historical Relation*, vol. 4, pp. 445, 499–500; HMC, *House of Lords Manuscripts, 1697–99* (London, 1905), pp. 358–61; Margaret Verney, ed., *Verney Letters of the Eighteenth Century*, vol. 1, p. 36; *Parliamentary History of England, 1688–1702* (London, 1809), vol. 5, p. 1197 (for Mohun's repentant behavior at the trial); *Journals of the House of Lords*, vol. 16, pp. 390, 396, 398, 400, 407, 411, 415–16, 418–19, 421–28; for the hangings used in the hall, *Calendar of Treasury Books*, vol. 17, pt. 1, p. 265.

2: EVIL INHERITANCE

1. *A True Narrative of the Proceedings in the Severall Suits in Law That Have Been Between the Right Honourable Charles Lord Gerard of Brandon, and Alexander Fitton, Esq.* (The Hague, 1663), p. 6.

2. *A True Account of the Unreasonableness of Mr. Fitton's Pretences Against the Earl of Macclesfield* (n.p., [1685]), p. 3; what seems more likely is that the Irish Fittons, with long experience of life in a turbulent society, were merely neutral, looking after their own interests.

3. *True Narrative*, p. 7.
4. Most of the details of Alexander's dealings with Lord Gerard are found in either the *True Narrative* or the *True Account*.
5. *True Narrative*, p. 41.
6. See Samuel Pepys, *The Diary of Samuel Pepys*, Robert Latham and William Matthews, eds. (Berkeley, Calif., 1970–83), vol. 5, p. 12, for a mention of Granger's skill as a forger.
7. *True Narrative*, p. 18.
8. *True Narrative*, p. 42.
9. Biographical details in *DNB;* Pepys, who despised Gerard, mentions his dishonesty at various points in the diary.
10. See *True Account*, p. 1.
11. For Gerard's temporary flirtation with James, see L.K.J. Glassey, "The Origins of Political Parties in Late Seventeenth Century Lancashire," *Transactions of the Historical Society of Lancashire and Cheshire* 136 (1987), p. 46.
12. For details of the settlement, see PRO, C9/179/61.
13. Sources for the Macclesfield divorce: HMC, *House of Lords Manuscripts*, N.S. (London, 1900–53), vol. 3, pp. 57–68.
14. Ibid.
15. See *DNB*, under "Richard Savage," and Richard Holmes, *Dr. Johnson and Mr. Savage* (New York, 1993).
16. H. J. Habakkuk, *Marriage, Debt, and the Estates System: English Landowner-ship, 1650–1950* (Oxford, 1994), pp. 234–38. See also Lawrence Stone, *Broken Lives: Separation and Divorce in England 1660–1857* (Oxford, 1993).
17. HMC, *House of Lords Manuscripts*, N.S., vol. 3, pp. 57–68.
18. *Topographer & Genealogist* 3 (1858), p. 494.
19. Manley's account of the first marriage is in Mary Delarivière Manley, *The New Atalantis*, Ros Ballaster, ed. (London, 1991), pp. 258–59. Robert Forsythe is skeptical of the story: *A Noble Rake: The Life of Charles, Fourth Lord Mohun* (Cambridge, Mass., 1928), pp. 18–21. Although no doubt Mrs. Manley's details cannot be trusted, the tale does ring true and fits with hints Mohun gave in some of his chancery bills against the Orbys— see PRO, C9/174/40, 42; 173/33.
20. See PRO, C9/174/40; Manley, *New Atalantis*, p. 258; Forsythe, *Noble Rake*, p. 20.
21. See Rosalind Marshall's account in *The Days of Duchess Anne: Life in the Household of the Duchess of Hamilton 1656–1717* (New York, 1973), chap. 10.
22. For details of the marriage settlement, see PRO, C9/156/63, and Marshall, *Days of Duchess Anne*, chap. 10.
23. Bernard Falk, *The Royal Fitzroys: Dukes of Grafton Through Four Centuries* (London, 1950), pp. 13–14; Philip Sergeant, *My Lady Castlemaine* (London, 1912), pp. 271, 317–18, 320.

24. Jonathan Swift, *Journal to Stella* (Oxford, 1974), vol. 2, pp. 473–74.

25. Narcissus Luttrell, *A Brief Historical Relation of State Affairs* (London, 1857), vol. 4, p. 457.

26. SRO, GD406/1/11804, Hamilton to Duchess Anne, January 20, 1702.

27. Habakkuk, *Marriage, Debt*, p. 192.

28. John Toland, *An Account of the Courts of Prussia and Hanover* (London, 1705), pp. 13–14. See also Ragnhild Hatton, *George I, Elector and King* (Cambridge, Mass., 1978), p. 75; for the unfavorable view of the embassy, see William Mure, ed., *Selections from the Family Papers Preserved at Caldwell* (Glasgow, 1854), pp. 216–17.

29. For Macclesfield's death, see HMC, *Cowper Manuscripts* (London, 1888–89), vol. 2, p. 446; Henry Hyde, Earl of Clarendon, *The Correspondence of Henry Hyde, Earl of Clarendon*, Samuel W. Singer, ed. (London, 1828), vol. 1, pp. 419–20; Thomas Heywood, ed., *The Norris Papers* (Chetham Society, vol. 9, 1846), p. 669; Luttrell, *Brief Historical Relation*, vol. 5, pp. 106–7; PRO, C9/344/49.

3: LAWYERS AND POLITICIANS

1. For details of the will and charges and countercharges about fraud, see PRO, C9/394/50; see also Raymond Richards, *The Manor of Gawsworth* (London, 1954), p. 31, note 4.

2. For information on burials in the Abbey, see *Collecteanea Topographica et Genealogica*, vol. 8 (London, 1843), pp. 9, 13.

3. For the size of the estate, see PRO, C9/204/11; HMC, *Cowper Manuscripts*, (London, 1888–89), vol. 2, p. 446; Narcissus Luttrell, *A Brief Historical Relation of State Affairs* (London, 1857), vol. 5, pp. 106–7; Henry Hyde, Earl of Clarendon, *The Correspondence of Henry Hyde, Earl of Clarendon*, Samuel W. Singer, ed. (London, 1828), pp. 419–20.

4. See Thomas Brockbank, *Diary and Letterbook of Thomas Brockbank*, Richard Trappes-Lomax, ed. (Chetham Society Publications, N.S., vol. 89 [1930]), p. 183 (August 1700), for Hamilton's poor reputation among his Lancashire neighbors. For maiming cattle, see SRO, GD406/1/5069.

5. SRO, GD406/1/7105, April 1702.

6. SRO, GD406/1/7858, September 1703.

7. For the Hamilton campaign to secure Fitton's support, see SRO, GD406/1/7403, 7574, 7131, January, March, December 1702.

8. SRO, GD 406/1/7131, December 24, 1702.

9. For details of the struggle over the third earl's leases and intrigues with the servants, see PRO, C9/179/61, 278/6; C22/995/3, 993/18; BL, Add. Ms. 36,148 (Hardwicke Papers), ff. 296–99, Add. Ms. 6,727 (Pengelly Papers), ff. 123–26; SRO, GD406/1/4903, 5174, 4923, 5144; Lennoxlove, Bdl. 3030 (unexecuted[?] power re the leases, by Duchess Elizabeth, March 1704).

296 *Notes*

10. Quoted in Paul Langford, *Public Life and the Propertied Englishman, 1689–1798* (Oxford, 1991), pp. 48–49. See also Henry Horwitz and Patrick Polden, "Continuity or Change in the Court of Chancery in the Seventeenth and Eighteenth Centuries?," *Journal of British Studies* 35 (1996), pp. 24–57.

11. Heneage Finch, Earl of Nottingham, *Lord Nottingham's Manual of Chancery Practice*, D.E.C. Yale, ed. (Cambridge, 1965), p. 15.

12. Nottingham, *Manual*, p. 51, note 4.

13. Quoted in Hilary St. George Saunders, *Westminster Hall* (London, 1951), p. 246.

14. See Nottingham, *Manual*, pp. 68, 217.

15. For details of the battle of the jewels, see PRO, C8/459/23; SRO, GD406/1/5048, 5054, 5055–61, 5064, 5143, 5148; HMC, *House of Lords Manuscripts*, N.S. (London, 1900–53), vol. 5, pp. 221–22.

16. SRO, GD406/1/8476, May 3, 1703.

17. See [Daniel Defoe?], *A Strict Enquiry Into the Circumstances of a Late Duel . . .* (London, 1713), p. 37.

18. P.W.J. Riley, *King William and the Scottish Politicians* (Edinburgh, 1979), pp. 146–47.

19. For some of these, and their recipients' reactions, see HMC, *Hamilton Manuscripts* (London, 1887–1932), vol. 2, pp. 149–55; Henry L. Snyder, ed., *The Marlborough-Godolphin Correspondence* (Oxford, 1975), vol. 1, pp. 131, 331.

20. Edward Ward, *The London Spy*, 4th ed. (London, 1709), p. 71; Swift, *Prose Works*, Herbert Davis, ed. (Oxford, 1939–74), vol. 5, pp. 295–320.

21. For this dispute, see George Lockhart, *The Lockhart Papers* (London, 1817), vol. 1, pp. 45–47; HMC, *Hamilton Manuscripts*, vol. 2, pp. 149–55; James Ogilvie, First Earl of Seafield, *Letters Relating to Scotland in the Reign of Queen Anne*, P. Hume Brown, ed. (Edinburgh, 1915), pp. 112–17; Snyder, ed., *Marlborough-Godolphin*, p. 131; Luttrell, *Brief Historical Relation*, vol. 5, p. 186.

22. SRO, GD406/1/7884, James to Duchess Anne, July 24, 1703.

23. NLS, Ms. 7021, Yester Manuscripts, f. 73, March 25, 1703.

24. W. C. Mackenzie, *Simon Fraser, Lord Lovat, His Life and Times* (London, 1908), p. 134.

25. For relations between Hamilton and the French, see Dorothy Middleton, *The Life of Charles, Second Earl of Middleton, 1650–1719* (London, 1957), p. 191; Mackenzie, *Lovat*, pp. 133–34; G. M. Trevelyan, *England Under Queen Anne* (London, 1930–34), vol. 1, p. 136; Nathaniel Hooke, *Correspondence*, William Dunn Macray, ed. (Roxburghe Club Publications, 1870), vol. 2, p. 138.

26. HMC, *Bath Manuscripts* (London, 1904–8), vol. 2, pp. 397–98, 412.

27. NLS, Ms. 7104, Tweeddale Letters, f. 66, Hamilton to Tweeddale, March 19, 1703; HMC, *Bath Manuscripts*, vol. 1, p. 57.

28. References to Hamilton's alleged royal ambitions are numerous. See, for example, Mackenzie, *Lovat*, p. 96; Trevelyan, *England Under Queen Anne*, vol. 2, p. 259; William Nicolson, Bishop of Carlisle, *The London Diaries*, Clyve Jones and Geoffrey Holmes, eds. (Oxford, 1985), p. 134; HMC, *Mar and Kellie Manuscripts* (London, 1904), p. 313. Gilbert Burnet, *History of My Own Times*, 2nd ed. (Oxford, 1825), vol. 5, p. 285.

29. HMC, *Portland Manuscripts* (London, 1891–1931), vol. 3, p. 198.

30. HMC, *Fourteenth Report* (London, 1894), App. 3 (Seafield Manuscripts), Godolphin to Seafield, p. 206.

31. For Hooke, see *Correspondence*, vol. 1, pp. 383–98, 406–9, 415–19; Middleton, *Life of . . . Middleton*, p. 192; for reports sent back to London, see HMC, *Portland Manuscripts*, vol. 4, pp. 171–234, passim.

32. HMC, *Portland Manuscripts*, vol. 4, p. 234.

33. Lockhart, *Lockhart Papers*, vol. 1, pp. 132–37.

34. Seafield, *Letters*, p. 46.

35. NLS, Ms. 1032, Hamilton Correspondence, f. 23, Duchess Anne to [Selkirk or Orkney], September 1705.

36. Hooke, *Correspondence*, vol. 1, pp. 280–81.

37. HMC, *Tenth Report* (London, 1885), App. 4, p. 340.

38. Sir John Clerk, *Memoirs of the Life of John Clerk*, John M. Gray, ed. (London, 1895), p. 57; NLS, Ms. 1032, f. 36.

39. Hooke, *Correspondence*, vol. 2, p. 170, Gordon to Lady Errol, March 1707.

40. HMC, *Portland Manuscripts*, vol. 8, pp. 256–66, Hamilton to Orkney; see also Seafield, *Letters*, p. 94.

41. HMC, *Portland Manuscripts*, vol. 8, p. 255.

42. See *DNB*.

43. HMC, *Mar and Kellie Manuscripts*, p. 309, Mar to D. Nairne, November 3, 1706; HMC, *Portland Manuscripts*, vol. 4, p. 345, Defoe to Harley, November 5, 1706.

44. HMC, *Mar and Kellie Manuscripts*, p. 300.

45. See Nathaniel Hooke, *The Secret History of Colonel Hooke's Negotiations in Scotland in 1707* (London, 1775), pp. 2–3, 29–30, 51; Middleton, *Life of . . . Middleton*, p. 199; HMC, *Bath Manuscripts*, vol. 1, p. 187; Hooke, *Correspondence*, vol. 2, pp. 138, 149–50, 268.

46. PRO, SP34/9/186.

47. William Coxe, ed., *Memoirs of the Duke of Marlborough* (London, 1847), vol. 2, p. 218.

48. Sir James Clavering, *The Correspondence of Sir James Clavering*, H. T. Dickinson, ed. (Gateshead, 1967), p. 3—I owe Charles Royster thanks for this reference; Snyder, ed., *Marlborough-Godolphin*, vol. 2, p. 957.

49. For Hamilton's letters relating his efforts in the government's behalf, see BL, Add. Ms. 61,628 (Blenheim Papers), ff. 80–124.

50. For dinners, see PRO, C104/113, part 2, Lord Ossulston's Diary, and Clyve Jones, "The London Life of a Peer in the Reign of Anne," *London*

Journal 16 (1991), pp. 140–55; for St. James's Square, see Arthur Dasent, *The History of St. James's Square* (London, 1895); C. R. Ashbee et al., eds., *Survey of London*, vol. 29 (London, 1960), pp. 61, 71.

51. For details on these cases, see BL, Add. Ms. 36,148 (Hardwicke Papers), ff. 297–303; Lennoxlove, Bdls. 3568, 4080; SRO, GD406/1/6926, 7042, 5454, 5459; PRO, C9/183/11, 381/3; C22/99/22.

52. See Thomas Macaulay, *History of England From the Accession of James II* (New York, 1892), vol. 4, p. 558.

53. Ward, *London Spy*, p. 197.

54. David Chandler, *The Art of Warfare in the Age of Marlborough* (New York, 1976), p. 37.

55. See John Childs, *The English Army of William III* (Manchester, 1987), pp. 36–37; see also R. A. Scouller, *The Army of Queen Anne* (Oxford, 1966).

56. J. W. Fortescue, *A History of the British Army* (London, 1910), vol. 1, p. 402.

57. HMC, *Ormonde Manuscripts*, N.S. (London, 1902–20), vol. 5, pp. 169–70.

58. HMC, *Seventh Report* (London, 1879), p. 777.

59. HMC, *Ormonde Manuscripts*, N.S., vol. 8, p. 226.

60. Snyder, ed., *Marlborough-Godolphin*, vol. 1, p. 576; vol. 2, p. 590.

61. Mohun did, at least, take an interest in military affairs. He regularly attended meetings of the Board of General Officers, which assisted in army administration and discipline. Army officers seldom missed an opportunity to offend, and meetings occasionally degenerated into shouting matches or brawls. See PRO, WO71/1, Proceedings of the Board of General Officers, 1706–10.

62. HMC, *Portland Manuscripts*, vol. 4, p. 490.

63. For a detailed description of the work of the Lords in the period immediately preceding Mohun's career, see Andrew Swatland, *The House of Lords in the Reign of Charles II* (Cambridge, 1996).

64. See *Journals of the House of Lords*, where committee assignments are printed.

65. Geoffrey Holmes, *British Politics in the Age of Anne* (London, 1967), p. 308.

66. A. S. Turberville, *The House of Lords in the XVIII Century* (Oxford, 1927), pp. 55–56; Nicolson, *London Diaries*, p. 254.

67. See Clyve Jones, "Godolphin, the Whig Junto, and the Scots: A New Lords Division List from 1708," *Scottish Historical Review* 58 (1979), pp. 160, 164, 168, 173.

4: THE REVOLUTION

1. For biographical information on Maccartney, see *DNB* and Charles Dalton, ed., *English Army Lists and Commission Registers, 1661–1714* (London, 1892–1904), vol. 3, pp. 44–45.

2. HMC, *Portland Manuscripts* (London, 1891–1931), vol. 4, p. 266, Major J. Cranstoun to Mr. Cunningham; J. Cartwright, ed., *The Wentworth Papers* (London, 1883), p. 86. See also Maccartney's 1706 letter to James Brydges asking for money to support his regiment, and A. Gordon's letter dated July 30, 1712, describing the "considerable debt" Maccartney left six years earlier. Huntington Library, Stowe Collection, ST 58, vol. 1, pp. 47–48; vol. 12, pp. 192–93. I am indebted to Charles Royster for transcribing these documents for me.

3. BL, Add. Ms. 31,143, f. 349v.

4. For details of the accusations against Maccartney at this point in his career, see *DNB;* [John Oldmixon], *A Defence of Mr. Maccartney, By a Friend* (London, 1713), p. 29; *Wentworth Papers*, pp. 85–86. Some of the details of the assault are omitted from the printed version of the Wentworth correspondence; for these, see BL, Add. Ms. 31,143, f. 349v. For Marlborough's defense of the general, see Henry L. Snyder, ed., *The Marlborough-Godolphin Correspondence* (Oxford, 1975), pp. 1252, 1294.

5. Snyder, ed., *Marlborough-Godolphin*, Godolphin to Marlborough, August 18 and 19, 1709, pp. 1346, 1348–49.

6. Ibid., p. 1294; *Wentworth Papers*, p. 92.

7. For Maccartney's dismissal, see Jonathan Swift, *Journal to Stella*, Harold Williams, ed. (Oxford, 1974), vol. 1, pp. 120–21; *Wentworth Papers*, pp. 162–63; BL, Add. Ms. 31,143, f. 619.

8. Swift, *Journal to Stella*, vol. 1, pp. 142–43.

9. BL, Add. Ms. 70,242, unfoliated, letters from F. Hoffman, dated November 7, 1704, and one undated, circa 1711.

10. Edward Ward, *The London Spy* (London, 1709), pp. 201, 15.

11. For news distribution at a number of London coffeehouses in 1707, see HMC, *House of Lords Manuscripts* (London, 1900–53), N.S., vol. 7, pp. 50–52.

12. Geoffrey Holmes, *British Politics in the Age of Anne* (London, 1967), pp. 22–23; Mohun's letter is in the Staffs. R.O., D(W) 1778/I/ii/181.

13. See Mary Delarivière Manley, *The New Atalantis*, Ros Ballaster, ed. (London, 1991), pp. 89–90, for a description.

14. Henri Misson, *Memoirs and Observations of His Travels Over England* (London, 1719), p. 126; Zacharias von Uffenbach, *London in 1710* (London, 1934), p. 15. For other descriptions of the park, see [James Macky], *A Journey Through England and Scotland* (London, 1714–29), vol. 1, p. 43.

15. Quoted in Neville Braybrooke, *London Green* (London, 1959), p. 62.

16. Alexander Pope, *The Twickenham Edition of the Poems of Alexander Pope*, John Butt, ed. (New Haven, Conn., 1939–67), vol. 4, p. 84, n. 125.

17. *Wentworth Papers*, p. 276.

18. Joseph Spencer, *Anecdotes*, S. W. Singer, ed. (London, 1964), pp. 196–97.

19. Holmes, *British Politics*, pp. 296–97.

20. See Brothers' Minute Book, BL, Add. Ms. 49,360.

21. Peter Drake, *Amiable Renegade: The Memoirs of Peter Drake*, S. A. Burrell, ed. (Stanford, Calif., 1960), pp. 212–15.

22. Manley, *New Atalantis*, pp. 255–56.

23. *Wentworth Papers*, p. 285.

24. For details of the wedding, see PRO, C9/344/61, 344/65, 482/49.

25. E. Beresford Chancellor, *The Romance of Soho* (London, 1931), p. 208.

26. Geoffrey Holmes, *The Trial of Dr. Sacheverell* (London, 1973), p. 157; for Sacheverell riots in general, see ibid., chap. 7. For Mohun's committee, see HMC, *House of Lords Manuscripts*, N.S., vol. 8, pp. 367–68.

27. Holmes, *Trial of Dr. Sacheverell*, p. 210, quoting George Lockhart.

28. Holmes, *Trial of Dr. Sacheverell*, p. 222; unfortunately, we do not know what the two lords said to each other. See Sir James Clavering, *The Correspondence of Sir James Clavering*, H. T. Dickinson, ed. (Gateshead, 1967), p. 72.

29. Holmes, *Trial of Dr. Sacheverell*, pp. 224–32.

30. Cowper's account of this meeting is in *Edward Lord Cowper's Private Diary*, Craven Hawtrey, ed., Roxburghe Club Publications (London, 1833), pp. 47–48; see also Mohun's letter arranging a meeting in October 1710; Staffs. R.O., D(W) 1778/I/ii/181.

31. For the new manor house at Gawsworth, see Raymond Richards, *The Manor of Gawsworth* (London, 1954); for Boconnoc, Nikolaus Pevsner, *The Buildings of England: Cornwall* (Harmondsworth, Middlesex, 1951), pp. 29–30.

32. See *Reports of Cases in Chancery* (London, 1826), Easter Term, 1710, pp. 117–22; for a copy of the order, see Lennoxlove, Hamilton Manuscripts, NRA (S) 2177, bdl. 3565. H. J. Habakkuk discusses the case in *Marriage, Debt, and the Estates System: English Landownership, 1650–1950* (Oxford, 1994).

33. BL, Add. Ms. 22,220, f. IV.

34. HMC, *Fourteenth Report* (London, 1894), App. 3, p. 210.

35. SRO, Mar and Kellie Manuscripts, GD, 124/15/17,18, September 12 and 14, 1710.

36. BL, Add. Ms. 70,026, f. 149. Sir M. Warton to Harley, September 5, 1710.

37. BL, Add. Ms. 70,197, unfoliated, Holt Elmes to Harley, March 24, 1711; Add. Ms. 70,026, f. 204, Hamilton to Harley, October 6, 1710; Daniel Szechi, *Jacobitism and Tory Politics* (Edinburgh, 1984), pp. 64–65.

38. Swift, *Journal to Stella*, vol. 1, p. 323.

39. HMC, *Fourteenth Report*, App. 3, p. 172, Lady Grizel Hume to Lord Marchmount, July 17, 1711.

40. HMC, *Polwarth Manuscripts* (London, 1916–61), vol. 1, p. 2, George Bailie to Alexander, Lord Polwarth, November 13, 1711.

41. See Harley's letter to Hamilton, dated January 16, 1712, where he assures the duke that he has done everything in his power to secure

Hamilton's seat. BL, Add. Ms. 70,278 (Harley Papers), unfoliated; HMC, *Portland Manuscripts*, vol. 5, p. 107, Hamilton to Oxford, November 9, 1711. See Geoffrey Holmes's essay "The Hamilton Affair of 1711–12: A Crisis in Anglo-Scottish Relations," in Geoffrey Holmes, *Politics, Religion, and Society in England, 1679–1742* (London, 1986), pp. 83–108.

42. For other letters commenting on the reaction to Hamilton's defeat, see Clyve Jones, ed., "Letters of Lord Balmerino to Harry Maule, 1710–13, 1721–22," *Miscellany of the Scottish History Society* 12 (1994), pp. 99–168.

43. NLS, Ms. 1032, Hamilton Correspondence, ff. 106–7, James to Selkirk, October 30, 1711.

44. William Nicolson, Bishop of Carlisle, *The London Diaries* (Oxford, 1985), p. 173. For a description of the interior of the house, see [Macky], *Journey Through England and Scotland*, p. 136.

45. See HMC, *House of Lords Manuscripts*, N.S., vol. 9, pp. 187–89, for the proceedings in this case. Nicolson mentions the vote in his *London Diaries*, p. 584; see also the Lords order for a hearing, February 4, 1711/12, in Lennoxlove, Hamilton Manuscripts, NRA (S) 2177, bdl. 3564, Hamilton attorney's notes in ibid., and the duke's petition to the Lords in ibid., bdl. 3565.

46. See *Wentworth Papers*, pp. 257–58, for rumors of Hamilton's possible appointment as Master of the Horse in January 1712.

47. HMC, *House of Lords Manuscripts*, N.S., vol. 9, pp. 187–89.

48. See Paul Langford's remark on this point in *Public Life and the Propertied Englishman, 1689–1798* (Oxford, 1991), p. 110.

49. SRO, Mar and Kellie Manuscripts, GD, 124/15/1947/4, Mar to Lord Grange, February 14, 1712. See also BL, Add. Ms. 31,144, f. 127 (Stafford Papers), Peter Wentworth to Strafford, misdated January 12 (for February 12), 1712.

50. Richards, *Manor of Gawsworth*, pp. 174, 189.

51. Kathleen Lynch, *Jacob Tonson, Kit Cat Publisher* (Knoxville, Tenn., 1971), p. 62; see also Swift, *Journal to Stella*, vol. 2, p. 415; HMC, *Earl of Dartmouth's Manuscripts* (London, 1887), pp. 309–10; G. M. Trevelyan, *England Under Queen Anne* (London, 1930–34), vol. 3, p. 208; Lorenzo Sabini, *Notes on Duels and Duelling* (Boston, 1856), pp. 238–39. For Lady Mohun's letter, see BL, Add. Ms. 61,454, f. 141.

52. For Cadogan's remarks, see Robert Pearman, *The First Earl Cadogan* (London, 1988), p. 74.

53. See *Wentworth Papers*, p. 277; John Timbs, *The Club Life of London* (London, 1866), vol. 1, p. 41; BL, Add. Ms. 36,772, Thomas Burnet Letters, f. 8v, March 15, 1712 (?); Swift, *Journal to Stella*, vol. 2, pp. 508, 511, 515; Nicolson, *London Diaries*, p. 595; BL, Add. Ms. 22,226 (Strafford Papers), f. 95.

54. HMC, *Bath Manuscripts* (London, 1904–8), vol. 1, p. 220; BL, Add. Ms. 31,144, f. 294v, August 26, 1712.
55. BL, Add. Ms. 31,144, f. 297v, Peter Wentworth to Lord Strafford, September 8, 1712.
56. BL, Add. Ms. 22,226, ff. 191v, 201. Lady Strafford to Lord Strafford, August 8 and 26, 1712; f. 225v, September 26, 1712.
57. *Evening Post*, no. 499, October 18, 1712.
58. Ibid., no. 503; for Chatelherault, see Rosalind Marshall, *The Days of Duchess Anne: Life in the Household of the Duchess of Hamilton 1656–1717* (New York, 1973).
59. Heneage Finch, Earl of Nottingham, *Lord Nottingham's Manual of Chancery Practice*, D.E.C. Yale, ed. (Cambridge, 1965), pp. 66–68, 217.
60. For the documents setting out the respective cases, see Lennoxlove, Hamilton Manuscripts, NRA (S) 2177, bdls. 3565, 3566.
61. Ibid., bdls. 3564, 3568.

5: THE DUEL

1. For details on Marlborough House, see E. Beresford Chancellor, *The Private Palaces of London* (Philadelphia, 1909), pp. 108–13. For the Queen's tortuous relationship with the Duchess of Marlborough, see Frances Harris, *A Passion for Government: The Life of Sarah, Duchess of Marlborough* (Oxford, 1991).
2. Philip Dormer Stanhope, Fourth Earl of Chesterfield, *Letters of Philip Dormer Stanhope, Fourth Earl of Chesterfield*, Bonamy Dobrée, ed. (London, 1932), p. 1969.
3. The most detailed (and sympathetic) treatment of Marlborough during this period can be found in W. S. Churchill, *Marlborough* (New York, 1933), vol. 5, passim. See also J. R. Jones, *Marlborough* (Cambridge, 1993).
4. For Chesterfield on Marlborough, see Chesterfield, *Letters*, pp. 1261–62.
5. For letters from Marlborough to Lord Treasurer Godolphin urging Maccartney's reinstatement, see Henry L. Snyder, ed., *The Marlborough-Godolphin Correspondence* (Oxford, 1975), vol. 2, pp. 1252, 1294. See also BL, Add. Ms. 61,283, f. 123; 61,298, f. 41, for letters from Maccartney to the duke.
6. Jonathan Swift, *The Portable Swift*, Carl Van Doren, ed. (Harmondsworth, Middlesex, 1986), p. 167.
7. See Churchill, *Marlborough*, vol. 5, p. 549; G. M. Trevelyan, *England Under Queen Anne* (London, 1930–34), vol. 3, p. 208; for the countess's letter and the council's action, see HMC, *Earl of Dartmouth's Manuscripts* (London, 1887), pp. 309–10.
8. See Churchill, *Marlborough*, vol. 5, chap. 31.
9. For Queen Mary's view, see Martin [Marian] Hailes, *Queen Mary of Modena: Her Life and Letters* (London, 1905), pp. 435–36; for Saint-Simon,

Louis, Duke of St. Simon, *Historical Memoirs of the Duc de St. Simon: A Shortened Version*, Lucy Norton, trans. and ed. (London, 1967), vol. 2, pp. 271–72; for Lockhart, see George Lockhart, *The Lockhart Papers* (London, 1817), vol. 1, pp. 407–9.

10. SRO, Mar and Kellie Manuscripts, GD 124/15/1024/20.

11. BL, Add. Ms. 22,226, ff. 191v, 201; for Swift, see Jonathan Swift, *Journal to Stella*, Harold Williams, ed. (Oxford, 1974), vol. 2, pp. 569–70.

12. BL, Add. Ms. 22,226, f. 207.

13. HMC, *Bath Manuscripts* (London, 1904–8), vol. 1, p. 223.

14. Quoted in Harris, *Passion for Government*, p. 182.

15. Churchill, *Marlborough*, vol. 6. p. 572.

16. See Robert Pearman, *The First Earl Cadogan 1672–1726* (London, 1988), pp. 78, 114–15, for details of these transactions. Typically, years later Sarah fell out with Cadogan and sued him over his stewardship of the money.

17. Charles Hamilton, *Transactions During the Reign of Queen Anne* (Edinburgh, 1790), p. 149.

18. In 1707, the value of a master's place was put at at least £1,500 per annum; William Sachse, *Lord Somers* (Manchester, 1975), p. 83, note 87.

19. Lennoxlove, bdl. 3565, deposition of John Morris dated November 7, 1711.

20. See above, chap. 2, and *A True Narrative of the Proceedings in the Severall Suits in Law That Have Been Between the Right Honourable Charles Lord Gerard of Brandon, and Alexander Fitton, Esq.* (The Hague, 1663), p. 67.

21. PRO, C9/204/11, Chancery bill dated April 27, 1708.

22. Quotes taken from *A Particular Account of the Trial of John Hamilton, Esq. . . .* (London, 1712), p. 6; *The Case at Large of Duke Hamilton and the Lord Mohun* (London, 1712), pp. 11–12.

23. Lockhart, *Lockhart Papers*, vol. 1, p. 403.

24. [George Maccartney,] *A Letter From Mr. Maccartney to a Friend of His in London* (London, 1713), pp. 7–8. This self-serving account of Maccartney's role in the affair must of course be treated with caution.

25. *Particular Account*, p. 2.

26. [Maccartney], *Letter*, p. 9.

27. Ibid.

28. See Williams's testimony in *Case at Large*, pp. 11–12.

29. See Lord Dartmouth's notes on the Privy Council inquiry into these events, HMC, *Earl of Dartmouth's Manuscripts*, pp. 311–15.

30. For information on the Bagnio, see Samuel Haworth, *A Description of the Duke's Bagnio* (London, 1683); Ralph Thoresby, *Diary* (London, 1830), vol. 2, p. 237; E. Beresford Chancellor, *The Annals of Covent Garden and Its Neighborhood* (London, 1930), p. 243.

31. *Particular Account*, p. 3.

32. BL, Add. Ms. 22,221 (Suffolk Papers), f. 156, Strafford to Duke of Beaufort, December 16, 1712.

33. *Case at Large*, pp. 1–2. Rich later married one of Mohun's two stepdaughters.

34. [Maccartney], *Letter*, p. 10.

35. *The Substance of the Depositions Taken at the Coroner's Inquest* . . . (London, 1712); sources vary on the barman's name: John or Isaac Sisson. Cf. *Particular Account*, p. 3.

36. [Maccartney,] *Letter*, p. 10; *Substance of the Depositions*.

37. BL, Add. Ms. 70,246, unfoliated, Francis Lee to Oxford, November 14, 1712.

38. [Abel Boyer], *A True Account of the Animosity, Quarrel, and Duel* . . . (London, 1712), p. 24.

39. *Memoirs of the Life and Family of the Most Illustrious James Late Duke of Hamilton* (London, 1717), p. 101.

40. *Particular Account*, p. 5; *True Account of the Animosity*, pp. 29–30; *Evening Post*, no. 523, p. 2.

41. *Memoirs of the . . . Duke of Hamilton*, pp. 111–12; *Evening Post*, no. 523, p. 2.

42. *Particular Account*, p. 4.

43. HMC, *Earl of Dartmouth's Manuscripts*, p. 312; *Particular Account*, p. 5.

44. *Particular Account*, p. 5.

45. *Substance of the Depositions*.

46. *Case at Large*, pp. 13–14.

47. *Substance of the Depositions*.

48. HMC, *Earl of Dartmouth's Manuscripts*, p. 313.

49. *Substance of the Depositions*. This account of the duel is compiled from several sources, the most important HMC, *Earl of Dartmouth's Manuscripts; Substance of the Depositions; Case at Large; True Account of the Animosity; Evening Post*, no. 523.

50. *Substance of the Depositions*.

51. *Case at Large*, p. 13.

6: THE AFTERMATH

1. Margaret Verney, ed., *Verney Letters of the Eighteenth Century* (London, 1930), vol. 1, p. 289. Thanks to Charles Royster for this citation.

2. George Lockhart, *The Lockhart Papers* (London, 1817), vol. 1, pp. 410–11.

3. Verney, *Verney Letters*, vol. 1, p. 289.

4. Jonathan Swift, *Journal to Stella*, Harold Williams, ed. (Oxford, 1974), vol. 2, pp. 570–71.

5. Ibid., pp. 473–74.

6. *A Full and True Account of a Desperate and Bloody Duel: Which Was Fought This Morning in High Park* (London, 1712).

7. Swift, *Journal to Stella*, vol. 2, p. 572.

8. *Notes and Queries*, 5th series, vol. 12, p. 131. In fact, Lady Mohun may still have been in the country when her husband died.

9. HMC, *Earl of Dartmouth's Manuscripts* (London, 1887), pp. 311–12.

10. Ibid., p. 312.

11. Lockhart, *Lockhart Papers*, vol. 1, pp. 402–3.

12. See *The Substance of the Depositions Taken at the Coroner's Inquest . . .* (London, 1712).

13. HMC *Portland Manuscripts* (London, 1891–1931), vol. 5, pp. 246–47. The coroner's deposition said that the blow to the duke's breast was on the right, rather than the left, side.

14. Lockhart, *Lockhart Papers*, vol. 1, pp. 402–3.

15. Sir David Hamilton, *Diary, 1709–14*, Philip Roberts, ed. (Oxford, 1975), p. 50.

16. See *DNB*, under Maccartney; for the duchess's wrangles with her relatives about the reward, see below.

17. Elizabeth Newton, ed., *Lyme Letters, 1660–1760* (London, 1925), p. 238; *Evening Post*, no. 520 (December 6–9, 1712), p. 3.

18. Hamilton, *Diary*, p. 45.

19. Swift, *Journal to Stella*, vol. 2, p. 588.

20. BL, Add. Ms. 70,282 (Portland Papers), unfoliated, Lord Buckley to Oxford, dated December 18, 1712.

21. *The British Mercury*, no. 451, p. 5. This was in fact the second time Maccartney had been reported captured in Man—there was a similar rumor in December. SRO, Hamilton Manuscripts, GD 406/1/8521.

22. Swift, *Journal to Stella*, vol. 2, pp. 588–89.

23. Sources for Richmond's role in Maccartney's getaway can be found at HMC, *Earl of Dartmouth's Manuscripts*, p. 314; BL, Add. Ms. 22,226, f. 235; 22,220, f. 41 (Strafford Papers); *Evening Post*, no. 515, November 25–27, 1712, p. 3. The council's messenger, after a search for Richmond, found him at Lady Mohun's house.

24. Swift, *Journal to Stella*, vol. 2, p. 595.

25. Ibid., p. 656.

26. These were *The Lives and Characters of James Duke of Hamilton . . . and Charles Lord Mohun; Who Were Unfortunately Kill'd by Each Other in Hyde Park* (London, 1712) (Read); *The Substance of the Depositions* (Baldwin); *A Particular Account of the Trial of John Hamilton, Esq.; For the Murder of Charles Lord Mohun and James Duke of Hamilton and Brandon* (London, 1712); *A Full and Exact Relation of the Duel Fought in Hyde Park on Saturday, November 15, 1712* (London, 1713) (Curll). Robert Forsythe gives a list of various accounts in *A Noble Rake: The Life of Charles, Fourth Lord Mohun* (Cambridge, Mass., 1928), App. D, pp. 268–72.

27. *The Examiner*, November 20, 1712.

306 *Notes*

28. [Daniel Defoe?], *A Strict Enquiry Into the Circumstances of a Late Duel* ... (London, 1713), p. 3.
29. Ibid., pp. 34, 37.
30. Thomas Hearne, *Reliquiae Hearnianae: The Remains of Thomas Hearne, M.A.*, Philip Bliss, ed. (Oxford, 1857), vol. 2, pp. 273–74.
31. BL, Add. Ms. 36,722, ff. 18–19.
32. Philip Dormer Stanhope, Fourth Earl of Chesterfield, *Letters of Philip Dormer Stanhope, Fourth Earl of Chesterfield*, Bonamy Dobrée, ed. (London, 1932), p. 2303. Chesterfield was present at Maccartney's trial.
33. SRO, Hamilton Manuscripts, GD 406/1/7243, Orkney to Lord Ruglen, December 16, 1712.
34. For the trial, see *Evening Post*, nos. 521, 522, 523; *Particular Account;* SRO, Hamilton Manuscripts, GD 406/1/8115, Orkney to Selkirk, December 11, 1712.
35. BL, Add. Ms. 35,988 (Hardwicke Papers), f. 178.
36. Hamilton, *Diary*, p. 50.
37. Verney, *Verney Letters*, p. 372.
38. See [Defoe], *Strict Enquiry*, passim; [John Oldmixon], *A Defence of Mr. Maccartney, By a Friend* (London, 1713), p. 1.
39. Hamilton, *Diary*, p. 47.
40. Verney, *Verney Letters*, p. 371; HMC, *Portland Manuscripts*, vol. 7, p. 114.
41. [George Maccartney], *A Letter From Mr. Maccartney to a Friend of His in London* (London, 1713), pp. 7, 9.
42. SRO, Hamilton Manuscripts, GD 406/1/7243; Orkney to [Ruglen], December 16, 1712.
43. Ibid., GD 406/1/7222/1, Lady Orkney to Ruglen, December 15, 1712.
44. Ibid., GD 406/1/6890, Elizabeth to James, February 1, 1705; 7086, same to same, October 12, 1710. A sample of her correspondence from 1708 contains this description from the Queen's birthday celebration: "for ye honour of North Brittaine," her anonymous friend wrote, describing one of Elizabeth's least-favorite peeresses, "her Grace of Argyle like a fatt hog in armour was very fine in yelow embroidered with silver." SRO, Hamilton Manuscripts, GD 406/1/5482.
45. Alexander Pope, *Correspondence*, George Sherburne, ed. (Oxford, 1956), vol. 1, pp. 404–5.
46. Swift, *Journal to Stella*, vol. 2, p. 513.
47. Quoted in Forsythe, *Noble Rake*, p. 137. Manley makes a similar remark in Mary Delarivière Manley, *The New Atalantis*, Ros Balaster, ed. (London, 1991), p. 259.
48. Elizabeth and Wayland Young, *London's Churches* (Topsfield, Mass., 1986), pp. 146–48.
49. For Elizabeth's age, see PRO, C9/382/1, where she is referred to as "about eighteen" in a Chancery bill dated November 18, 1713.

50. BL, Add. Ms. 61,454 (Blenheim Papers), ff. 152v–153r; Lady Mohun to Duchess of Marlborough, undated, c. 1713–14.

51. PRO, C9/344/61.

52. PRO, C9/467/35; what appears to be the original copy of this will is in the British Library, Add. Ms. 39,923, f. 29, dated March 23, 1711.

53. Mohun's principal creditor, Hugh Fortescue, had lent him nearly £30,000, and other debts brought the grand total to nearly £70,000. For Mohun's debts, see PRO, C9/381/1; BL, Add. Ms. 61,454, ff. 166–67.

54. PRO, C9/344/65, 344/61.

55. BL, Add. Ms. 61,454 (Blenheim Papers), f. 143.

56. Ibid.; ff. 151–54.

57. Ibid., ff. 166–67.

58. HMC, *Cowper Manuscripts* (London, 1888–89), vol. 3, p. 181.

59. BL, Add. Ms. 70,283 (Portland Papers), unfoliated, Lady Mohun to Oxford, dated November 7, [1713].

60. BL, Add. Ms. 36,152 (Hardwicke Papers), ff. 41–42.

61. HMC, *Portland Manuscripts*, vol. 10, pp. 486–88.

62. BL, Add. Ms. 70,283 (Portland Papers), unfoliated, Charlotte Orby to Oxford, May 7, 1714; Thomas Orby to Oxford, November 12, 1713.

63. Ibid., Elizabeth Mohun to Oxford, June 7, [1714?].

64. William Nicolson, Bishop of Carlisle, *The London Diaries*, Clyve Jones and Geoffrey Holmes, eds. (Oxford, 1985), p. 610.

65. BL, Add. Ms. 70,250 (Portland Papers), unfoliated. Report of Edward Northey, Attorney General.

66. BL, Add. Ms. 70,283 (Portland Papers), unfoliated, Charlotte Orby to Oxford, May 18, 1714.

67. BL, Add. Ms. 70,250 (Portland Papers), unfoliated, Order in Council dated December 6, 1714; HMC, *Portland Manuscripts*, vol. 5, pp. 502–3.

68. Lockhart, *Lockhart Papers*, vol. 1, p. 404.

69. *The Review*, No. 34, November 29, 1712.

70. Malachy Postlethwait, *The Universal Dictionary of Trade and Commerce*, 4th ed. (London, 1774; reprint, New York, 1971), vol. 1, under "bankrupt." I owe Charles Royster thanks for this reference.

71. See Forsythe, *Noble Rake*, for a detailed examination of the use Thackeray made of the historical facts of Mohun and Hamilton's lives.

72. *The Lord M——n's Ghost to the D—— of R——nd On Sunday Night Last* (n.p., 1712?); "The Embassy," printed in *The Roxburghe Ballads* (reprint, New York, 1966), vol. 8, p. 827.

73. Jonathan Swift, *The Complete Poems*, Pat Rogers, ed. (New Haven, Conn., 1983), p. 159, "The First Ode of the Second Book of Horace Paraphrased and Addressed to Richard Steele, Esq.," ll. 91–92; Alexander Pope, *The Twickenham Edition of the Poems of Alexander Pope*, John Butt, ed. (New Haven, Conn., 1939–67), v. 4, p. 85, "Imitations of Horace," serm. I, ii, ll. 124–25.

74. *Duke Hamilton and Lord Moon* (n.p., 1760?); other versions of this ballad can be found in NLS, Manuscript 17,799 (Saltoun Papers), f. 150, and *Notes and Queries*, 6th series, vol. 12, p. 331.

75. Nicholas Tindal, *The Continuation of Mr. Rapin de Thoryas' History of England*, 2d ed. (London, 1751), vol. 4, p. 299.

76. *Duke Hamilton and Lord Moon.*

77. HMC, *Stuart Manuscripts* (London, 1902–23), vol. 2, p. 242.

78. See *DNB;* HMC, *Stuart Manuscripts*, vol. 4, p. 525; HMC, *Polwarth Manuscripts* (London, 1916–61), vol. 1, p. 39; HMC, *Townshend Manuscripts* (London, 1887), p. 138; HMC, *Portland Manuscripts*, vol. 5, p. 554; Charles Dalton, ed. *English Army Lists and Commission Registers, 1661–1714* (London, 1892–1904), vol. 3, pp. 44–45.

79. For Maccartney's post-1714 career, see A. J. Guy, *Oeconomy and Discipline: Officership and Administration in the British Army, 1714–63* (Manchester, 1985), pp. 138–39.

80. Pope, *Correspondence*, vol. 1, pp. 404–5, 436–39, 450.

81. John Hervey, Lord Hervey, *Some Materials Towards Memoirs of the Reign of George II*, Romney Sedgwick, ed. (London, 1931), pp. 594–95. Elizabeth had seven children, three boys and four girls; two of the girls died young. See George Hamilton, *A History of the House of Hamilton* (Edinburgh, 1933), pp. 444–50.

82. Mary Cowper, *Diary of Mary, Countess Cowper, 1714–20* (London, 1864), pp. 32–33; Pope, *Correspondence*, vol. 1, p. 407.

83. Lewis M. Wiggin, *The Faction of Cousins: A Political Account of the Grenvilles, 1733–63* (New Haven, Conn., 1958), p. 60, n. 40; see also Tresham Lever, *The House of Pitt: A Family Chronicle* (London, 1947), pp. 47–48.

84. The Pitt diamond weighed no less than 410 carats; Pitt sold it to the Regent of France for 2 million livres. See Zacharias von Uffenbach, *London in 1710*, W. H. Quarrell and Margaret Mare, eds. and trans. (London, 1934), p. 178.

85. Though Elizabeth never paid a debt willingly; she struggled with the Virginian William Byrd over a long-standing debt to Byrd's deceased father-in-law. See William Byrd, *The London Diary*, Louis B. Wright and Marion Tinling, eds. (New York, 1958), pp. 62, 65, 98, 328.

86. Henrietta, Countess of Suffolk, *Letters to and from Henrietta, Countess of Suffolk, and Her Second Husband, the Honourable George Berkeley, from 1712–1767* (London, 1824), vol. 1, p. 91.

87. BL, Stowe Manuscript 750 (Letters of Thomas Parker, Earl of Macclesfield), f. 178.

88. BL, Add. Ms. 69,374 (Dropmore Papers), unfoliated, indenture dated March 26, 1717.

89. For the Griffith girls' dowries, see BL, Add. Ms. 36,148 (Hardwicke Papers), f. 298v.

90. See GEC, under "Doneraile;" HMC, *Stuart Manuscripts*, vol. 7, p. 621.
91. The duchess harassed even those tangentially connected to Lady Mohun, including one of her trustees, the dramatist Congreve. See William Congreve, *William Congreve: Letters and Documents*, John C. Hodges, ed. (New York, 1964), pp. 136–39, 142–45.
92. For some of the documents relating to the suits the Duchess pursued after 1720, see Lennoxlove, Hamilton Manuscripts, Bdls. 3031, 3567, 3568; BL, Add. Ms. 35,584 (Hardwicke Papers), ff. 302, 338; 36,148, ff. 298–303; 36,152, ff. 41–44; HMC, *House of Lords Manuscripts*, N.S. (London, 1900–53), vol. 12, pp. 192–95, 310–14.

BIBLIOGRAPHY

MANUSCRIPT SOURCES

British Library, London

Additional Manuscripts
6,722, 6,727: Pengelly Papers
23,904: Political Poems, in the Reign of Queen Anne
22,220, 22,226, 31,143–44: Strafford Papers
22,627, 22,221, 22,629: Suffolk Papers
29,575–76: Hatton-Finch Papers
34,195: Official Papers
35,584, 35,988, 36,148, 36,152: Hardwicke Papers
36,772: Thomas Burnet Letters
38,141: William Dugdale's Heraldic Collections
38,855: Hodgkin Papers
39,188: Mackenzie Letters
39,923: Jacobite Letters
49,360: Minute Book, Board of Brothers
61,136, 61,283, 61,298, 61,454, 61,609, 61,611, 61,628: Blenheim Papers
69,374: Dropmore Papers
70,026, 70,081, 70,197, 70,242, 70,246, 70,250, 70,278, 70,282, 70,283: Portland Papers

Stowe Manuscripts
750: Letters of Thomas Parker, Earl of Macclesfield

Public Record Office, London
SP 34: State Papers, Domestic, Queen Anne
C 22, C 8, C9: Chancery Bills
C 104/113; 116: Chancery Master's Exhibits, Lord Ossulston's Diary
WO 71/1: Proceedings of the Board of General Officers, 1706–10
WO 71/13: General Courts Martial

Scottish Record Office, Edinburgh
GD 406/1: Hamilton Manuscripts
GD 124/15: Mar and Kellie Manuscripts

National Library of Scotland, Edinburgh
Ms. 1032: Hamilton Correspondence
Ms. 2092: Political Poems
Ms. 7020–21: Yester Manuscripts
Ms. 7104: Tweeddale Letters
Ms. 8262: Stuart Stevenson Papers
Ms. 17,799: Saltoun Papers (Political Poems)

Lennoxlove House, Haddington, Scotland
Hamilton Manuscripts

Huntington Library, San Marino, California
LO 8973: Loudon Papers
ST 58: Stowe Manuscripts

PRINTED PRIMARY SOURCES
Ashmole, Elias. *Diary.* C. H. Josten, ed. 5 vols. Oxford, 1966.
Bellingham, Thomas. *Diary.* Anthony Hewitson, ed. Preston, Lancashire, 1908.
Blackader, John. *Select Passages from the Diary and Letters of John Blackader.* Edinburgh, 1806.
Boswell, James. *Life of Samuel Johnson.* Oxford, 1953.
[Boyer, Abel.] *A True Account of the Animosity, Quarrel, and Duel Between the Late Duke of Hamilton, and the Lord Mohun.* London, 1712.
The British Mercury, 1713–16. London.
Brockbank, Thomas. *Diary and Letterbook of Thomas Brockbank.* Richard Trappes-Lomax, ed. Chetham Society Publications, New Series, vol. 89 (1930).
Burnet, Gilbert. *History of My Own Times.* 2nd ed. 6 vols. Oxford, 1823.
Byrd, William. *The London Diary.* Louis B. Wright and Marion Tinling, eds. New York, 1958.
Calendar of Treasury Books. 32 vols. London, 1904–57.
Cartwright, J., ed. *The Wentworth Papers.* London, 1883.
The Case at Large of Duke Hamilton and the Lord Mohun. London, 1712.
Clavering, Sir James. *The Correspondence of Sir James Clavering.* H. T. Dickinson, ed. Gateshead, 1967.
Clerk, Sir John. *Memoirs of the Life of John Clerk.* John M. Gray, ed. Roxburghe Club Publications. London, 1895.
Congreve, William. *William Congreve: Letters and Documents.* John C. Hodges, ed. New York, 1964.
Cowper, Edward, Lord. *Edward Lord Cowper's Private Diary.* Craven Hawtrey, ed. Roxburghe Club Publications. London, 1833.
Cowper, Mary. *Diary of Mary, Countess Cowper, 1714–20.* London, 1864.
Coxe, William, ed. *Memoirs of the Duke of Marlborough.* 3 vols. London, 1847.

Cust, Elizabeth. *Records of the Cust Family*. Series 2: The Brownlows of Belton. London, 1909.

The Daily Courant, 1702–7. London.

Dalton, Charles, ed. *English Army Lists and Commission Registers, 1661–1714*. 3 vols. London, 1892–1904.

Defoe, Daniel. *Memoirs of Captain George Carleton*. Oxford, 1840.

[Defoe, Daniel?] *The Secret History of the White Staff, Part One*. 4th ed. London, 1714.

[Defoe, Daniel?] *A Strict Enquiry into the Circumstances of a Late Duel, With Some Account of the Persons Concern'd on Both Sides, Being a Modest Attempt to Do Justice to the Injur'd Memory of a Noble Person Dead, and to the Injur'd Honour of an Absent Person Living*. London, 1713.

Dilke, Thomas. *The Lover's Luck: A Comedy*. London, 1696.

Douch, H. L., ed. "The Household Accounts of Warwick Mohun of Luney, 1705–14." *Journal of the Royal Institution of Cornwall*, New Series, vol. 11 (1984), pp. 226–303.

Drake, Peter. *Amiable Renegade: The Memoirs of Peter Drake*. S. A. Burrell, ed. Stanford, Calif., 1960.

D'Urfey, Thomas. *Love for Money: Or, the Boarding School*. London, 1691.

Farquhar, George. *Works*. Shirley Strum Kenny, ed. 2 vols. Oxford, 1988.

Finch, Heneage, Earl of Nottingham. *Lord Nottingham's Manual of Chancery Practice*. D.E.C. Yale, ed. Cambridge, 1965.

Fraser, Simon, Lord Lovat. *Memoirs*. London, 1797.

Freke, Elizabeth. *Elizabeth Freke: Her Diary 1671–1714*. Mary Carbery, ed. Cork, 1913.

A Full and Exact Relation of the Duel Fought in Hyde Park on Saturday, November 15, 1712. London, 1713.

A Full and True Account of a Desperate and Bloody Duel: Which Was Fought This Morning in High Park. London, 1712.

Gay, John. *Poetry and Prose*. Vinton Dearing, ed. Oxford, 1974.

Hamilton, Charles. *Transactions During the Reign of Queen Anne*. Edinburgh, 1790.

Hamilton, Sir David. *Diary, 1709–14*. Philip Roberts, ed. Oxford, 1975.

Haworth, Samuel. *A Description of the Duke's Bagnio*. London, 1683.

Hearne, Thomas. *Reliquiae Hearnianae: The Remains of Thomas Hearne, M.A.* Philip Bliss, ed. 2 vols. Oxford, 1857.

Hervey, John, Lord Hervey. *Some Materials Towards Memoirs of the Reign of George II*. Romney Sedgwick, ed. London, 1931.

Heywood, Thomas, ed. *The Norris Papers*. Chetham Society Publications, vol. 9 (1846).

Historical Manuscripts Commission. *Fourth Report*. London, 1874.

Historical Manuscripts Commission. *Fifth Report*. London, 1876.

Historical Manuscripts Commission. *Seventh Report*. London, 1879.

Historical Manuscripts Commission. *Eighth Report*. London, 1881.

Historical Manuscripts Commission. *Ninth Report*, Appendix, Part 2. London, 1884.

Historical Manuscripts Commission. *Tenth Report*, Appendix 4. London, 1885.

Historical Manuscripts Commission. *Twelfth Report*, Appendix 8. London, 1891.

Historical Manuscripts Commission. *Thirteenth Report*, Appendix 6. London, 1893.

Historical Manuscripts Commission. *Fourteenth Report*, Appendix 3. London, 1894.

Historical Manuscripts Commission. *Bath Manuscripts*. 3 vols. London, 1904–8.

Historical Manuscripts Commission. *Cowper Manuscripts*. 3 vols. London, 1888–89.

Historical Manuscripts Commission. *Earl of Dartmouth's Manuscripts*. London, 1887.

Historical Manuscripts Commission. *Fortescue Manuscripts*. 10 vols. London, 1892–1915.

Historical Manuscripts Commission. *Hamilton Manuscripts*. 2 vols. London, 1887–1932.

Historical Manuscripts Commission. *Hastings Manuscripts*. 4 vols. London, 1928–47.

Historical Manuscripts Commission. *Hodgkin Manuscripts*. London, 1897.

Historical Manuscripts Commission. *House of Lords Manuscripts, 1677–88*. London, 1887.

Historical Manuscripts Commission. *House of Lords Manuscripts, 1688–93*. 4 vols. London, 1894.

Historical Manuscripts Commission. *House of Lords Manuscripts, 1697–99*. London, 1905.

Historical Manuscripts Commission. *House of Lords Manuscripts*, New Series, 12 vols. London, 1900–53.

Historical Manuscripts Commission. *Kenyon Manuscripts*. London, 1894.

Historical Manuscripts Commission. *Laing Manuscripts*. 2 vols. London, 1914–25.

Historical Manuscripts Commission. *LeFleming Manuscripts*. London, 1890.

Historical Manuscripts Commission. *Mar and Kellie Manuscripts*. London, 1904.

Historical Manuscripts Commission. *Ormonde Manuscripts*. New Series, 8 vols. London, 1902–20.

Historical Manuscripts Commission. *Polwarth Manuscripts*. 5 vols. London, 1916–61.

Historical Manuscripts Commission. *Portland Manuscripts*. 10 vols. London, 1891–1931.

Historical Manuscripts Commission. *Rutland Manuscripts.* 4 vols. London, 1888–1905.

Historical Manuscripts Commission. *Stuart Manuscripts.* 7 vols. London, 1902–23.

Historical Manuscripts Commission. *Townshend Manuscripts.* London, 1887.

Hooke, Nathaniel. *Correspondence.* William Dunn Macray, ed. 2 vols. Roxburghe Club Publications, 1870.

———. *The Secret History of Colonel Hooke's Negotiations in Scotland in 1707.* London, 1775.

Hope, Sir William. *A Vindication of the True Art of Self-Defence.* Edinburgh, 1724.

Hyde, Henry, Earl of Clarendon. *The Correspondence of Henry Hyde, Earl of Clarendon.* Samuel W. Singer, ed. London, 1828.

Jackson, James, ed. *Three Elizabethan Fencing Manuals.* Delmar, N.Y., 1972.

Journals of the House of Lords. London, 1767– .

The Lives and Characters of James Duke of Hamilton . . . and Charles Lord Mohun; Who Were Unfortunately Kill'd by Each Other in Hyde Park. London, 1712.

Lockhart, George. *The Lockhart Papers.* 2 vols. London, 1817.

Luttrell, Narcissus. *A Brief Historical Relation of State Affairs.* 6 vols. London, 1857.

[Maccartney, George.] *A Letter From Mr. Maccartney to a Friend of His in London.* London, 1713.

[Macky, James.] *A Journey Through England and Scotland.* 3 vols. London, 1714–29.

Macky, James. *Memoirs of the Secret Services of James Macky.* London, 1733.

Magalotti, Lorenzo. *Lorenzo Magalotti at the Court of Charles II.* W. E. Knowles Middleton, ed. Waterloo, Ont., 1980.

Manley, Mary Delarivière. *The New Atalantis.* Ros Ballaster, ed. London, 1991.

Mary II. *Memoirs of Mary, Queen of England.* Richard Doebner, ed. London, 1886.

Memoirs of the Life and Family of the Most Illustrious James Late Duke of Hamilton. London, 1717.

Misson, Henri. *Memoirs and Observations of His Travels Over England.* London, 1719.

Mure, William, ed. *Selections from the Family Papers Preserved at Caldwell.* Glasgow, 1854.

Newcombe, Henry. *The Autobiography of Henry Newcombe, M.A.* Richard Parkinson, ed. Chetham Society Publications, vols. 26–27 (1852–53).

Newton, Elizabeth, ed. *Lyme Letters, 1660–1760.* London, 1925.

Nicolson, William, Bishop of Carlisle. *The London Diaries.* Clyve Jones and Geoffrey Holmes, eds. Oxford, 1985.

Ogilvie, James, First Earl of Seafield. *Letters Relating to Scotland in the Reign of Queen Anne.* P. Hume Brown, ed. Edinburgh, 1915.

[Oldmixon, John.] *A Defence of Mr. Maccartney, By a Friend*. London, 1713.

Parliamentary History of England, 1688–1702. London, 1809.

A Particular Account of the Trial of John Hamilton, Esq.: For the Murder of Charles Lord Mohun and James Duke of Hamilton and Brandon. London, 1712.

Pepys, Samuel. *The Diary of Samuel Pepys*. Robert Latham and William Matthews, eds. 11 vols. Berkeley, Calif., 1970–83.

Pope, Alexander. *Correspondence*. George Sherburne, ed. 5 vols. Oxford, 1956.

———. *The Twickenham Edition of the Poems of Alexander Pope*. John Butt, ed. 10 vols. New Haven, Conn., 1930–67.

Postlethwait, Malachy. *The Universal Dictionary of Trade and Commerce*, 4th ed. 2 vols. London, 1774; reprint, New York, 1971.

Reports of Cases in Chancery. London, 1826.

Rogers, James E. Thorold, ed. *A Complete Collection of the Protests of the Lords*. 3 vols. Oxford, 1875.

The Roxburghe Ballads. 9 vols. London, 1871–99; reprint, New York, 1966.

Ryder, Dudley. *The Diary of Dudley Ryder, 1715–16*. William Matthews, ed. London, 1939.

Savile, George, First Marquis Halifax. *The Life and Letters of Sir George Savile, First Marquis Halifax*. H. C. Foxcroft, ed. 2 vols. London, 1898.

Snyder, Henry L., ed. *The Marlborough-Godolphin Correspondence*. Oxford, 1975.

Stanhope, Philip Dormer, Fourth Earl of Chesterfield. *Letters of Philip Dormer Stanhope, Fourth Earl of Chesterfield*. Bonamy Dobrée, ed. London, 1932.

Stanning, J. H., ed. *Royalist Composition Papers*. Record Society for the Publication of Original Documents Relating to Lancashire and Cheshire. Vol. 29 (1896).

The Substance of the Depositions Taken at the Coroner's Inquest the 17th, 19th, and 21st November. London, 1712.

Suffolk, Henrietta, Countess of. *Letters to and from Henrietta, Countess of Suffolk, and Her Second Husband, the Honourable George Berkeley, from 1712–1767*. 2 vols. London, 1824.

Swift, Jonathan. *The Complete Poems*. Pat Rogers, ed. New Haven, Conn., 1983.

———. *Journal to Stella*. Harold Williams, ed. 2 vols. Oxford, 1974.

———. *The Portable Swift*. Carl Van Doren, ed. Harmondsworth, Middlesex, 1986.

———. *Prose Works*. Herbert Davis, ed. 16 vols. Oxford, 1939–74.

Thoresby, Ralph. *Diary*. 2 vols. Joseph Hunter, ed. London, 1830.

Tindal, Nicholas. *The Continuation of Mr. Rapin de Thoryas' History of England*. 2nd ed. 4 vols. London, 1751.

Toland, John. *An Account of the Courts of Prussia and Hanover*. London. 1705.

A True Account of the Unreasonableness of Mr. Fitton's Pretences Against the Earl of Macclesfield. n.p., [1685?].

A True and Impartial Account of the Murder of His Grace the Duke of Hamilton and Brandon. London, 1712.

A True Narrative of the Proceedings in the Severall Suits in Law That Have Been Between the Right Honourable Charles Lord Gerard of Brandon, and Alexander Fitton, Esq. The Hague, 1663.

The Tryal of Charles Lord Mohun Before the House of Peers in Parliament. London, 1693.

Uffenbach, Zacharias von. *London in 1710.* W. H. Quarrell and Margaret Mare, eds. and trans. London, 1934.

Verney, Margaret, ed. *Verney Letters of the Eighteenth Century.* 2 vols. London, 1930.

Ward, Edward. *The London Spy.* 4th ed. London, 1709.

Warrand, Duncan, ed. *More Culloden Papers.* Inverness, 1925.

The Whole Lives, Characters, Actions, and Fall of D. Hamilton and L. Mohun. London, 1712.

PRINTED SECONDARY SOURCES

Ashbee, C. R., et al., eds. *Survey of London.* 37-plus vols. London, 1900–   .

Bahlman, D.W.R. *The Moral Revolution of 1688.* New Haven, Conn., 1957.

Beattie, John M. *The English Court in the Reign of George I.* Cambridge, 1967.

Beckett, J. V., and Clyve Jones. "Financial Improvidence and Political Independence in the Early Eighteenth Century: George Booth, Second Earl of Warrington." *Bulletin of the John Rylands Library* 65 (1982–83).

Bennett, G. V. *White Kennett, 1660–1728, Bishop of Peterborough.* London, 1957.

Bickley, Francis. *The Cavendish Family.* London, 1911.

Blewett, David. "Changing Attitudes Towards Marriage in the Time of Defoe: the Case of Moll Flanders." *Huntington Library Quarterly* 44 (1980–81).

Braybrooke, Neville. *London Green.* London, 1959.

Brett-Jones, Norman. *The Growth of Stuart London.* London, 1935.

Britton, J., and E. W. Brayley. *Devonshire and Cornwall Illustrated.* London, 1832.

Bucholz, R. O. *The Augustan Court: Queen Anne and the Decline of Court Culture.* Stanford, 1993.

Callow, Edward. *Old London Taverns.* London, 1899.

Chancellor, E. Beresford. *The Annals of Covent Garden and Its Neighborhood.* London, 1930.

———. *The Private Palaces of London.* Philadelphia, 1909.

———. *The Romance of Soho.* London, 1931.

Chandler, David. *The Art of Warfare in the Age of Marlborough.* New York, 1976.

Childs, John. *The English Army of William III.* Manchester, 1987.

Churchill, W. S. *Marlborough.* 5 vols. New York, 1933.

Clode, Charles. *The Military Forces of the Crown.* 2 vols. London, 1869.

Collecteanea Topographica et Genealogica. 8 vols. London, 1843.

Coward, T. A. *Cheshire: Traditions and History.* London, 1932.

Crossley, F. H. "The Post-Reformation Effigies and Monuments of Cheshire." *Transactions of the Historical Society of Lancashire and Cheshire* 91 (1959).

Croston, James. *Nooks and Corners of Lancashire and Cheshire.* London, 1882.

Cruickshanks, Dan, and Neil Burton. *Life in the Georgian City.* London, 1990.

Dalton, Cornelius. *The Life of Thomas Pitt.* Cambridge, 1915.

Dasent, Arthur. *The History of St. James's Square.* London, 1895.

Davies, Godfrey. "The Seamy Side of Marlborough's War." *Huntington Library Quarterly* 15 (1951–52).

Dearing, Vinton. "A Walk Through London With John Gay and a Run With Daniel Defoe." In J. H. Plumb and Vinton Dearing, eds. *Some Aspects of Eighteenth Century England.* Los Angeles, 1971.

Dickinson, H. T. *Bolingbroke.* London, 1970.

———. "The Mohun-Hamilton Duel: Whig Conspiracy or Sham Plot?" *Durham University Journal* 57 (1967).

Dickinson, William C. *Sidney Godolphin, Lord Treasurer, 1702–1710.* Lewiston, N.Y., 1990.

Ellis, Aytoun. *The Penny Universities: A History of the Coffee Houses.* London, 1956.

Eves, Charles. *Matthew Prior: Poet and Diplomatist.* New York, 1939.

Falk, Bernard. *The Royal Fitzroys: Dukes of Grafton Through Four Centuries.* London, 1950.

Figueiredo, Peter de, and Julian Treuherz. *Cheshire Country Houses.* London, 1988.

Fishwick, Henry. *The History of the Parish of Garstang.* 2 vols. Chetham Society Publications 104–5 (1878–79).

Fitzroy, Sir Almeric. *Henry, Duke of Grafton, 1663–1690.* London, 1921.

Forsythe, Robert. *A Noble Rake: The Life of Charles, Fourth Lord Mohun.* Cambridge, Mass., 1928.

Fortescue, J. W. *A History of the British Army.* London, 1910.

Francis, A. David. *The First Peninsular War 1702–1713.* London, 1975.

Gastrell, Francis. *Notitia Cestriensis, Or Historical Notices of the Diocese of Chester.* F. R. Raines, ed. Chetham Society Publications 8 (1845).

Geduld, Harry M. *Prince of Publishers: A Study of the Work and Career of Jacob Tonson.* Bloomington, Ind., 1969.

Gilmour, Ian. *Riot, Risings, and Revolution: Governance and Violence in Eighteenth Century England.* London, 1992.

Glassey, L.K.J. "The Origins of Political Parties in Late Seventeenth Century Lancashire." *Transactions of the Historical Society of Lancashire and Cheshire* 136 (1987).

Guy, A. J. *Oeconomy and Discipline: Officership and Administration in the British Army, 1714–63.* Manchester, 1985.

Habakkuk, H. J. "Daniel Finch, Second Earl of Nottingham: His House and Estate." In J. H. Plumb, ed., *Studies in Social History.* London, 1955.

————. *Marriage, Debt, and the Estates System: English Landownership, 1650–1950.* Oxford, 1994.

Hailes, Martin [Marian]. *Queen Mary of Modena: Her Life and Letters.* London, 1905.

Hainsworth, D. R. *Stewards, Lords, and People: the Estate Steward and His World in Later Stuart England.* Cambridge, 1992.

Hamilton, Elizabeth. *The Mordaunts: An Eighteenth Century Family.* London, 1965.

Hamilton, George. *A History of the House of Hamilton.* Edinburgh, 1933.

Harris, Frances. *A Passion for Government: The Life of Sarah, Duchess of Marlborough.* Oxford, 1991.

Hart, A. Tindal. *The Life and Times of John Sharp, Archbishop of York.* London, 1949.

Hatton, Ragnhild. *George I, Elector and King.* Cambridge, Mass., 1978.

Holdsworth, W. S. *A History of English Law.* 3 vols. London, 1903.

Holmes, Geoffrey. *British Politics in the Age of Anne.* London, 1967.

————. *Politics, Religion, and Society in England, 1679–1742.* London, 1986.

————. *The Trial of Dr. Sacheverell.* London, 1973.

Holmes, Richard. *Dr. Johnson and Mr. Savage.* New York, 1993.

Hooker, Edward. "Humor in the Age of Pope." *Huntington Library Quarterly* 11 (1947–48).

Horwitz, Henry. *Revolution Politicks: The Career of Daniel Finch Second Earl of Nottingham 1647–1730.* Cambridge, 1968.

————, and Patrick Polden. "Continuity or Change in the Court of Chancery in the Seventeenth and Eighteenth Centuries?" *Journal of British Studies* 35 (1996).

Jacobsen, Gertrude Ann. *William Blathwayt: A Late Seventeenth Century English Administrator.* New Haven, Conn., 1932.

Jenkins, Simon. *Landlords to London: The Story of a Capital and Its Growth.* London, 1975.

Jones, Clyve. "Godolphin, the Whig Junto, and the Scots: A New Lords Division List from 1708." *Scottish Historical Review* 58 (1979).

————. "The London Life of a Peer in the Reign of Anne." *London Journal* 16 (1991).

————. "The Parliamentary Organization of the Whig Junto in the Reign of Queen Anne: The Evidence of Lord Ossulston's Diary." *Parliamentary History* 10 (1991).

————, ed. "Letters of Lord Balmerino to Harry Maule, 1710–13, 1721–22." *Miscellany of the Scottish History Society* 12 (1994).

Jones, J. R. *Marlborough.* Cambridge, 1993.

Jordan, Robert. "George Farquhar's Military Career." *Huntington Library Quarterly* 37 (1973–74).

Kent, Anthony. *Weapons and Equipment of the Marlborough Wars.* Poole, Dorset, 1980.

Kiernan, V. G. *The Duel in European History.* Oxford, 1988.

Klein, Lawrence. *Shaftesbury and the Culture of Politeness.* Cambridge, 1994.

Langford, Paul. *Public Life and the Propertied Englishman, 1689–1798.* Oxford, 1991.

Lever, Tresham. *The House of Pitt: A Family Chronicle.* London, 1947.

Lynch, Kathleen, *Jacob Tonson, Kit-Cat Publisher.* Knoxville, Tenn., 1971.

Macaulay, Thomas. *History of England From the Accession of James II.* 5 vols. New York, 1892.

Mackenzie, W. C. *Simon Fraser, Lord Lovat, His Life and Times.* London, 1908.

Marshall, Rosalind. *The Days of Duchess Anne: Life in the Household of the Duchess of Hamilton 1656–1717.* New York, 1973.

Maurice, Sir Francis. *The History of the Scots Guards.* 2 vols. London, 1934.

Middleton, Dorothy. *The Life of Charles, Second Earl of Middleton, 1650–1719.* London, 1957.

Mingay, G. E. *English Landed Society in the Eighteenth Century.* London, 1963.

Montague, W. D., Duke of Manchester. *Court and Society From Elizabeth to Anne.* 2 vols. London, 1864.

Newton, Elizabeth. *Lyme Letters, 1660–1760.* London, 1925.

Nicholson, T. C., and A. S. Turberville. *Charles Talbot, Duke of Shrewsbury.* Cambridge, 1930.

Oakeshott, Ewart. *European Weapons and Armour.* London, 1980.

Parnell, Arthur. *The War of the Succession in Spain.* London, 1905.

Pearman, Robert. *The First Earl Cadogan 1672–1726.* London, 1988.

Pevsner, Nikolaus. *The Buildings of England: Cornwall.* Harmondsworth, Middlesex, 1951.

Plumb, J. H. *Sir Robert Walpole: The Making of a Statesman.* London, 1956.

———, ed. *Studies in Social History.* London, 1955.

———, and Vinton Dearing, eds. *Some Aspects of Eighteenth Century England.* Los Angeles, 1971.

Redding, Cyrus. *An Illustrated Itinerary of the County of Cornwall.* London, 1842.

Richards, Raymond. *The Manor of Gawsworth.* London, 1954.

Riley, P.W.J. *King William and the Scottish Politicians.* Edinburgh, 1979.

Robbins, Christopher. *The Earl of Wharton and Whig Party Politics 1679–1715.* Lewiston, N.Y., 1991.

Sabini, Lorenzo. *Notes on Duels and Dueling.* Boston, 1856.

Sachse, William. *Lord Somers.* Manchester, 1975.

St. Simon, Louis, Duke of. *Historical Memoirs of the Duc de St. Simon: A Shortened Version.* 2 vols. Lucy Norton, trans. and ed. London, 1967.

Saunders, Hilary St. George. *Westminster Hall.* London, 1951.

Scouller, R. A. *The Army of Queen Anne.* Oxford, 1966.

Sergeant, Philip. *My Lady Castlemaine.* London, 1912.

Shelley, Henry C. *Inns and Taverns of Old London.* London, 1909.

Spencer, Joseph. *Anecdotes.* S. W. Singer, ed. London, 1964.

Spurr, John. "The Church, the Societies, and the Moral Revolution of 1688," in John Walsh, Colin Haydon, and Stephen Taylor, eds. *The Church of England 1689–1833: From Toleration to Tractarianism.* Cambridge, 1993.

———. *The Restoration Church of England.* New Haven, Conn., 1991.

Stockdale, F.W.L. *Excursions in the County of Cornwall.* London, 1824.

Stone, Lawrence. *Family and Fortune: Studies in Aristocratic Finance in the Sixteenth and Seventeenth Centuries.* Oxford, 1973.

———. *Broken Lives: Separation and Divorce in England 1660–1857.* Oxford, 1993.

Swatland, Andrew. *The House of Lords in the Reign of Charles II.* Cambridge, 1996.

Szechi, Daniel. *Jacobitism and Tory Politics.* Edinburgh, 1984.

Timbs, John. *The Club Life of London.* 2 vols. London, 1866.

Trevelyan, G. M. *England Under Queen Anne.* 3 vols. London, 1930–34.

Truman, Ben C. *The Field of Honor.* New York, 1884.

Turberville, A. S. *The House of Lords in the XVIII Century.* Oxford, 1927.

Voitle, Robert. *The Third Earl of Shaftesbury, 1671–1713.* Baton Rouge, La., 1984.

Weatherill, Lorna. *Consumer Behaviour and Material Culture in Britain, 1660–1760.* London, 1988.

Weber, Harold. "Rakes, Rogues, and the Empire of Misrule." *Huntington Library Quarterly* 47 (1984).

Wiggin, Lewis M. *The Faction of Cousins: A Political Account of the Grenvilles, 1733–63.* New Haven, Conn., 1958.

Wilson, John. *A Rake and His Times: George Villiers, Second Duke of Buckingham.* New York, 1954.

Young, Elizabeth and Wayland. *London's Churches.* Topsfield, Mass., 1986.

SOURCES OF ILLUSTRATIONS

1. By Sir Godfrey Kneller. Reproduced with the permission of the Duke of Hamilton.
2. Author's collection.
3. F.W.L. Stockdale, *Excursions in the County of Cornwall* (London, 1824).
4. Robert Forsythe, *A Noble Rake: The Life of Charles, Fourth Lord Mohun* (Cambridge, Mass., 1928).
5. Daniel Defoe, *A Tour Through London* (New York: Beny Blom, 1969).
6. Author's collection.
7. John Ireland, ed., *Hogarth's Works* (Edinburgh, 1883).
8. Author's collection.
9. Walter Besant, *London, North of the Thames* (London: Adam and Charles Black, 1911).
10. By Peter Tillemans. © Her Majesty Queen Elizabeth II, reprinted by permission from Royal Collection Enterprises Ltd.
11. Edward Welford, *Old and New London*, vol. 4 (London: Lasseu, Petter and Galpin, n.d. [c. 1850s]).
12. Daniel Defoe, *A Tour Through London* (New York: Beny Blom, 1969).
13. A. S. Turberville, *English Men and Manners in the Eighteenth Century*, 2nd ed. (Oxford: Clarendon Press, 1929).
14. Author's collection.
15. *The Memoirs of the Duke of Hamilton* (London, 1717).
16. W. S. Churchill, *Marlborough* (New York, 1933).
17. Edward Welford, *Old and New London*, vol. 4 (London: Lasseu, Petter and Galpin, n.d. [c. 1850s]).
18. J. D. Aylwand, *The English Man at Arms* (London: Routledge, Kegan, and Paul, 1956).
19. Daniel Defoe, *A Tour Through London* (New York: Beny Blom, 1969).
20. Edward Welford, *Old and New London*, vol. 4 (London: Lasseu, Petter and Galpin, n.d. [c. 1850s]).
21. Robert Forsythe, *A Noble Rake: The Life of Charles, Fourth Lord Mohun* (Cambridge, Mass., 1928).
22. Walter Besant, *London, North of the Thames* (London: Adam and Charles Black, 1911).

Allsup, Diana, 88
Almanza, Battle of, 155, 217
Anglesey, Arthur, Earl of, 16–18, 37
Anglesey, Countess of, 5–6
Anglican Church, *see* Church of England
Anne, Queen, 32, 101, 118–22, 126, 140–42, 145–46, 151, 161–63, 169, 171, 185–88, 193, 196–98, 216, 271, 273, 284; accession of, 118, 127, 129, 130; and aftermath of Hamilton-Mohun duel, 248, 249, 255, 256; death of, 4, 8, 131, 268–69; doctors of, 172; duels abhorred by, 221; favorites of, 159–60, 174; Jacobites and, 129–34, 209–12; and Junto Whigs, 173, 178–80; Maccartney dismissed from command by, 156–58; Marlborough and, 147, 203, 205, 207–9; Order of Garter awarded to Hamilton by, 220; petitioned by Orbys, 266, 267; proclamation against Mohawks issued by, 195; and Scottish Parliament, 124, 125
Argyll, Duchess of, 268, 306*n44*
Argyll, Duke of, 268, 269
Arran, James, Earl of, *see* Hamilton, James Douglas-Hamilton, fourth Duke of

Balmerino, Lord, 185
Bamford, Elizabeth, 264
Baptists, 151
Berkeley, Lord, 184
Birmingham, Edward, 21
Board of Brothers, 168–69, 284
Board of General Officers, 298*n61*
Bolingbroke, Henry St. John, first Viscount, 195–96, 219, 244–45, 247, 267
Boussier, Paul, 226, 228

Bracegirdle, Anne, 42–49, 57, 58, 94

Bradford, Lord, 143

Bridgewater, Earl of, 192

Buckingham, George Villiers, second Duke of, 14, 17, 22

Buckley, Lord, 249

Burnet, Gilbert, Bishop of Salisbury, 5, 91

Burnet, Thomas, 194, 253

Byrd, William, 308*n85*

Cadogan, William, 194, 303*n16*

Capel, Lord, 61

Carmarthen, Thomas Osborne, Marquess of, 56, 58–61

Caroline, Queen (wife of George II), 277

Catholics, 7, 12, 20, 29, 31, 81, 174

Cavendish, William, Lord, 20–21

Chaboner, John, 227, 229

Chancery, Court of, 53, 214

Charles I, King, 6, 9, 65–66, 279, 283

Charles II, King, 4, 5, 6, 11, 13, 20, 27, 28, 29, 31*n*, 37, 71, 79, 80–81, 98–99

Chesterfield, Philip Dormer Stanhope, fourth Earl of, 205, 253

Churchill, John, *see* Marlborough, John Churchill, first Duke of

Churchill, Col. Joseph, 217, 218, 221, 225

Church of England, 20, 31, 87, 91, 151, 169, 175, 179

Clarendon, Edward Hyde, first Earl of, 190, 192

Clark, Andrew, 228–30, 232, 237

Clement XI, Pope, 128

Clerk, Sir John, 136

Cleveland, Barbara Villiers, Duchess of, 98

Cleveland, Duke and Duchess of, 178

Clydesdale, Marquess of, 225–26

Coke, Vice Chamberlain, 265

Common Pleas Court, 53

Congreve, William, 309*n92*

Coote, Capt. Richard, 62–63, 111

Cowper, Lady, 278

Cowper, William Cowper, first Earl, 177, 180–84, 189, 201, 256

Cromwell, Oliver, 6, 71, 132

Darien Company, 4, 121, 131, 286

Dartmouth, Lord, 244

Davenport, Capt. John, 70

Defoe, Daniel, 138, 252, 256, 258, 270

Dissenters, Protestant, 151, 174

Dixon, William, 45, 46, 57

Dolben, John, Bishop of Rochester, 15

Doneraile, Viscount, 280

Dorchester, Lord, 143

Douglas-Hamilton, James, *see* Hamilton, James Douglas-Hamilton, fourth Duke of

Drake, Peter, 169–71

Duppa, Sir Thomas, 51, 53, 56

Elizabeth I, Queen, 68, 130

Elrington, John, 266

Exclusion Crisis (1679–81), 7, 81

Fitton, Alexander, 72–82, 103
Fitton, Sir Edward (father of
    William), 68
Fitton, Sir Edward, second
    baronet, 65–70, 71, 72, 75, 82
Fitton, Felicia, 68–71
Fitton, Jane, 68
Fitton, William, 68–72
Fitzroy, Barbara, 98–99

George, Prince of Denmark, 118
George I, King (Elector of
    Hanover), 8, 101, 269, 270, 275
Gerard, Anne, *see* Macclesfield,
    Anne Gerard, Countess of
Gerard, Charles, Lord, *see*
    Macclesfield, Charles Gerard,
    first Earl of; Macclesfield,
    Charles Gerard, second Earl of
Gerard, Charlotte, *see* Orby,
    Charlotte, Lady
Gerard, Digby, Lord, of Bromley,
    83, 97, 167, 182, 201
Gerard, Elizabeth, Lady, 83, 97,
    99, 101, 108, 115, 182–84, 200,
    214, 215
Gerard, Elizabeth (daughter), *see*
    Hamilton, Elizabeth, Duchess
    of
Gerard, Fitton, *see* Macclesfield,
    Fitton Gerard, third Earl of
Gerard, Ratcliffe, 70
Gloucester, William, Duke of, 118
Godolphin, Sidney, first Earl of,
    122, 125, 137, 141, 147, 148,
    150, 160, 162, 182, 185; and
    Anne's accession, 118; dismissal
    as Lord High Treasurer, 180;

Jacobites and, 127, 136; and
    Junto Whigs, 143, 152, 173–75,
    178; Maccartney and, 156, 157;
    during Sacheverell's trial, 176,
    178, 179; and war with France,
    142–43
Gordon, Duchess of, 136
Grafton, Duke of, 6
Graham, Col. James, 133
Granger, Abraham, 75–79, 287
Griffith, Col. Edward, 172
Griffith, Elizabeth (née
    Lawrence), *see* Mohun,
    Elizabeth, Lady
Griffith, Elizabeth (daughter), 264
Guilford, Lord Keeper, 81
Gulliver's Travels (Swift), 114
Gunpowder Plot, 174

Halifax, Charles Montague, Earl
    of, 105*n*, 143
Hamilton, Anne, Duchess of
    (mother), 11–13, 23–25, 29, 31,
    107–9, 119, 144, 187*n*, 198, 221,
    259, 260, 277
Hamilton, Anne, Duchess of (née
    Spencer; first wife), 98
Hamilton, Archibald (brother),
    180, 213, 259, 275
Hamilton, Charles (illegitimate
    son), 99
Hamilton, Charles (illegitimate
    grandson), 212
Hamilton, Charlotte, Lady
    (daughter), 277
Hamilton, Elizabeth, Duchess of
    (née Gerard; second wife), 83,
    126, 136, 141, 145, 192, 198,

Hamilton, Elizabeth, Duchess of (*cont.*)
200, 201, 251, 259–60, 269–78, 306*n44*, 308*n81*, 309*n91*; and Colonel Hamilton's trial, 253–55; death of father of, 167, 182–83; and husband's death, 240–41; in lawsuit against Lady Mohun, 266, 268, 281; London house of, 143; and Macclesfield estate, 83, 104–6, 110, 113; marriage of, 97, 99, 108, 119, 140, 183, 289; in public brawl, 168, 194; reward for Maccartney's capture offered by, 248

Hamilton, James Douglas-Hamilton, fourth Duke of (Earl of Arran), 9–10, 64, 283–89; and Act of Security, 131; aftermath of death of, 245–81; and Anne's accession, 118–21; appointment as ambassador to France of, 197–98, 209–11; attempted assassination of, 33–34, 75; birth of, 23; British dukedom granted to, 187–89; at Charles II's court, 25–29; on day of duel, 228–36, 282; death of, 236–37, 239–41, 244–45; education of, 23–25; events leading to duel of Mohun and, 212–28; family background of, 11–13; as favorite of James II, 29–31; financial problems of, 108–9; and Godolphin's fall from power, 179–80; imprisonment in Tower of, 34–35; Jacobite activities of, 127–30, 140–41; legal battles of Mohun and, 113,

115–17, 119–20, 126, 143, 145, 148, 181–85, 189–93, 196, 198, 200–2, 211, 212; and local elections of 1710, 185–86; London life of, 143–44, 161, 163, 166–69; and Macclesfield estate, 67, 100, 107–8, 110–13, 187; marriage of, 83, 97–99, 183; Queensberry and, 121–22, 124–26; and Sacheverell trial, 177–79; as Scottish representative in Union Parliament, 142–43, 152–53; and Union treaty, 132–40; and William III's accession, 31–33

Hamilton, Col. John, 217, 223, 228, 230, 232, 234, 236–8, 242–48, 251–59, 269–70, 273, 274

Hamilton, Susan, Lady (daughter), 277

Hamilton, William, third Duke of (father), 25, 30–31, 34

Hamond, John, 113

Hanoverian succession, 101, 130, 171, 196, 207, 210, 268, 269; *see also* George I, King; Sophia, Electress of Hanover

Harley, Robert, *see* Oxford, Robert Harley, first Earl of

Harte, Capt., 147

Harvey, William, 21

Hearne, Thomas, 253

Henrietta Maria, Queen, 11

Henry VIII, King, 87, 91

Henry Esmond (Thackeray), 271

Hill, Capt. Richard, 42–50, 56–59

Hill, Capt. William, 62, 93, 284, 285

Hipsley, John, 219, 221, 240

Hoffman, Frances, 162
Hogarth, William, 98
Holt, Lord Chief Justice, 50, 156
Honeywood, Col., 157
Hooke, Nathaniel, 133, 135, 140,
 141
House of Commons, 137, 149,
 150, 152, 186, 283
House of Lords, 15–16, 48–49, 62,
 79, 149–52, 283; divorce granted
 to Macclesfield by, 91–93;
 Mohun/Hamilton lawsuits in,
 189–93, 266, 268, 281; murder
 trials of Mohun in, 51–61, 63,
 83, 284; Scottish peers in, 137,
 188–89
Hudson, John, 57

Inns of Court, 287

Jacobites, 7, 10, 64, 100, 128, 131,
 133, 140, 141, 152, 188, 220,
 269, 270, 272, 288; and Anne's
 accession, 127, 129; and
 Hamilton's appointment as
 ambassador to France, 197,
 209–12, 284; and Hamilton's
 death, 239, 253; 1745 rebellion
 of, 281; Tories and, 158, 177,
 267; and Union treaty, 132,
 134–36
James I, King, 66*n*, 132, 159, 160
James II, King, 7, 9, 20, 27, 35, 80,
 81, 82, 83–84, 129, 210;
 accession of, 29, 81; Arran as
 favorite of, 29–31; exile of, 33,
 101, 127, 289; Marlborough and,

146, 205; revolution against,
 31–32, 82, 154, 283
Jekyll, Sir Joseph, 190, 191
Johnson, Esther, 250
Johnson, Samuel, 5, 90*n*
Johnston, Lady, 139
Johnston, Sir Patrick, 139
Joseph I, Holy Roman Emperor,
 205

Kennedy, John, Lord, 41, 51
Kincardine, Earl of, 126–27
King's Bench, Court of, 53, 77–78,
 269–70
Kit-cat Club, 168–69, 175, 193–94,
 284, 287
Kneller, Godfrey, 287

La Fage, Mr., 241
Lawrence, Sir Thomas, 172, 260
Lee, Francis, 224, 244
Leinster, Lord, 56, 60
Lesley, John, 228–30, 232, 237
Lo (coroner), 243–45
Lockhart, George, 134–35, 209,
 211, 216, 239, 243, 248, 270
London, Bishop of, 156
Louis XIV, King of France, 7, 8,
 28, 31, 128, 130, 140, 209
Love, Anne, 35–37
Lovelace, Lord, 17

Maccartney, Gen. George, 161,
 171, 194, 202, 210, 217–23, 225,
 227, 271–77; Col. Hamilton's
 charges against, 246–48, 251–58,

Maccartney, Gen. George (*cont.*) 274; dismissed by Queen Anne, 157–58; at duel of Mohun and Hamilton, 229–37; as fugitive, 242, 243, 249, 250, 256, 269; Marlborough and, 154–57, 205–6, 212–13; trial of, 269–70, 285

Macclesfield, Anne Gerard, Countess of (née Mason), 85–93, 95, 196

Macclesfield, Charles Gerard, first Earl of, 69–84, 87, 215

Macclesfield, Charles Gerard, second Earl of, 83–93, 96, 97, 99–107, 113, 119, 120, 145–47, 182, 183, 281, 284

Macclesfield, Fitton Gerard, third Earl of, 92–93, 103, 104, 105, 107, 110, 111

Manley, Mary Delarivière, 95, 96, 171, 251, 260

Mar, Earl of, 138, 185, 193

Marlborough, John Churchill, first Duke of, 99, 118, 122, 125, 142, 150, 162, 169, 170, 203–11, 246, 260, 276; and accession of George I, 269; and events leading to duel of Mohun and Hamilton, 217–19, 223–24*n*, 254, 257; and Jacobites, 127; and Junto Whigs, 173; Maccartney and, 154–57, 205–6, 212–13; and Mohun's military career, 146–48, 170; and overthrow of James II, 32; Poulett challenged to duel by, 208, 252; Swift's attacks on, 207, 250; in war with France, 141, 147, 175, 195

Marlborough, Sarah, Duchess of, 159–60, 172–74, 194, 203, 207, 211, 213, 264–66, 269, 303*n16*

Mary, Princess (mother of William III), 31*n*

Mary II, Queen, 5, 8, 31*n*, 59, 61, 193

Mary of Modena, Queen of England, 140, 209

Masham, Abigail, 160, 174, 178

Mason, Anne, *see* Macclesfield, Anne Gerard, Countess of

Mason, Gavin, 110, 116–17, 214

Mason, Sir Richard, 85

Meredith, Col., 157

Merry, William, 48, 57

Middleton, Lord, 127

Mohawks, 194–95, 288

Mohun, Catherine, Lady (grandmother), 11–13, 40, 51

Mohun, Charles Mohun, third Baron (father), 13–24, 27, 32, 81, 261

Mohun, Charles Mohun, fourth Baron, 9–10, 64, 283–89; aftermath of death of, 245–81; and Anne's accession, 118; birth of, 22; on day of duel, 229, 232–36, 282; death of, 236–37, 239–42; early life of, 35, 37–42; events leading to duel of Hamilton and, 212–28; family background of, 11–22; first marriage of, 82–83, 93–96, 165; at Hanoverian court, 101–2; Junto and, 151–53, 175–80; legal battles of Hamilton and, 113, 115–17, 119–20, 126, 143, 145, 148, 181–85, 189–93, 196, 198, 200–2, 211, 212; London

life of, 161, 163, 166–71;
Maccartney's friendship with,
154, 156, 158, 194; and
Macclesfield estate, 67, 83, 93,
100, 103, 104–8, 110–13, 187;
Marlborough as patron of, 205,
208, 210, 252; military career of,
145–49; murder charges against,
42–64; second marriage of,
172–73
Mohun, Charlotte, Lady (née
Orby; first wife), 83, 93–96, 105,
165, 261, 263
Mohun, Elizabeth (daughter), 95,
96, 261–65, 267, 279–80
Mohun, Elizabeth (sister), 23, 35
Mohun, Elizabeth, Lady (née
Lawrence; second wife), 172–
73, 216, 241, 253, 259–61, 264–
69, 272, 278–81, 308n85
Mohun, James (uncle), 95
Mohun, Phillippa, Lady (mother),
16–18, 21–23, 35–37, 41, 51, 84
Mohun, Warwick, Baron, 12
Monmouth, James Scott, Duke of,
7, 29–30, 31, 80
Mordaunt, Charles, 278
Mordaunt, Lord, 20, 27
Morris, William, 231–33, 236,
247
Mountford, William, 43–50, 56–
60, 83, 94
Mountjoy, Lady, 250

Nicholson, John, 233, 234, 236–37,
245
Nicolson, William, Bishop of
Carlisle, 190, 194–95, 268
Nottingham, Earl of, 60, 61

Oldmixon, John, 256
Orby, Sir Charles, 37, 40, 82,
93–94
Orby, Charlotte, Lady (née
Gerard), 82, 89, 93, 104, 107,
110–12, 180–81, 215, 262, 263,
266–68
Orby, Sir Thomas, 82, 93, 262,
263, 265–66, 268
Order of the Garter, 220
Order of the Thistle, 220
Orford, Edward Russell, Earl of,
105, 143
Orkney, Earl of, 253, 259
Orkney, Lady, 259
Orlebar, John, 198, 200–2, 214,
218, 245, 246, 254, 257
Ormonde, James, Duke of, 16,
147, 195
Oxford, Robert Harley, first Earl
of, 141, 162, 165, 196, 224, 274,
284; and Hamilton-Mohun
lawsuits, 180–81, 184–85, 187,
264–68; and Hamilton's
appointment as ambassador to
France, 197, 209–12, 216, 239;
investigation of duel by,
244–48; Junto Whigs' enmity
toward, 142, 160, 173, 174; Kit-
cat Club celebrations banned
by, 194; and Maccartney's
dismissal, 157–58, 213;
Marlborough and, 204, 206–9,
212; overthrow of Godolphin
by, 176, 178–80;
and Scottish members of
Parliament, 186, 188–89,
193; Swift and, 186, 195, 224,
240; and Union treaty, 133,
138

Page, Gawen, 46–47, 57
Page, Mrs., 46–47, 57
Parliament, 12, 40, 41, 66, 131, 137, 140, 142, 147, 149, 153, 187, 267, 283; *see also* House of Commons; House of Lords; Scottish Parliament
Peisly, William, 261–64
Pennington, John, 229, 231–33, 237, 245
Pepys, Samuel, 16
Peter the Great, Czar of Russia, 115
Pitt, Thomas, 4, 279, 283, 308n84
Pope, Alexander, 259–60, 272, 276, 278
Portlock, Anne, 90
Postlethwait, Malachy, 271
Poulett, Earl, 208, 252
Poulett, Lady, 208
Powell, George, 57
Power, John, 20–21
Pratt, Serjeant, 190
Presbyterians, 11, 12, 24, 29, 137, 151
Protestants, 7, 31, 80, 101, 129, 151, 174, 194; *see also specific denominations*

Queensberry, James Douglas, second Duke of, 121–26, 133, 143, 152, 153, 184, 186, 188

Restoration, of Charles II, 4, 13
Reynolds, John, 232–34, 236
Rich, Sir Robert, 221, 225

Richardson, Sarah, 88–89
Richmond, Charles Lennox, first Duke of, 178, 225, 250, 253, 264, 271
Rivers, Richard Savage, fourth Earl, 87–90, 196
Rochester, Lawrence Hyde, first Earl of, 61, 91, 92, 151, 152, 258, 288
Rogers, John, 46, 57
Ronjat, Dr., 241
Rowe, Sergeant, 76–77
Roxburghe, Duke of, 253–54
Rupert of the Rhine, Prince, 65

Sacheverell, Dr. Henry, 174–79, 191, 193
St. John, Henry, *see* Bolingbroke, Henry St. John, first Viscount
St. Leger, Arthur, 280
St. Leger, Arthur Mohun, 280
Saint-Simon, Duke of, 209
Sandys, Elizabeth, 45
Savage, Anne, 89
Savage, Richard (Richard Smith), 89–90
Scobell, Francis, 61
Scottish Parliament, 100, 109, 122–25, 128, 129, 131, 133, 134, 137
Seafield, Earl of, 135, 185
Security, Act of (1704), 131
Sedgemoor, Battle of, 7, 29
Selkirk, Charles, Earl of, 136
Settlement, Act of (1701), 8, 101, 130
Shaftesbury, Earl of, 20, 22, 29, 80, 81

Societies for the Reformation of Manners, 5
Somers, John Somers, Baron, 63–64, 105, 117
Somerset, Duke of, 156
Sophia, Electress of Hanover, 101, 130, 171
Spanish Succession, War of the, 120, 130, 195, 267
Stanley, Thomas, Lord, 8
Steele, Richard, 272
Strafford, Earl of, 155, 220, 244
Strafford, Lady, 194, 195, 197
Stuart, Charles Edward, 273
Stuart, James Edward (James III; the Pretender), 7, 131, 188, 195, 207, 210, 244, 267, 272–73, 286; and accession of Anne, 127, 129, 130; Hamilton as leader of Scottish support for, 128–30, 133, 135–36, 139–42; and Hamilton's appointment as ambassador to France, 197, 212, 213, 282; Junto Whigs' opposition to, 151–52
Stuarts, 8, 9, 11, 31n, 130, 141, 202, 207, 239; *see also specific monarchs*
Suffolk, Countess of, 279
Sunderland, Charles Spencer, third Earl of, 105n, 141, 174, 177, 256
Swift, Jonathan, 34, 114, 166, 196, 210, 249, 250, 252, 253, 258, 260, 272, 287; in Board of Brothers, 168; Elizabeth, Duchess of Hamilton, and, 99, 259, 276; Marlborough ridiculed by, 207; Oxford and, 186, 195, 224, 240; Scots denounced by, 122

Thackeray, William Makepeace, 271, 273
Tonson, Jacob, 168
Tories, 6–9, 107, 110, 154, 173, 179–81, 188, 194, 206, 245, 250, 271–73, 279, 284, 286, 287; during aftermath of duel, 243, 248, 251, 252, 254–56; and Anne's accession, 118; in Board of Brothers, 168–69; coffee-houses patronized by, 163; and Hamilton-Mohun lawsuits, 192, 213, 266, 268; Hanoverian, 269; High Church, 150–52; Jacobite, 100, 127, 158, 211; and Macclesfield's divorce, 91, 92; Marlborough and, 206–9; at Mohun's murder trial, 61; and peace with France, 195, 207, 267; and Sacheverell trial, 174–78; in 1710 elections, 185, 186; taverns catering to, 167
Tudors, 8, 130; *see also specific monarchs*

Uffenbach, Zacharias von, 164–65
Union, Act of (1707), 139, 285
Utrecht, Treaty of, 267

Vanburgh, Sir John, 205

Walker, Elizabeth, 58, 59
Walpole, Sir Robert, 272
Ward, Ned, 146, 162–63
Warwick, Earl of, 62–63
Wentworth, Peter, 155, 156, 196–97, 211

Wharton, Thomas Wharton, Earl of, 20, 105n, 148, 173, 177, 288

Whigs, 7–9, 64, 97, 100, 110, 153, 157, 172, 188, 194, 202, 217, 225, 260, 271–72, 276, 278, 279; during aftermath of duel, 244, 248, 250–55, 270; coffeehouses patronized by, 163; and Hamilton's appointment as ambassador to France, 197, 210–11; and Hamilton-Mohun lawsuits, 117, 181, 189, 192, 268; Hanoverian succession supported by, 101, 196, 210, 212, 269; Junto, 105, 111, 118, 136, 142, 148, 150–53, 160, 169, 171, 173–80, 186, 256; in Kit-cat Club, 168–69, 284; and Macclesfield's divorce, 91; at Mohun's murder trials, 61, 62; and Oxford's fall from power, 274; and peace with France, 195–96, 207, 267; in 1710 elections, 185–86; taverns catering to, 167

Whitworth, Richard, 105, 215–17

William III, King (William of Orange), 8, 34, 41, 127, 128, 129, 132, 141, 283; accession of, 7, 9, 31–33; death of, 122, 130; Macclesfield and, 82, 84, 91, 93, 101–2; and murder charges against Mohun, 55, 62, 117, 284, 285; Scottish antagonism toward, 120–21

Williams, Rhys, 216, 218, 225, 229, 230, 237, 254

Wren, Sir Christopher, 53, 55, 63, 203

Wright, Elizabeth, 89–90

York, James, Duke of, *see* James II, King